D1577322

IN SEARCH OF

ANNE
BRONTË

IN SEARCH OF
ANNE
BRONTË

NICK HOLLAND

First published 2016

The History Press
The Mill, Brimscombe Port
Stroud, Gloucestershire, GL5 2QG
www.thehistorypress.co.uk

British Library Cataloguing in Publication Data.
A catalogue record for this book is available from the British Library.

ISBN 978 0 7509 6525 5

Typesetting and origination by The History Press
Printed in Great Britain

CONTENTS

ACKNOWLEDGEMENTS

There are many people and organisations without whom this work would not have been possible, so alongside the support of family and friends I must give special thanks to the following people: Sophie Bradshaw, a pleasure to work with, and the team at The History Press; Julie Shaw and all at the Hollybank Trust (formerly Roe Head School), a wonderful charity that can be supported via www.hollybanktrust.com; Sylvie Lain and Arthur Sansam; Dave Zdanowicz, for his stunning photography; Amanda White, whose love for the Brontës and other writers is reflected in her art; Mark de Luca, proprietor of 'Emily's by De Luca' on the site of the Brontë birthplace; Diana Chaccour, National Portrait Gallery; Sylvia Thomas, President of the Yorkshire Archaeological Society; Charles Chambers, the Vina Cooke Museum; and Kit Shorten, expert on the Moravian church in Yorkshire.

Many thanks also to the British Library, Leeds City Library, Leeds University Library, Bradford City Library, Royal & Pavilion Museums, Durham University, and Julie and Steve at Ponden Hall. Special thanks must go to the Brontë Society, and especially Ann Dinsdale for her help and support. Final thanks, and without whom this labour of love really would not have been possible, to Anne Brontë herself, the courageous woman whose work continues to bring joy to me and many others.

PROLOGUE

Shielded by my own obscurity, and by the lapse of years,
and a few fictitious names, I do not fear to venture;
and will candidly lay before the public what I would
not disclose to the most intimate friend.

Agnes Grey

It is 28 May 1849 in a room in Wood's Lodgings, a guest house in
the northern resort of Scarborough. A thin, pale-faced woman gazes
out at the sea far below. Beads of sweat shine on her forehead as she
tries to draw in one more painful breath. Watching on despairingly are
her sister Charlotte and her friend Ellen. They are in tears, but the young
woman smiles as best she can. After a lifetime of regrets and fears, punctuated by brief, golden moments of love and triumph, she is completely
at peace. These are the last moments of Anne Brontë. She is 29 years old.

A month earlier Anne had written to Ellen Nussey, stating that she
wasn't afraid to die, but she regretted that she could not live longer, as
she longed to do something good and worthwhile in life, even if little.
Anne was dying, as she had lived, in total obscurity. Nobody who saw

her could have guessed that she was the much talked about Acton Bell, whose novel *The Tenant of Wildfell Hall* had become such a cause célèbre. Nor could they have guessed that the woman alongside her was the famed Currer Bell.

In her last days, Anne was confident that the literary success that she and her elder sisters, Emily and Charlotte Brontë, had found in the last two years would be fleeting. The names of Acton, Currer and Ellis Bell would soon be forgotten, like marks in the sand that are washed away by an incoming tide. It did not trouble her: she was, after all, a woman who scorned fame and the trappings of success. Little did she know that over a century and a half later, she and her sisters would be loved and lauded across the world.

Anne, the youngest of the Brontë sisters, was in many ways the most enigmatic. Quiet and thoughtful in real life, she could seem mysterious even to those closest to her. In a letter to W.S. Williams, one of her publishers, on 31 July 1848, Charlotte wrote of Anne, 'She does not say much for she is of a still, thoughtful nature, reserved even with her nearest of kin.'[1]

Nevertheless, Anne hid deep and powerful feelings within her and had led a life that was full of joys and sorrows, even though short of days. She was a woman who was always committed to the truth, however painful it could be to others.

Anne Brontë has for too long been the 'forgotten Brontë', an epithet that is unbecoming of her great talents as a poet and novelist. She deserves to be sought out by new readers and revisited by those who are already familiar with her work.

When we go in search of Anne Brontë we inevitably meet with difficulties. All of her youthful prose writing, in itself a prodigious output, has been lost. Only five letters by Anne are currently known to exist, although she was a keen letter writer. Nevertheless we still have more than enough source material to construct a meaningful and accurate life.

Piecing together a biography of Anne Brontë is in some ways like being a lawyer working on a case before the courts. There are lots of clues, if we choose to see them, and from these clues we can piece together a fuller picture of the truth itself. This may in some cases have to lead to supposition as to what Anne would have said, done or felt, but by examining the clues of her life we can do so with some degree of confidence, even certainty.

To a large extent we are reliant upon the testimony of others, most notably Charlotte Brontë and Ellen Nussey, but this can be very revealing, particularly when we know how to read many of Charlotte's opinions and pronouncements. The greatest evidence of all, however, is contained within Anne's writing itself. Yes, these are works of fiction, but as every fiction writer knows, there will always be elements of truth contained within them. Whether an author is a first-rate writer like Anne or a tenth-rate scribbler, every book will contain pieces of the person who created it. To discard this is to wilfully misunderstand the art of creating prose and poetry. Anne particularly used her novels to unburden the feelings that she was normally so careful to hide. In *Agnes Grey* alone, in itself quite a slender novel, we find sixty instances that are drawn directly from her actual life. To examine Anne's writing, then, is not only rewarding, it is fruitful too, although of course we must be careful to extract the facts from the fiction.

We can now embark upon a remarkable life story. To seek out the real Anne Brontë, we must go back to the very beginning. Back twenty-nine years and four months before the scene that is playing out in Scarborough, to the village of Thornton, near Bradford, in the West Riding of Yorkshire.

1

IN THE BEGINNING

My father was a clergyman of the north of England;
deservedly respected by all who knew him.

Agnes Grey

The month of January 1820 was an exceptionally cold one in the north of England, and conditions were very hard for the workers of Yorkshire's West Riding. Crops of wheat and corn had failed, peat farmers were left with nothing, and the moors and fields lay covered by a thick blanket of snow. Rivers and canals were frozen, and supplies of food and fuel were brought to a standstill.

The harvest of 1819 had been the poorest in memory, and the harsh January weather promised little respite in the year to come. People with little means and little hope were starving and freezing to death. Bodies were found in the streets, with nobody to mourn them. Families were left without breadwinners or broken up as men left the countryside and headed into the burgeoning new urban centres that offered jobs and at least a little hope for the future.

England was entering an age of increased automation, the Industrial Revolution was reaching its height and machines made by one were doing the work of many. It was a period of civil unrest, and discord hung in the air. Groups of people gathered together and plotted acts against the machines and the mill owners who used them. These men became known as Luddites, and the West Riding was a hotbed for them. They would break into factories at night, smashing machines before vanishing into the darkness, or they would intimidate mill owners and workers with threats that were sometimes bloodily carried out.

Others were taking an interest in the political sphere and agitated for suffrage for men of all social classes. Just five months previously, 80,000 people had gathered in St Peter's Field, across the Pennines in Manchester. They had come to see Henry Hunt, a famous orator who was calling for political and social reform. Unrest grew in the crowd as the day progressed, and soon the local militia were called. These militia, not caring who was in the way, drew sabres and charged into the crowd, cutting down men, women and children. In an ironic comparison to the Battle of Waterloo that had taken place four years before, this infamous event became known as the Peterloo Massacre; it is in this world of change and unrest that Anne Brontë's story begins.

Her father, the Reverend Patrick Brontë, was a priest in the Church of England. He had been born into very inauspicious circumstances in Emdale, near the village of Drumballyroney, in County Down, Ireland. Despite spending the majority of his life in England, his Irish accent remained undimmed. Due to their very particular circumstances, most of Anne's formative days were spent in his company, so it is little surprise that contemporary accounts state that both she and her sisters spoke with an Irish accent,[1] although Charlotte was the only one who would ever see the country of her forebears.[2]

Through determination and the kindness of benefactors such as local landowner Reverend Thomas Tighe, Patrick secured an education at Cambridge University and was then ordained into the Anglican priesthood. Patrick saw entering Cambridge as the start of a new life, and a new life required a new name. In Ireland, his family was known by the name Brunty, but from the time of his arrival in England, he called himself Brontë. A Latin scholar, he knew that Brontë translates as thunder, and he was also aware of the castle that Lord Nelson, a hero of his,[3] had near the town of Brontë in the foothills of Sicily. These factors influenced his adoption of the name that was to become so famous. It is worth noting that neither he nor his children used the familiar diaeresis, the two dots above the letter 'e', from the beginning.[4] Patrick often used a plain 'e', and in their early years the sisters frequently used the French accented 'é' in their surname. Only later in their lives was the 'Brontë' we know today uniformly adopted.

After positions as an assistant curate in the south of England, Patrick was offered the role of chaplain to the Governor of Martinique. He was a very inquisitive man, whose mind thrilled at the thought of new ideas and new places. A situation in the West Indies must have seemed highly appealing to him, but it was then that fate took a hand.

The vicar of Dewsbury, John Buckworth, was looking for an enthusiastic and evangelical cleric to help him in his parish. Dewsbury, like many parishes across the West Riding of Yorkshire, was growing rapidly, and priests were in short supply. Patrick recognised this calling, and in December 1809 he headed north to a new life.

By 1810 Patrick was curate at a village parish called Hartshead, near Dewsbury. On the moor near Hartshead is a marker point known as the Dumb Steeple. It was here, on 11 April 1812, that a bloody and terrible event had its beginning. A large crowd of Luddites from the region gathered at the steeple. Their target was to be Rawfolds Mill in nearby Cleckheaton.

The mill owner was a Mr William Cartwright, a man who saw progress only in terms of the revenue that entered his coffers, and who had replaced many of his men with cropping machines that worked tirelessly day and night. Cartwright had been targeted before, and as a consequence of this he slept in his mill along with five soldiers and four armed guards.

On this particular night a crowd of over 200 Luddites headed across the moor towards the mill. Patrick watched them march past his rented home at Lousy Thorn Farm, and, guessing their intentions, made his way to Hartshead church to pray for their souls. When the men reached Cartwright's mill they tried to gain access but were met by a hail of rifle fire from within. A group of Luddites approaching from Leeds turned and fled at this sound, and soon the fields around Rawsfold turned red with blood and were scattered with the bodies of groaning men. Two were left dead and seventeen more were later executed after the York assizes.

That same night, Patrick heard a scraping and shovelling noise. Looking out of the church window, he saw by moonlight men digging at the earth. Having heard the shots carrying across the night-time stillness, Patrick realised that they were burying others who'd been injured at the mill and had succumbed to their injuries. He left them in peace to bury the dead, and later said a prayer over the unmarked graves.[5] Patrick Brontë knew what it was like to struggle with poverty.

Later that year another event took place, and it was to have the most direct impact upon Anne's story. One of Patrick's earliest curacies had been at Wellington in Shropshire. It was there that he made friends with a schoolmaster called John Fennell. By 1812, Mr Fennell was also in Yorkshire, and he was running a boys' school in Rawdon, near the growing city of Leeds. Knowing his friend's skill at Greek and Latin, John asked if he would inspect the boys in the classics. Patrick had always taken a special interest in education – he had already served as a teacher while a teenage boy in County Down – so he readily agreed to his friend's request, and in July he commenced his role.

Patrick spent a lot of time at Woodhouse School, but the pupils weren't his only interest. It was there that he met, and fell quickly in love with, a woman, then 29 years old, by the name of Maria Branwell. Maria was the niece of John Fennell and had come to the school from Penzance, leaving behind her sisters Elizabeth and Charlotte, to assist her cousin Jane with the domestic duties of the establishment.

Eros cast his spell upon them both. It was a whirlwind romance, such as that which can rapidly consume two lonely souls a long way from home and family. They sent each other frank and loving letters, in which Maria playfully referred to Mr Brontë as her 'saucy Pat'. On 29 December of that year they were married in the parish church of Guiseley. On the same day, and at the same ceremony, Maria's cousin Jane Fennell married William Morgan, a curate who was an established friend of Patrick Brontë. The two friends performed the ceremonies for each other, sealing bonds that would last a lifetime.

Anne would later lament that she was unable to remember anything of her mother, but she was left in no doubt that she had been a very pious and intelligent woman, and indeed she had written an essay entitled 'The Advantages of Poverty, in Religious Concerns'.[6]

The Branwells were a well-established family in Cornwall society and were staunch supporters of the Methodist cause, which was at the time having a revolutionary impact on the Church of England, from which it hadn't as yet split. Her father, Thomas, was a wealthy merchant with a keen love of music, but both he and his wife, Anne, had died before Maria came to Yorkshire. As the title of Maria's essay shows, she was predisposed to love a poor clergyman like Patrick Brontë, despite her own more exalted background.

It may seem strange that her wealthy relatives did nothing to help her transition into married life, but it is likely that they disapproved of the match and so cut her out of any inheritance or financial help that she could otherwise have expected. Years later Anne Brontë was to hint at this on the very first page of her novel *Agnes Grey*, where Agnes reveals a family background very much like that of the author. After revealing that her father was a northern clergyman, she continues:

> My mother, who married him against the wishes of her friends, was a squire's daughter, and a woman of spirit. In vain it was represented to her, that if she became the poor parson's wife, she must relinquish her carriage and her lady's-maid, and all the luxuries and elegance of affluence … but she would rather live in a cottage with Richard Grey than in a palace with any other man in the world.[7]

Whilst Anne exaggerated the wealth and position of the Branwell family here, there is more than an element of truth to this portrait.

From a surviving portrait we can see that Maria Brontë, née Branwell, had long, curly hair, like Anne, and striking eyes, like Charlotte, above a long aquiline nose. Despite their lack of monetary resources, and a life very different to the one left behind in Cornwall, she and Patrick were very much in love. It was during this first year of their marriage that Patrick wrote and published his first volume of poems, *The Rural*

Minstrel, setting down his belief in a loving God and the importance of a life without sin.

At the beginning of 1814 their first child, Maria, was born, and from her earliest days she seemed to be an exceptional child. A year later, a sister, Elizabeth, arrived. They were now a happy band of four, but it was a struggle for Patrick to meet the needs of his growing family, especially as his incumbency at Hartshead included no parsonage, leaving him to pay the rent for his little cottage at Lousy Thorn Farm out of his small annual stipend.

Providence was to shine upon them, however. Shortly after Elizabeth's birth, Patrick received a very timely and most interesting proposal from Reverend Thomas Atkinson, the curate of Thornton. Reverend Atkinson was a man of independent means, not reliant on the larger income that Thornton offered, but he had his eyes on a very different prize. He was in love with Frances Walker of Lascelles Hall near Huddersfield. He'd met Frances on many occasions at Kipping House in Thornton, home of the Firth family who were related to the Walkers. Thomas believed that by moving closer to Lascelles Hall, he could form stronger ties with her. In this he was not wrong, as they would later be married.

It was for this reason that Reverend Atkinson suggested to Patrick Brontë that they swap parishes. Thornton offered an increased income and came with a rent-free parsonage building. Patrick, of course, quickly accepted, and once the archbishop gave his assent, the Brontë family made the move to Thornton in May of 1815.

Thornton is a semi-industrial village on the outskirts of the city of Bradford. Its church, of which Patrick had now been made incumbent, was known as the Old Bell Chapel and was positioned at the southern end of the village, in a remote aspect surrounded by fields. The Church of England was not strong in Thornton, and most of the populace attended the dissenting chapels and schools, a problem that he was to face in his next parish as well and one that was becoming increasingly common across the West Riding of Yorkshire as a whole.

Other than the church, the main building of Thornton was Kipping House, home to the aforementioned Firth family who were to become so important to the Brontës. Kipping House is a very beautiful and imposing building, dating from the seventeenth century but largely rebuilt and extended in the eighteenth century. The Firths were the undoubted leaders of Thornton society and keen Church of England supporters. At the time Patrick arrived, with his wife and two young children, only John Firth and his daughter Elizabeth lived at the house, Mrs Firth having been killed in a tragic accident a year earlier when thrown from a horse.

The Firth family made the Brontës very welcome, and as Elizabeth Firth's diary entries reveal, they spent much time at Kipping House.[8] Soon after arriving in Thornton, Maria's sister, also called Elizabeth, came to help look after the children. She would stay for a year at first, but she then returned at regular intervals; in later years, she made her permanent home with the family, a move that would have a profound effect on all of them, particularly Anne.

On 21 April 1816, another girl was born into the Brontë family. She was christened Charlotte after Maria's sister. At this time, and with Aunt Elizabeth no longer in residence, further help was needed, and Nancy Garrs was taken on as a nanny. Nancy and her sister Sarah were to remain friends and helpers of the family from then on, even after they were no longer employed by them. They were the first of a succession of servants who would form a close bond above and beyond the call of duty with the Brontës.

In June 1817, Patrick and Maria were at last blessed with a boy. He was christened Patrick but would always be known by his middle name Branwell; taking on the name his mother had given up on her wedding day. The parents felt blessed: at last a boy to take their name forward. They hatched great plans for him and prayed for a glorious future for one whose duty it would be to take the Brontë name forward into the world.

On 30 July 1818 the fifth child was born, Anne's dear, beloved sister Emily Jane. By now, things were again becoming difficult for Patrick and Maria. Thornton Parsonage was a terraced building in the middle of Market Street, on a hilly trajectory, far away from the church itself, with a small walled garden at the back. The building was often in need of repair, and Patrick wrote to the Archbishop of York, and to a friend named Richard Burn, calling it a 'very ill constructed and inconvenient building'.[9] He now had a family of seven in the house, as well as Nancy Garrs, and suffered much from lack of space and resources.

Nevertheless, the family was not yet finished. On 17 January 1820, Maria was to deliver another child, in front of the roaring fire at Thornton Parsonage, with the village midwife in attendance. Patrick was at the church, offering up thanks and prayers. The Brontë children had been taken for the day to Kipping House, where they were entertained by Elizabeth Firth. She kept a detailed diary of this time, and from it we get glimpses of how Maria, just turned 6 years old, was already ordering the younger children around and how Charlotte acted like quite the young lady, taking great care over her manners. Elizabeth, Branwell and young Emily would have stood transfixed by the sight of snow falling outside of the large windows that looked out on to extensive grounds stretching out on to the Thornton moors.[10]

It was on that day that Anne was born. A small and delicate child at birth, all who saw her in those first days fell in love with the tiny and quiet baby. Anne was later baptised, as her brother and sisters had been, by Reverend William Morgan. She was named after her maternal grandmother, and her godmothers were Elizabeth Firth and Miss Fanny Outhwaite, Elizabeth's close friend, a pillar of polite society and well known to Anne's parents. How well chosen they were, for although they were soon to be distanced from Anne, they would provide acts of kindness on her behalf throughout her life. It was thanks to Miss Outhwaite, and a legacy that she left to her god-daughter, that Anne was able to make her final journey to Scarborough.

On that day in January 1820 the family was complete, and complete in their happiness. Maria and Patrick, and their children, Maria, Elizabeth, Charlotte, Branwell, Emily Jane and Anne were not wealthy by any standards, but they had an abundance of love and a belief in a bright future stretching out ahead of them.

2

EARLY LOSS

In all we do and hear, and see,
Is restless Toil and Vanity,
While yet the rolling earth abides,
Men come and go like ocean tides;
And ere one generation dies;
Another in its place shall rise;
That, sinking soon into the grave,
Others succeed, like wave on wave.

Vanitas Vanitatum, Omnia Vanitas

Anne was not to stay in Thornton long. Just three months after her birth, the Brontës were making a trip across the moors to Haworth. A new life awaited them, a life full of hope, tragedy, laughter and loss. One wagon carried their meagre possessions, and another carried the family. Always a keen walker, Patrick walked alongside the carriage the whole way. From time to time Anne would have been passed down from her mother within the carriage to her father, to be carried safely in his arms. At other times, Emily would be passed to him and would ride piggyback on her father's shoulders. It is a journey of only 8 miles, yet full of undulations, steep inclines and unfirm ground. Progress was slow before they reached the steep Kirkgate, today known as Main Street, which would lead to their new home. The carriage ride took a full day, but for Patrick it was the culmination of a journey that had lasted months.

Patrick had already complained of the inadequacies of the Thornton Parsonage and was looking for a new, larger parish to meet the demands of his growing family. When the incumbency of Haworth became available, it was offered to Patrick; however, problems quickly arose. Haworth was, and is, a parish like no other. From ancient times Haworth council of elders had held the right to select its own curate, rejecting the choice of the vicar of Bradford, at this time Reverend Henry Heap, who would ordinarily control the rights to the parish. This would normally have been a formality, but the vicar was a man unused to having his actions questioned and had not consulted the council of Haworth elders before announcing the choice of Reverend Brontë as the new priest. They immediately let it be known that they would not accept this priest who had been foisted upon them.[1]

In this they were not expressing any slight against Patrick himself but merely exercising their powers. They were hardy and stubborn, although kind-hearted, folk, and when roused they would not back down. Recognising this, and mindful of stirring up any real enmity, Patrick politely declined the offer of the Haworth curacy.[2]

A new choice was needed, but once more the vicar of Bradford chose not to consult the elders and instead appointed Reverend Samuel Redhead to the position. Redhead had often officiated at Haworth during the prolonged illness of the previous incumbent, Reverend Charnock, and had been well liked by the congregation, so it is likely that Heap foresaw no problem with this appointment. The Haworth men, however, saw it as a great affront; at Reverend Redhead's first Sunday service, the parishioners stamped on the stone floor with their clogs until he could not be heard, before walking out en masse.[3]

The second week was much worse. As the sermon commenced, a great uproar was heard. A drunk chimney sweep, seemingly oblivious to what was happening, had ridden into the church on a donkey. He was facing backwards and shouting as if he could feel the fires of hell. The sweep was then sat in the front pew; he stared at the poor curate all the time, swaying from side to side occasionally. At last he rose unsteadily to his feet, climbed to the pulpit and fell on to Reverend Redhead, to general hilarity from the stalls. The atmosphere then grew worse still, and the reverend had to wrestle his way through the crowd. He managed to reach the safety of the Black Bull Inn next to the church, but a mob had gathered outside and were threatening his very life. By luck and intrigue, Mr Redhead made good his escape by way of the inn's back door and a nearby horse, but it was clear that his curacy at Haworth could not continue. In later years, Redhead occasionally acted as a guest preacher at Haworth, often joking about the incident, and he was well received by the locals, who had once been much less welcoming to him.

An impasse had been reached. Patrick acted as a mediator of sorts, with assistance from the Bishop of Ripon, and after speaking to the parish elders they agreed to nominate him to the position of curate, which the vicar would then accept. In this way, pride and tradition were restored, and Patrick Brontë found himself the new curate at Haworth after all, a position he held until the end of his life.

Thus, on 20 April 1820, the Brontë family, along with Nancy Garrs and her sister Sarah, moved into the Haworth Parsonage. It is a lovely Georgian building, set apart from the rest of the village, although it proved somewhat cold in winter. The parsonage was built in 1775; it had, and indeed still has, a not overly spacious garden to the front, where currant and lilac bushes, along with laburnum and cherry trees, grew. In day time, at that period, it was infused with light, as Patrick would not allow any curtains in the windows because of a morbid fear of fire, in part due to the many funerals he had presided over for victims of conflagrations.

Anne could remember nothing, of course, of those first few days, but her father often spoke of them as the happiest of his life. His family were all around him, and his days were full. The parish was large and flourishing, and every week brought baptisms, weddings and funerals. At this point he was at the height of his physical and mental powers, and he met the challenge head on.

Anne's mother was happy too. Maria had a large house to manage and a loving brood around her at all hours. Her presence was much in demand among the wives of the elders and merchants of Haworth, and she remained in correspondence with her good friends from Thornton. As Anne lay burbling in her cradle, arms outstretched for the happy although as yet unrecognisable faces that gazed down at her, Haworth Parsonage was full of noise and full of life. It was not to last long.

The day was 29 January 1821. The Brontës had been in Haworth for less than a year. Nothing had presaged the event. A day earlier, Maria had been her usual self, tidying, cleaning and organising. Ensuring that everything was in its rightful place.

In the morning she came downstairs, but her face was paler than before. She tried to reach the dining table, but fell with a thud to the floor, where she screamed in pain. Maria was Patrick's whole world; he ran for the local doctor, but when the doctor came he said that she was eaten by a cancer of sorts and would not last the day. It would have been less cruel for Maria if that had indeed been true.

Maria Brontë was strong and determined: she clung to her new family for as long as she could, enduring torments that could not be borne by many. For Patrick this was a dreadful trial, but it was also a portent of what was yet to come. At times, his wife would cry out in pain and shout, 'There can be no God that lets me suffer like this!'[4] Then later she would be full of terror and curse herself for having spoken against her Lord. For many days, she could not speak at all, could not move.

In May her sister Elizabeth came to stay to help nurse the sibling that she loved so much. Nobody knew at the time that Haworth was now to be her home until her dying day. Aunt Branwell, as she became known to Anne and her siblings, was greatly affected by what she saw happen to her sister and by the sacrifice that she later had to make. Later biographers, including Elizabeth Gaskell, would make much of her stern aspect,[5] but to Anne and Branwell at least, she was always loved and respected as a second mother.

Patrick refused to give up hope; as always, he turned to the faith that told him anything was possible. He hired a succession of specialists to see Maria, and when they said there was nothing to be done, he dismissed them and turned to others. His wife lingered terribly for eight months, until she left this world on 15 September 1821.

Anne was just 18 months old, and yet she still felt somehow to blame whenever she heard the tale. Maria was already 30 when she had her first child; within seven years, she gave birth to six children, Anne being the last. People whispered that it was this that proved too much for her and caused the cancer that ate her away. Anne must have wondered whether her mother would have lived a full life if she herself had never been born.

It is commonly related today that Maria died of uterine cancer, and yet in the early 1970s a medical expert came up with a different and convincing diagnosis.[6] Professor Philip Rhodes was not only a Brontë lover, he was also a professor of obstetrics and gynaecology at the University of London's St Thomas' Hospital Medical School. In his opinion, it is very unlikely that a woman would die of uterine cancer after giving birth healthily six times, including one birth just a year and a half earlier. It is also highly unusual for this cancer to occur in women under the age of 40, and Maria was 38 at the time of her death. Professor Rhodes diagnosed the cause of death as chronic pelvic sepsis with anaemia, resulting in extreme pain and blood poisoning that would lead to a fatal cardiac arrest. The cause of this deadly infection was poor antenatal care after the birth of Anne, at a time when gynaecological knowledge was very limited.

From an early age Anne was a deeply thoughtful person, who would consider whether her actions, all of her actions, were right or wrong. As a child, when the bed chamber candles were snuffed out she would think of the mother that she could not remember, and she would wonder how different things could have been. She added it to the list of sins that she stored and carried around within her for the rest of her life, until she finally reached the destination that would free her from sin forever.

Patrick was now 44, with a family of six children, a job that took up every moment of his time and not a penny to his name. All the savings he had gathered had been spent, in vain, on medical treatment for Maria. The Brontës were now rescued from the very real threat of poverty by the power of friendship, and the kindness of their fellow man, as Patrick's friends rallied around him and his family. The Firths, Outhwaites, Fennells, Morgans and more proved good and true. Between them, and despite his protestations, they paid off all of Patrick's not inconsiderable debts.[7]

Patrick Brontë's marriage had not been one of convenience, as so many were in his day, but a match of true love. He had no desire to marry again, but he knew that it was expected of him, and he also recognised that it would be beneficial to his young family. His sister-in-law Elizabeth encouraged him in this endeavour too. She herself had hopes of securing a husband one day, but time's winged chariot was moving on. Elizabeth Branwell had made a promise to her sister to look after her children for as long as it was needed. In Elizabeth's mind, this meant until Patrick took a new bride, at which point she could leave Haworth behind and resume her search for a husband.

Eventually, worn down by these arguments, Patrick asked Anne's god-mother, Elizabeth Firth, to marry him. The year was 1822, and by now Elizabeth's father had died, leaving a fortune to her alone. She was young, rich, in good health, held Patrick in great esteem and both knew and loved the Brontë children. Alas, for Patrick and his family, she had her heart set elsewhere. She declined in the kindliest manner and was later to marry a Reverend James Franks of Huddersfield.

Mr Brontë made two more attempts to find a bride, and one in particular was most forthright, not to say hurtful, in her rejection. This was Mary Burder, a young woman he knew from his days as a curate in Essex. Patrick had briefly been engaged to her, but had broken the engagement off when he was offered the curacy in Wellington. She was now to let him know, via a brutally honest letter telling him that his contact was not remotely welcome, that all had not been forgiven.[8] A new plan was needed. It became clear that although Patrick was much respected as a clergyman of some repute, his age and lack of wealth, and the burden of a large family dependent upon him, meant he would never find a woman who would consent to be his bride. You may wonder why Patrick did not enter into a marriage of convenience with his late wife's sister? Such marriages had been common, even expected, in earlier centuries, but by this time unions of that nature were specifically prohibited by law.

Elizabeth Branwell had a deep belief in the importance of accepting God's will, and in putting it before any longings or needs of one's own. She locked away all hopes of married life and confined herself for evermore to what would become to her the prison of Haworth Parsonage. Although she had once hoped, even expected, to be married, this abandonment of her original plan may have come as some relief, especially when she considered what marriage and child bearing had brought her sister. Patrick too, put all such plans aside. From now on, his mission in life would be to do his best for God, and for his daughters and only son.

Branwell was, from birth, the true hope of the family. He was a precocious boy who loved to talk and laugh, and Patrick dreamed of a life for him as an officer in the king's army (King George IV being then on the throne). Nevertheless, Patrick Brontë was a man of enlightened views on many subjects. He saw education as being important for daughters as well as sons, and he believed that women could make strong and worthwhile careers for themselves, if given the encouragement and tools to do so. This view was at odds with that commonly held in the early nineteenth century, where girls were trained to do housework and little else, or given the skills that would help them attract a husband in later life.

Patrick devised a teaching plan for all of the children except for Emily and Anne, who were still too young at the time, although they soon longed to be included. Aunt Branwell would teach sewing, cookery and household management during the day, as well as reading from the scriptures, but in the afternoon the elder sisters were permitted to join Branwell in their papa's study, where Patrick would give them lessons on more learned themes, from history to politics and languages.

It soon became evident that one child in particular had a rather brilliant aptitude for learning. The eldest Brontë sister Maria had a remarkable mind. Once something had been said to her, she could remember it forever. That was true with the lessons she learned from her father, and with the lessons she learned when she was later sent away to school. She was ever of a forthright, though kindly, nature and was quick to form her opinions on subjects and to explain her point of view to others.

Patrick would later say how he cherished every moment that he spent teaching his eldest daughter and looked forward to it as a bright spot in the day. He boasted proudly that he could converse with Maria, then only 9 years of age, on any of the leading topics of the day as freely, and with as much pleasure, as with any adult.

Maria took great care of her younger brother and sisters, so that by 10 years old she had become as another mother to them, and it was a role she was happy to fulfil.[9] She would sit Anne on her knee, and as her youngest sister gazed up into her kindly hazel eyes, she would read the papers to her siblings and explain the situation in countries across the globe.

Throughout their lives, the surviving sisters would often wonder how things would have been if Maria had lived and whether she would have joined them in their writing endeavours. What works have been lost to history we shall never know, but the contemplation of it grieved Charlotte in particular, before she paid tribute to her twenty-two years after her death. Helen Burns, that kindest, most courageous young girl in *Jane Eyre*, was a fitting portrait of their loved and lost sister Maria. Years after she had last seen her, Charlotte still recalled her fortitude and calm spirit, as well as the way she was mistreated by her teachers:

> Burns immediately left the class, and going into the small inner room where the books were kept, returned in half a minute, carrying in her hand a bundle of twigs tied together at one end. This ominous tool she presented to Miss Scratcherd with a respectful curtsey; then she quietly, and without being told, unloosened her pinafore, and the teacher instantly and sharply inflicted on her neck a dozen strokes with the bunch of twigs. Not a tear rose to Burns' eye; and, while I paused from my sewing, because my fingers quivered at this spectacle with a sentiment of unavailing and impotent anger, not a feature of her pensive face altered its ordinary expression.[10]

Charlotte later confirmed to Elizabeth Gaskell that these sections had been drawn from real life, and that Maria had been the constant and undeserving recipient of punishment from one particularly brutal teacher, insisting that 'not a word of that part of *Jane Eyre* but is a literal repetition of scenes between the pupil and the teacher'.[11]

Patrick was a keen believer in the power of education. It had taken him from a poor village in Ireland, via Cambridge University, to a position of great respect. For these reasons, he spent many summers campaigning to build a Sunday school in Haworth, and at last he succeeded. The school building is still in place alongside the parsonage, and all his children taught there from time to time. It was this same love of education that made him decide to send his daughters to school.

He and his sister-in-law were dedicated to their didactic cause, but if his daughters were to gain roles as governesses or teachers, those being the careers most suited to ladies of their social position, they would need a broader education. Anne's godmothers, Elizabeth and Fanny, recommended a school called Crofton Hall, near Wakefield. They had both been scholars there and found it to be a perfect stimulus for young minds, and a school where the spiritual and temporal needs of the pupils were taken care of.

Maria and Elizabeth were sent there in the summer of 1823. Elizabeth did not possess the intellectual brilliance of Maria, but she had a kind soul and seemed full of vigour and health. If anything practical needed to be done, Elizabeth would be the first to volunteer her help. She liked nothing more than cleaning and tidying, just as her mother had done; in contrast her elder sister preferred reading to housework.

The two sisters enjoyed their first term at school and were making good progress both in their lessons and in terms of making friends. Maria and Elizabeth were the most gregarious and outgoing of the Brontë girls. They, like their brother, would have been happy to look anyone in the eye and talk to them, whereas even from a young age Charlotte, Emily and Anne were crippled by shyness. Maria and Elizabeth had everything needed to be a success in life, but when they returned home at Christmas 1823, their days were already running out.

Patrick was happy with the schooling they received, but the fees for Crofton Hall reflected its excellent reputation. The cost was £28 per pupil per year. Anne's wealthy godmother Elizabeth was subsidising this cost but Patrick knew that she could not be asked to pay for the three further sisters who would also need schooling in their turn.

It was at this point that he heard of another school that had been newly formed, and it seemed perfect for his girls. It was called the Clergy Daughters' School, and it offered schooling on reduced terms for daughters of curates such as Patrick. This seemed a heaven-sent opportunity, but how he would later curse the day that it opened. Charlotte, still grief stricken at the things she saw there, reproduced it faithfully in the harrowing portrayal of Lowood, a school where death was dispensed along with lessons.

The beginning of 1824 saw epidemics of whooping cough and measles sweep through Haworth, and the Brontës were not immune. All of the Brontë children caught it, although the consequences were not as serious as they were for some of the village's young, who by then lay buried in the graveyard beyond the parsonage's garden gate. For this reason, the entry of Maria and Elizabeth to their new school was delayed until July of 1824. Their destination was Cowan Bridge, in Westmorland, and their father journeyed with them, keen to inspect the school himself. He stayed a night and shared a meal with his daughters before returning home, professing himself happy with the establishment.[12] In September, Elizabeth Firth, or Franks as she was by then called, having just married her reverend suitor, also visited Cowan Bridge and found no cause for concern.[13] If only they could have known that the proprietor, a Reverend Carus Wilson, put on a rather different show for visitors than could be expected during the school's normal daily routine.

Mr Wilson believed that fear and want were better teachers than love and comfort, and his school was perfect in every way for his hypothesis. It was a cold and desolate place, subject to the freezing winds of the north, and unhealthy in every aspect. Food was scarce and lacking any kind of sustenance, and harsh punishments were exacted for sins and offences that were never explained. He was a Calvinist through and through, and he believed that want and suffering were the rightful way of this world that provides but a temporary shelter.

Charlotte joined her older sisters on 24 August, having taken longer to recover from her whooping cough. What she saw and heard would stay with her forever and was later to be poured out into the opening of her famous novel.

Emily was sent to them on 25 November. At just 6 years old, she was the youngest pupil and had been given special dispensation to attend.

In the months preceding this, being the only girls at home, Anne and Emily had grown even closer to each other, and both wept as Emily left for the coach that would carry her to Westmorland.

Emily was the darling of the school, and she was shielded from some of the harsh treatments that were handed out to others not so fortunate. Sickness would spread through Cowan Bridge at regular intervals, and typhus and cholera were frequent visitors. The sick slept side by side with the healthy, with inevitable consequences.

Charlotte and Patrick were both vehement in later life that the descriptions of Lowood in *Jane Eyre* were studies drawn from real life:

> That forest-dell, where Lowood lay, was the cradle of fog and fog-bred pestilence; which, quickening with the quickening spring, crept into the Orphan Asylum, breathed typhus through its crowded schoolroom and dormitory, and, ere May arrived, transformed the seminary into a hospital.[14]

Charlotte often asked herself why she, or her sisters, never wrote to their father to reveal the true nature of the Clergy Daughters' School. In truth they were frightened to do so, and they may not have believed that the letters would be sent, as all mail was opened and inspected before being placed into eager hands. This was, in fact, set in stone by the 8th rule of the official Cowan Bridge regulations that stated, 'All letters and parcels are inspected by the superintendent'.[15]

By 14 February 1825, it was already too late. Maria Brontë was sent home from Cowan Bridge in 'ill health', as the school register records. Once she reached Haworth it was apparent to her father and the physicians that she was in an advanced and hopeless state of consumption, or tuberculosis. The happy beaming girl, bright in every sense, had been replaced by a living skeleton without the strength to smile. Four other girls were also sent home from the school on the same day, and two of them had reached their heaven before Maria was called there on 6 May. By this date, twenty-eight of the seventy-seven pupils at Cowan Bridge were recorded as being in 'ill health'.

On 31 May, Elizabeth was also sent home in this all-encompassing 'ill health'. She was accompanied by the school housekeeper, who promptly presented Patrick with a bill upon her arrival. Elizabeth died on 15 June, and she was buried by her father, next to her mother and elder sister.

By now, even Reverend Wilson had to acknowledge the truth: if the children remained at his school, not one would survive. Cowan Bridge was closed temporarily, and on the day that Elizabeth was sent home, the children were transferred to a lodging that Reverend Wilson owned near to Morecambe on the Lancashire coast.

From the moment the heartbroken Patrick had set eyes on his second dying daughter, however, he had decided to take action of his own. On the day after Elizabeth's arrival, he took a coach to Morecambe and collected Charlotte and Emily. From now on he was determined to keep an eye on his daughters, come what may, and hold them in the safety of his own keeping. We can only surmise what words he had for Reverend Wilson, but Patrick Brontë was a very forthright man when sorely tried. From that day on, whenever their paths would cross, Reverend Carus Wilson would try to thwart whatever Patrick was doing.

One of Anne's earliest memories was lining up with her brother and two, now only two, sisters to look into Elizabeth's open casket.[16] We can imagine how Aunt Branwell lifted Anne up and said to her the words that would often be spoken during Maundy Thursday services: 'Your sister suffers no more, Anne, but look on this and remember, that dust thou art, and to dust thou will return.' 'I remember, Aunt,' she would say for the rest of her days, 'I remember.'

Where were the bards to offer up an elegy to the sisters, so untimely taken? Who would remember them? Their brother, who had adored his eldest sister, wrote the poem 'Caroline', which is actually about Maria, in her memory. His reference to 'mother' is the role played by his aunt. The many sufferings he endured as a young child would have a dreadful effect on his later life.

> I stooped to pluck a rose that grew
> Beside this window waving then;
> But back my little hand withdrew,
> From some reproof of inward pain;
> For she who loved it was not there

To check me with her dove-like eye,
And something bid my heart forbear
Her favourite rose-bud to destroy.
Was it that bell – that funeral bell,
Sullenly sounding on the wind?
Was it that melancholy knell
Which first to sorrow woke my mind?
I looked upon my mourning dress,
Til my heart beat with childish fear,
And frightened at my loneliness,
I watched, some well-known sound to hear ...
My father's stern eye dropt a tear,
Upon the coffin resting there.
My mother lifted me to see,
What might within that coffin be;
And to this moment I can feel
The voiceless gap – the sickening chill –
With which I hid my whitened face
In the dear folds of her embrace ...
There lay she then, as now she lies –
For not a limb has moved since then –
In dreamless slumber closed, those eyes
That never more may wake again.
She lay, as I had seen her lie
On many a happy night before,
When I was humbly kneeling by –
Whom she was teaching to adore;
Oh, just as when by her I prayed,
And she to heaven sent up her prayer,
She lay with flowers about her head –
Though formal grave-clothes hid her hair![17]

So it was that Charlotte, having just turned 9, became the oldest child, and she changed from that moment. Despite being close to her brother and sisters in age, she herself acted like a mother as well as a sister, with all that entails. Charlotte made decisions for them, always doing what she felt was best, however others may judge her actions, but the cost to her was too great. Anne would see how she suffered and understand the reason why. Charlotte's wild flashes of temper, the dark moods that often overtook her, were the external symptoms of the grief that had been growing within her since she lost the three people she loved most in such quick succession. She had to sit through lessons, suffer chastisements and punishments, while nearby her sisters were perishing before her eyes. 'Dear Lord God,' pleaded Anne as she spent her last hours in Scarborough, 'please let Charlotte find peace after I've gone.'

3

THE BRONTË TWINS

That I might simply fancy there
One little flower – a primrose fair,
Just opening into sight;
As in the days of infancy,
An opening primrose seemed to me,
A source of strange delight.

'Memory'

'Papa, come quickly! Papa, please come, there's an angel standing next to Anne's cradle!'

Charlotte tugged at her father's sleeve as he sat behind his writing desk.

Patrick looked at her incredulously. He was a man who valued his privacy, and all his children were taught to knock and wait before entering his study. Yet here was his 5-year-old daughter in a state of agitation, her eyes wide with excitement.

'Please come quickly, there's an angel looking over Anne', Charlotte insisted.

A smile broke out on her father's face: he would humour his daughter this time.

'Come on then, dear Charlotte, we can't keep an angel waiting can we?'

When they reached Anne's cradle they found her smiling contentedly as usual, quietly observing the world around her.

'He's gone! You were too late, and the angel is gone!', shouted Charlotte, and she stamped her feet in frustration.

Patrick laughed heartily at this, which only served to make Charlotte even angrier and more frustrated.

Whether an angel was looking over Anne or not in her childhood we leave you to determine, but it is a tale of Anne's infancy that both Patrick Brontë and Nancy Garrs would repeat.[1] If nothing else, it is a testament to how calm, contented and angelic Anne herself was as a baby.

The loss of Anne's mother and two eldest sisters irrevocably changed the life she could have had, but she was so young when they happened that she did not comprehend the first loss and soon recovered from the next two. Branwell and especially Charlotte would carry the pain around with them to a much greater measure for the rest of their lives.

Strange as it may sound, then, Anne's early childhood was a very happy one, you could say idyllic. It was a period that she would look back on with great fondness, as of a time before the sky took on a darkened hue and when she forged the close friendship with a sister that sustained her through all the suffering that was to come.

Aunt Branwell had taken the place of the mother Anne had never fully known, and although of contrasting characters, they were suited to each other's ways. Aunt Branwell was a woman of very peculiar and precise thinking. After coming to Haworth she put away her make-up and paints, and sold the fancy clothes that she'd worn with pleasure in Penzance and Bradford. Instead, she dressed from head to foot in dark greys and black, as if in perpetual mourning. She clothed herself in the fashion of twenty years before, and therefore all who saw her thought her to be much older than she actually was.

As in all she did, there was method in her madness. Aunt Branwell believed that children should be raised with discipline, first and foremost. By projecting a fierce exterior, she aimed to create obedient and unquestioning young women who would be perfectly suited to a future life as a governess. It did not quite work out like that.

Their surrogate mother was as cold with Emily and Charlotte as the easterly winds that rolled in off the moors around them, but she was much more indulgent with Branwell. She, like Patrick, saw him as the great hope for the Brontë family, and consequently she allowed him many more liberties than she would extend to his sisters.

There was one member of the family, however, that she could be said to have truly loved. Aunt Branwell doted on Anne with as much fervour as the rigidity that she showed to Charlotte and Emily. Who can say why one person loves another? Perhaps it was because Anne bore the name of the mother Elizabeth had loved, or perhaps Anne's infant helplessness evoked the maternal spirit in her? An even more powerful possible reason for her affection is that of all the Brontës, Anne most obviously had the Branwell family blood flowing through her.

From an early age it was clear that she looked unlike her sisters. Charlotte and Emily shared the same mouth, the same strong facial features, with dark hair and hazel eyes. Although there was a great difference in height between them – Emily growing to be the tallest in the family at over five and a half feet tall, while Charlotte would be several inches shy of five feet, and very conscious of it – it was obvious that they were sisters. Anne took her looks from her mother's family, having light brown hair that fell in curls and violet eyes that looked out from a fair and delicate complexion. Her frame would always be slim and short, although a little taller than Charlotte's.

It may be that when Aunt Branwell watched Anne growing up she saw a reminder of her own sisters and for this reason gave her smiles and loving words that were denied to others. For her own part, Anne doted on her aunt like the mother she'd never really known, and would take great interest in everything she had to say, with later consequences that she could not have foreseen.

Aunt Branwell was a very firm follower of the Methodist faith that was then having such an impact on Cornwall and in the north of England. Her spirituality tended more to that favoured by George Whitefield, an early leader of the movement, rather than the more moderate Wesleys.

She believed Whitefield's creed that we live in a harsh and cruel world, and that once we fall into sin we are lost to the fires of hell forever. She would delight in telling Anne about the punishments that such sinners could expect in the afterlife, and her scripture readings would focus on the wrath of God, rather than any hope of redemption. To Aunt Branwell there was no redemption and no loving Father in the heavens. All that was to be done was to strive every day to avoid the temptations that would lead to the devil himself.

So unflinching was she in her views that even the preaching of Patrick, who held a very different idea of his maker, could have no effect on her. Despite her declamations of hellfire and damnation, however, Anne loved her aunt dearly. They shared a room throughout much of Anne's early life, and she would refuse to sleep until her aunt had planted a goodnight kiss on her forehead. In such ways, the bonds of affection were strengthened between them.

Anne recalls this time in her lines from *Agnes Grey*, with the word 'mother' substituting for aunt:

> In my childhood I could not imagine a more afflictive punishment than for my mother to refuse to kiss me at night: the very idea was terrible. More than the idea I never felt, for, happily, I never committed a fault that was deemed worthy of such penalty; but once I remember, for some transgression of my sister's, our mother thought proper to inflict it upon her: what *she* felt, I cannot tell; but my sympathetic tears and suffering for her sake I shall not soon forget.[2]

This illustrates not only Anne's tender feelings for her aunt but also the characteristic sympathy for others that would continue throughout her life. She could never bear to see another person, or creature, suffering.

The Brontë family were soon to gain a new servant who would become very dear to them all. It was at the time that Maria, Elizabeth, Charlotte and Emily were at school. Nancy Garrs had announced that she was to marry, and Patrick, taking advice from his sister-in-law, decided that an old servant was better than a young one such as Sarah Garrs. Nancy and Sarah would continue to be a presence in the parsonage whenever needed, but their permanent place was taken by Tabitha Aykroyd.

Tabby, as she became known to the Brontë children, was then in her 50s, and as typical a model of Yorkshire woman as you could find. She was as broad as she was tall, with hands that always seemed covered in flour. Her black hair was tied back tightly, away from a round face that had the lines of a life well lived. Her accent at first seemed impenetrable to the children, but they soon had great fun imitating her. At this she would call them 'divil's childer', but a smile was never far from her face, and always in her warm heart.

Tabby held great affection for all the children, but as with Nancy and Sarah, she looked most smilingly upon the youngest. She was always 'dear Anne' or 'pretty little Anne'. If left with these temptations alone, she could perhaps have grown up a self-loving or vainglorious child, but Aunt Branwell would guard against that with her constant warnings of how the sins of pride and vanity are punished.

One reason that Anne was so prized was because she was so very frail and delicate. In the same way that our eyes are drawn to a tiny snowdrop that is surrounded by a blanket of grander flora, so all eyes looked to Anne. She was never to have the physical strength that her sisters possessed, and she suffered with asthma from the earliest age. A sudden draught, such as would often blow through the parsonage, would send her shivering to the nearest chair accompanied by wheezing and gasps for air. At these times she would often feel five fingers intertwine with hers.

Emily, although an infant herself, had decided that Anne needed to be cared for and that she was the person to do it. She would wrap her cloak around her younger sister and rock her gently backwards and forwards until the attack subsided. With tears of gratitude, Anne would look up at the face that meant more to her than any other at that time. With Emily beside her, Anne knew she was safe, as did everyone who came near her. Within her woman's body, Emily had a strength and power that could not be denied, and that would ever refuse to be cowed.

For three months, the time between Charlotte leaving for Cowan Bridge and Emily being sent after her, Anne and Emily barely left each other's side. Childlike promises were made that nothing would ever come between them. They took to holding hands everywhere they went, or Emily would have one arm draped protectively around her sister's shoulder, and they became the whole universe to each other.

It may seem strange that a girl who was so strident with those she knew, could be so timid in the presence of others, but this is how it came to pass. Emily had all she needed in her sister and the land around her home that she loved, and she feared the intrusion of anything else. This increased Anne's own natural timidity, until they found it hard to speak to anybody they did not know. At times, when visitors came to the parsonage to see Reverend Brontë, Emily and Anne would hide under tables or in closets, arms huddled around each other for protection against the terror that was other people.

Emily's departure for the school in Westmorland was a dreadful thing for the sensitive young Anne to endure. She was left solely to the teachings of her aunt and would go to bed at night praying that she would not die and be cast into the pits of hell. Without Emily to comfort her, everything seemed oppressive, and she felt a cold melancholia creep over her.

How Anne's heart leaped when her father brought Charlotte and Emily home from Morecambe. Her childish thoughts were too undeveloped to understand the true cost of the loss of her eldest sibling Maria and the impending loss of Elizabeth, but they revelled in an ecstasy at seeing Emily again and feeling her hand once more in her own.

Their temperaments were alike in every way, and people talked of them being inseparable like twins, despite the difference in their appearances. Nothing delighted them more than nature itself, and in Haworth they were truly blessed. Some people revel in lush greenness, in a superabundance of plants and flowers or in tall majestic trees towering as far as the eyes can see. Emily and Anne had none of that. They had bleak moors that stretched all around them, covered in moss, heather or mud, depending upon the seasons, and bedecked by hardy little flowers in the brief summer. Nothing could have been more magical to them or more suited to their character. It was simple, it had no pretence, it had the power of magic about it.

As young children they were taken for a daily walk on the moors that lay directly at the foot of the parsonage. Their aunt did not like to walk, having no appreciation for nature, so they were instead taken by Tabby, Nancy or Sarah – or even Branwell when no one else could be found. He liked to think of himself as a man about the house, the great protector, even though he was a child still and much smaller in stature than Emily. As he marched in front of his troop, he imagined he was the Duke of Wellington surveying Waterloo. These were happy, carefree times that Anne would remember with fondness and clarity.

Sarah Garrs later recalled these early excursions on the moors. 'Their afternoon walks, as they all sallied forth, each comfortably clad, were a joy. Their fun knew no bounds. It was never expressed wildly. Bright and often dry, but deep, it occasioned many a merry burst of laughter. They enjoyed a game of romps, and played with zest.'[3]

On the moors the girls were at one with the world, completely at ease with nature's power in a way that they would never feel in the company of people. On one day in particular, they felt its strength in a way that would mark them forever.

It was 2 September 1824. Although just 4½ at the time, the power and devastation Anne was about to witness would have been a memory that stayed with her throughout her life. The morning had seen heavy rain, as indeed had the week leading up to it. Emily and Anne were feeling miserable at their enforced incarceration, two young girls who longed to be allowed out to play. At last the rains stopped, and they begged to be allowed out. Their aunt would hear nothing of it, but Patrick, a keen walker himself, took their side and said that exercise and fresh air was good for children. Dressed against the elements, they strode forth: Nancy and Sarah Garrs, Anne, Emily, Charlotte and Branwell.

They had walked nearly 2 miles across the moors towards Ponden when the skies suddenly darkened. A great rolling roar could be heard and was then silent. A shower of hailstones came from nowhere and pinged off the children's skin but then vanished as quickly as it started. By now, the sky was as dark as if it was night-time. Nancy and Sarah realised that something was terribly wrong, and they rushed the children towards a building on the horizon. As they got closer they heard a voice calling from the building, urging them to run as fast as they could. This would be Anne's first encounter with Ponden Hall, a building that was to play a central part in her second novel.

Their father too sensed that all was not well. He was at an upstairs window in the parsonage, looking out at the moors and longing to see his family return, but instead he was to see something that nobody in Haworth had seen before or since. It is now recorded as the Crow Hill Bog Burst, although at the time people referred to it as an earthquake.[4]

There was another huge roar, followed by a sound as if the earth was being torn apart. It was heard as far away as Leeds. A violent storm erupted all around the children, and then a huge torrent of mud and water took to the sky, 7ft in height. It rolled onwards, consuming all in its path. Boulders that had seemed great and immovable were lifted up and hurled a mile from where they had started. Thankfully they had found the shelter of a porch just in time. Sarah Garrs covered the children in her cloak and warned them not to watch. Only one pair of eyes disobeyed her. Emily was staring out at the dreadful storm and the destruction it was bringing, with wonder and happiness. Now she saw what nature could do, she loved it even more. What had been silent and still could possess a power within it that was unstoppable. This was how she wanted to be.

The landslip, and subsequent explosion, were caused by the recent storms and flooding eroding the moorland landscape. *The Leeds Mercury* reported the 7ft-high torrent of peat, mud and water that plunged from Crow Hill towards Ponden and added, 'Somebody gave alarm, and thereby saved the lives of some children who would otherwise have been swept away.' The damage caused by the explosion can still be seen on the scarred and cratered moors today.

The great storm passed as quickly as it began, and the group walked home as swiftly as they could over the rain sodden and difficult terrain, realising the distress their absence would be causing their father. Indeed, before they reached Haworth, Patrick ran to them and embraced his children with tears rolling down his cheeks. Unable to watch any longer, he too had braved the storm, and he was now covered in mud from head to foot. The whole party shed tears of relief, except for Emily. A wide smile still played on her face, and her dark eyes sparkled as Anne had never seen before. We can imagine Emily whispering to her beloved sister, 'I did that.'

As they grew older, they were allowed to go out on to the beautiful moors, where Anne would spend so many happy times with the sister she loved so much, in their own company. Emily had by then become a free spirit that nobody could dissuade from doing what she thought was right. Sometimes they would walk up to 20 miles in a day, but Emily knew every stone and every stream of the landscape. Anne's hand held in hers, they were invincible children of nature. As Anne left Haworth on her final journey to Scarborough, she knew that she would never see those moors again, but in her mind she wondered whether Emily saw them still. In her heart she knew that if Emily could leave her celestial home and roam them again, that would be her choice.

A year after the death of her sisters, on 22 May 1850, Charlotte wrote, in a letter to W.S. Williams:

> I am free to walk on the moors – but when I go out there alone everything reminds me of the time when others were with me and then the moors seem a wilderness, featureless, solitary, saddening. My sister Emily had a particular love for them, and there is not a knoll of heather, not a branch of fern, not a young bilberry leaf not a fluttering lark or linnet but reminds me of her. The distant prospects were Anne's delight, and when I look round, she is in the blue tints, the pale mists, the waves and shadows of the horizon. In the hill-country silence their poetry comes by lines and stanzas into my mind: once I loved it – now I dare not read it – and am driven often to wish I could taste one draught of oblivion and forget much that, while mind remains, I never shall forget.[6]

4

YOUTHFUL EXPLORATIONS

The other was a slender girl,
Blooming and young and fair,
The snowy neck was shaded with
The long bright sunny hair
And those deep eyes of watery blue
So sweetly sad they seem'd
And every feature in her face
With pensive sorrow teem'd
The youth beheld her saddened air
And smiling cheerfully
He said 'How pleasant is the land
Of sunny Araby!'

'Alexander and Zenobia'

Anne was the youngest of the Brontë children, but she was much loved by her siblings, her father and her aunt, and they did all they could to make sure that she was included in the older children's games. With no mother to learn from, Anne turned instead to her sisters and brother for inspiration, and she would hang on every word they said, while striving to emulate all they did. In this way she grew quickly in mind if not in body.

From an early age she showed a prodigious intellect that was well beyond her years. This is demonstrated by a recollection that her father gave to Mrs Gaskell at the time when she was writing her celebrated biography of Charlotte Brontë. Patrick was a very busy man, spending much of his day carrying out church services, baptisms and funerals or locked in his study. He believed that his children were too timid to share their true feelings with him, and so he came up with an ingenious way to break down the barriers between them and find out who they really were and how they felt. This is how he explained the scene:

When my children were very young, when as far as I can remember, the oldest was about ten years of age, and the youngest about four, thinking that they knew more than I had yet discovered, in order to make them speak with less timidity, I deemed that if they were put under a sort of cover I might gain my end; and happening to have a mask in the house, I told them all to stand and speak boldly from under the cover of the mask.

I began with the youngest (Anne, afterwards Acton Bell) and asked what a child like her most wanted; she answered, 'Age and experience'. I asked the next (Emily, afterwards Ellis Bell) what I had best do with her brother Branwell, who was sometimes a naughty boy; she answered, 'Reason with him, and when he won't listen to reason, whip him'. I asked Branwell what was the best way of knowing the difference between the intellects of men and women; he answered, 'By considering the difference between them as to their bodies'. I then asked Charlotte what was the best book in the world; she answered, 'The Bible'. And what was the next best; she answered, 'The Book of Nature'.[1]

Patrick then questioned his two eldest children, who were soon to meet their untimely end. He asked the practical Elizabeth what was the best form of education for a woman, to which she answered, 'That which would make her rule her house well'. To his eldest child, Maria, he asked what was the best way of spending time, to which she replied, touchingly under the circumstances, 'By laying it out in preparation for a happy eternity'.

This brief insight into the young Brontës told their father a lot about them, and it's very revealing for us too. We can glean Charlotte's love of reading, even at an early age, which is why Patrick asked what her favourite book was. We also get evidence of Branwell's independent streak and inherent naughtiness at just 7 years old. In opposition to that, we have Emily's common sense and high moral standards. And then, of course, we come to Anne. At just 4 years old she is a bright and precocious girl with a longing for the two things that fate decreed she would never be allowed to receive: age and experience.

We also learn something about the Brontë children as a whole, their love of drama and performance. Patrick realised that many of his children were taciturn by nature and prone to keeping secrets, traits that would remain with them all their lives. He also recognised that they could not resist the chance to perform, and this is the opportunity that a simple prop in the form of a mask gave them. They discovered the thrill that many actors down the centuries have experienced, the chance to set down their normally reserved characters and become someone completely different. Hidden behind the mask they could become like other people: confident, proud, ready to speak the truth come what may. It was something they would later bring to fruition under the masks of Acton, Currer and Ellis Bell.

It is easy to think of the young Brontës as scholarly children, sitting silently over books, somehow out of touch with the reality around them, but in fact they were as lively and fun loving as any other youngsters. Whilst books and magazines certainly did play a big part in their lives, as we shall see, it was their sense of fun and love of playing together that really lit the spark beneath their creativity.

The Reverend Patrick Brontë could be a very serious man, and to the end of his life he preferred spending long hours serving the church or reading and writing about political and social matters of the day to mixing in general society. Nevertheless he delighted in seeing his children happy, and he would often buy them toys, including ninepins, dolls and play houses.

One day he returned from a business journey to Leeds with presents for all his children. It was 5 June 1826, and his present was to change the course of literary history forever. It was late at night when he arrived back at the parsonage, and so the children would not get their gifts until the morning. For the 6-year-old Anne there was the delightful present of a dancing doll, crafted out of paper and with pins jointing the arms and legs allowing it to dance, but it was the present selected for Branwell that was to prove life changing for the whole family. Three years later, Charlotte recollected this day:

> Papa bought Branwell some wooden soldiers at Leeds. When Papa came home it was night, and we were in bed, so next morning Branwell came to our door with a box of soldiers. Emily and I jumped out of bed, and I snatched up one and exclaimed: 'This is the Duke of Wellington! This shall be the Duke!' when I had said this Emily likewise took one up and said it should be hers; when Anne came down, she said one should be hers. Mine was the prettiest of the whole, and the tallest, and the most perfect in every part. Emily's was a grave-looking fellow, and we called him 'Gravey'. Anne's was a queer little thing, much like herself, and we called him 'Waiting-boy'. Branwell chose his, and called him Buonaparte.[2]

It's no surprise that Charlotte should choose the Duke of Wellington's name for her soldier. She had grown up listening to tales of the great war hero, and her obsession with him would last a lifetime. For 10-year-old Charlotte, the Iron Duke and his sons Arthur and Charles Wellesley were as the latest boy band would be to a young girl today. We can only imagine her excitement when she finally met him in London's Chapel Royal nearly a quarter of a century later. In a letter to Ellen Nussey dated 12 June 1850 she described him as a 'real grand old man'.

We should also not be surprised at Branwell's choice of Napoleon, at an early age taking delight in being an anti-hero rather than doing what was expected of him. The names that Charlotte and Branwell bestowed on their sisters' soldiers are also telling. Even at this young age Emily could be gravely serious and quiet, and Anne was small and delicate, even if far from 'queer looking' by the accounts of others.

The soldiers grabbed the attention of all four children, yet we all know how quickly a child can grow tired with what has been their favourite toy. In this instance, however, it was to be an enduring love and one that would kindle the creative spark growing within them. All twelve were given names and their own individual characters. Together they were known as The Young Men or The Twelve, and in the children's minds they were soldiers returning from the Peninsular War and seeking new adventures.

The Peninsular War lasted from 1807 to 1814 and formed part of what we now call the Napoleonic Wars. After years of fighting across Spain and Portugal, the Duke of Wellington, with his Iberian allies, defeated Napoleon and pushed him back to France. Whilst the war was over before any of the Brontë children were born they would have heard all about it from their father, who held a keen interest in all things relating to the military and was also a huge fan of his fellow Irishman, Wellesley.

The children would have also read recollections of the duke's exploits in the newspapers that were taken at the parsonage. In 1829, Charlotte proudly revealed, 'We take 2 or 3 newspapers a week. We take the Leeds Intelligencer, Tory, and the Leeds Mercury, Whig, and see the John Bull: it is high Tory, very violent.'[3]

The girls took after their father's political leanings, becoming passionate Tories themselves. From the earliest age they took an interest in the cut and thrust of British politics, and would discuss matters with each other and with their father. After the death of their sister Maria, it was Branwell who would sit and read to the girls on occasions when their father was too busy or when he was resting his weak eyes. From these papers they not only learned about the political world but also about Britain's military campaigns and the exciting adventures of explorers, like Mungo Park and his successors, who had opened up new continents to British eyes.

These stories were so exciting to the Brontë children that they began to re-enact them using their beloved set of twelve soldiers. It was a small step from here to letting their imagination take flight, and they first did this through the creation of plays. This was a daily occurrence. The four children would gather together for an hour in the evening and use their soldiers as inspiration for tales of heroism and romance which they would then re-enact. By 1829, Charlotte proudly revealed in her 'History of the Year' for 1829 that they had created three great plays entitled *The Young Men, Our Fellows* and *The Islanders*.[4] These were the three plays that were not secret, although she also wrote of 'bed plays' that she composed with Emily and which must remain secret.

Charlotte and Emily were at this time sharing a bed, as was common in this era and necessitated by the lack of space provided by the parsonage. These bed plays show that even when they had retired to bed and were supposed to be sleeping, they were really composing new plays, verbally, well into the night. This was a secret, of course, that had to be kept from their strict Aunt Branwell, whilst the daytime plays could be revealed to all.

Anne was sharing a room with her aunt, so of course there was no hope of any night-time playing there. How she must have yearned for the evening hour when she could join her brother and sisters in inventing their fantastic tales. At any and every opportunity they acted out their wild stories, as shown by one incident when their father and aunt had both left the house, leaving the children in the care of Tabitha Aykroyd.

The children immediately began to act out one of their plays, and they were so immersed in their characters that Tabby had to run screaming from the house to fetch help from her nephew William. The story was later recounted by Francis Leyland, a friend of Branwell who had heard the story from eyewitnesses to the event. He has her saying, 'William! William! Yah mun goa up to Mr Brontë's for aw'm sure yon chiller's all gooin mad, and I dar'nt stop ith house ony longer wi'em; and aw'll stay here woll yah come back!'[5]

Seeing how frightened his Aunt Tabitha was, William marched off to the parsonage, only to be greeted by a 'great cackling of laughter' when he came in sight of the children. They were delighted at how effective their playing and acting had been.

We have a record of another such event. The cemetery of St Michael and All Angels' church lies at the foot of the parsonage garden and is today shaded all round by trees. The garden was very different in the 1820s, however, bare and barren, which is why Patrick Brontë took such pride in the cherry tree growing outside the parsonage. One day, during the course of their playing, the children decided to re-enact the flight of King Charles I after the Battle of Worcester. It was Emily who displayed typical fearlessness and climbed into the tree to act as the king in hiding. Alas one of the branches snapped off, leaving the children less worried about Emily's fall than about what their father would say when he saw the damage.

Showing great ingenuity, they ran to the house next to the parsonage, which was home to John Brown, the young village sexton who had recently succeeded his father in the role. Amused by the girls' antics, he was easily persuaded to paint the damaged area brown in an attempt to cover up the missing branch. Their efforts were to no avail, however, as their father spotted the missing branch immediately upon his return. Nancy Garrs told Patrick that it was she who had accidentally broken the branch, but he must have known the handiwork of his mischievous, fun-loving children.[6]

From this we can see the affection and loyalty to the children of those who knew them, in the way that John Brown and Nancy Garrs attempted to cover for them, but also how boisterous the young Brontës could be. In contrast to their bookish, cloistered image, they loved to play as much as any other children then or now. It's a heartening image when we consider that by this point they had already lost two sisters and a mother.

Patrick Brontë was an enlightened man for the time, and he indulged his children in both their playing and their learning. He had an extensive library himself, and he allowed his children to read any book that they wanted from it rather than saying that some books were unsuitable for girls, as many other fathers would have done. He also passed on the magazines that were to have such an important influence on the next stage of their creative development.

As well as the patriotic *John Bull* magazine, Patrick received a new periodical called *Blackwood's Edinburgh Magazine*, which was lent to him by a parishioner called Dr Driver and then passed on to his children. This magazine featured some of the greatest writers of the day, including James Hogg, known as the Ettrick Shepherd, and Thomas de Quincey, known as the Opium Eater. The magazine featured political and philosophical discussions, as well as reviews of all the latest literary works, often including lengthy extracts from them. Nothing was as eagerly anticipated by the Brontë children as a new edition passed into their eager hands. From 1832, the parsonage also took a subscription to *Fraser's Magazine*, another source of literary news and opinion.

There were some books in the parsonage library that were especially prized by the children's young eyes and minds. *Tales from the Arabian Nights* was read on an almost daily basis, as was *Tales of the Genii* by James Ridley, writing under the pen name of Sir Charles Morrell, and *Aesop's Fables*. They also loved *Gulliver's Travels* and *Pilgrims Progress*, along with the poetry of Lord Byron and Sir Walter Scott. In Christmas 1828 they received Scott's *Tales of a Grandfather* from Aunt Branwell, showing that she did indeed have a thoughtful and caring side. It's a book that recounts a series of tales around episodes of Scottish history, featuring characters such as Mary, Queen of Scots. It was a big hit in the parsonage, and it sparked a lifelong love of Sir Walter Scott and all things Scottish among the Brontës.

Fiction wasn't the only thing that caught their imagination. One particularly cherished book was the beautifully illustrated *A History of British Birds* by Thomas Bewick. We can tell the impact that it had on the children by the fact that it features in two Brontë novels. Bewick's history is the book that Jane Eyre is reading as a child, hidden behind the curtains, before being found and attacked by her monstrous cousin.[7] It is also the book that Helen Huntingdon, the eponymous tenant of Wildfell Hall, gives her son Arthur to read to distract him while she discusses matters of love with Gilbert Markham.[8] We can here read Anne Brontë's own opinion of the book, put into the mouth of the young boy after he runs excitedly towards Gilbert: 'Look, Mr Markham, a natural history with all kinds of birds and beasts in it, and the reading as nice as the pictures!'[9]

As well as Bewick's history, they also delighted in studying the *Grammar of General Geography* by J. Goldsmith (a pen name of Sir Richard Phillips). This collection of maps and drawings showed the growing understanding of the world around Britain as the extent of its military and trade influence grew. Nevertheless, there were vast swathes of land that were still unknown, and it was these that captured the children's imagination. They added details of explorations reported by *Blackwood's*, but there was soon a new land added to the maps: the land that was to become known as the Great Glass Town Confederacy. The Brontës' imaginations had now taken a leap from verbal enactments to the written word.

In their new collaborative adventure, The Twelve had become shipwrecked at the delta of the Niger River and had headed into the heart of Africa to form their own lands. The chief characters were once again the four soldiers that they had snatched so eagerly on that day in 1826. Charlotte's soldier was given control of 'Wellingtonsland'. Branwell's soldier was now called 'Sneaky', from which we again get an early insight into his character, and he formed 'Sneakysland'. Emily and Anne's soldiers had by now taken on the name of two Arctic explorers who had caught their imagination, and Emily was in charge of 'Parrysland' while Anne's soldier founded 'Rossesland'.[10]

At the heart of each land was a capital made of glass, the mighty glass towns themselves, and the lands were populated by lords and ladies, politicians and poets, sorcerers and adventurers. By 1829 their adventures were being chronicled in exquisitely written books that were the size of postage stamps. Examples of the tiny books can be seen today at the Brontë Parsonage Museum, readable only through a powerful magnifying glass.

These famous little books aren't the first example of Brontë writing that we have, however. That honour goes to a charming little story that a 10-year-old Charlotte wrote for her 6-year-old youngest sister, and it begins, 'There was once a little girl and her name was Ane'.[11] The short story is illustrated by the author as well, and it tells of how the little girl explores a castle in London and then sails off on an adventure with her parents, who are very rich. It's a touching story designed to delight young Anne's heart, helping her imagine how life would be if she were from a rich family and still had a mother to love her. It is noted in the story that 'Ane's Mama was very sick and Ane attended her with so much care. She gave her medicine.' Charlotte also gives us a portrayal of Anne as 'not too much indulged' and says that 'by and by she became a good girl'. Charlotte wasn't the only one to produce drawings to please little Anne. Branwell too would draw elaborate pictures of fairy-tale castles and thatched cottages that he inscribed 'for Anne'. It was a brotherly kindness that Anne would always cherish and remember.

Charlotte's composition skills increased immeasurably in the years after this first tale, as we can tell from the little books that she contributed to. Each tiny book was stitched together by hand beneath a brown paper cover, and they tell the complex stories of Glass Town, which would become known as Verdopolis, and then later focused on the nearby land of Angria. Whilst other children in the same era, John Ruskin being a notable example, also produced little books, none possessed the sheer sophistication, wit and flair that the Brontës brought to theirs. Alongside the stories themselves, there are songs, maps and illustrations, as well as miniature adverts for imaginary products that are both satirical and comical.

The smallness of the books served two purposes. Firstly, they were designed to be small enough for the soldiers to read, and secondly, they provided a veil of secrecy, as they would have been completely unreadable to their short-sighted father.

This gave the children free reign over what they wrote, and they made the most of it. Their tiny books were imagined along the lines of *Blackwood's* magazine and were originally titled *Branwell's Blackwoods Magazine*, after the first editor. A year later Branwell relinquished editing duties to Charlotte, although still contributing, and she changed the title to *Young Men's Magazine*. The four children themselves often appeared in the stories under their guises as the four genii that dwelled on Mount Aornos and ruled the kingdoms with a rod of iron.

Branwell is the 'Chief Genius Brannii' who is a 'gloomy giant' who sits enthroned in the clouds. Charlotte is 'Chief Genius Tallii', revealing that her childhood nickname must have been Tally, who 'like a dire eagle flies'. We then learn that 'Emmii and Annii with boding cry, famine and war foretell and mortal misery'.

A vast range of characters spring up throughout the tales of Glass Town and Angria, and soon the stories were gathered on sheets of paper as well as in the self-made books and magazines. All of these tales were written by either Charlotte or Branwell, but it's clear that the younger children Emily and Anne provided stories which were then set down by the older siblings. Tales set in Parrysland and Rossesland have a character of their very own, and indeed the books are full of light-hearted rivalries between the four authors, with Charlotte attacking Emily's Parrysland for being too like Yorkshire and lacking the exciting African feel of Wellingtonsland and Sneakysland.[12]

These early stories saw the development of themes that Charlotte would carry through into her adult novels, and the four young Brontës would eagerly gather around their dining table before bed discussing new tales and relating the latest news from the kingdom, just as if it was a real place. In 1831 this was to come to an abrupt end. Charlotte's godparents, the Atkinsons, had offered to pay to send her to boarding school again. The school suggested was very different to Cowan Bridge, and eventually an initially reluctant Patrick agreed that it was for the best if Charlotte was to become properly equipped for a future career as a governess. On 17 June 1831 she made the journey to Roe Head school at Mirfield, around 14 miles from Haworth. No more would the four Brontës sit around their table composing thrilling stories about the kingdom of Angria.

Although parted, the children would still continue to compose escapist prose and poetry in their own way. Branwell would use the name of his Angrian counterpart Northangerland for poetry that would later be printed in local newspapers. For Anne and Emily, the event marked a liberation and an opportunity finally to unleash their own creativity to the full.

Once more, Anne and Emily were thrust into each other's company, and they revelled in it. During their daily walks on the moors they would continue to conjure up stories about Angria, but before long they decided that this new beginning needed a new kingdom. They wanted a blank canvas to populate with people, towns and events completely of their own choosing, and they soon settled on a name for it: Gondal.

As if to emphasise the break with the African setting of Angria, Gondal was an island in the North Pacific and had a rivalry with the neighbouring island kingdom of Gaaldine. It was now, at last, that the youngest Brontës put pen to paper, initially in their own little books, none of which survive today, and then in prose and poetry that together made up complex and interweaving tales of the heroes and heroines of the islands.

These poems were written under the pseudonyms of Gondalian characters, but then signed and dated by either Anne or Emily. The first surviving poem that we have of Anne's is from December 1836 and is titled 'Verses by Lady Geralda'. It begins:

Why when I hear the stormy breath,
Of the wild winter wind,
Rushing o'er the mountain heath,
Does sadness fill my mind?
For long ago I loved to lie
Upon the pathless moor,
To hear the wild wind rushing by
With never ceasing roar;
Its sound was music then to me
Its wild and lofty voice
Made my heart beat exultingly
And my whole soul rejoice
But now, how different is the sound?
It takes another tone
And howls along the barren ground
With melancholy moan. [13]

We can see here that while Gondal was ostensibly a Pacific paradise, its landscape greatly resembled that which Anne and Emily loved to explore around their home. Readers may also find it strange that Anne talks of how 'long ago I loved to lie upon the pathless moor' at a time when she was only 16 years old.

The truth is that Anne immersed herself in the Gondalian characters, imagining how she would feel if in their shoes. Thus we read in her poetry of this time of love thwarted, people in exile longing for their former lives and people trapped in dungeons reminiscing about the landscapes and people they have left behind.

Lady Geralda was just one of the recurring characters in the Gondal chronicles, alongside women such as Olivia Vernon and Marina Sabia. Anne's main heroine, however, was Alexandrina Zenobia who was embroiled in a complicated love affair with Alexander Hibernia. Such love lay at the very heart of the many intrigues that ran throughout Gondal. Confinement was another common theme in both Emily and Anne's poetry, representing both the confinement of their characters and the physical and mental confinement of the young writers. We can find an example of this in the 17-year-old Anne's 'A Voice From The Dungeon', in which miseries and woes weigh the narrator down.[14]

Like any developing writer, Anne and Emily tended to focus on dramatic events and deeper feelings, which is why grand love and even grander despair feature so heavily in their Gondal poetry. Nevertheless, there are hints of the inner turmoil that Anne was beginning to experience, and this composition dates from the time that Anne herself, by then as we shall see also at Roe Head School, was about to experience a physical and mental breakdown.

Although composed solely by Anne and Emily, these writings were also shared with Charlotte whenever she was back in Haworth, but as the years went by, Emily became more secretive about her own Gondal compositions. Whilst both Anne and Emily would continue to write on Gondal themes into their adulthood, Anne was no longer always privy to Emily's work. In a diary paper written on 30 July 1841, Anne looks ahead to the next diary paper that she planned to write in four years' time and writes: 'I wonder whether the Gondaliland will still be flourishing and what will be their condition? I am now engaged writing the 4th volume of Sofala Vernon's life.'[15]

Sofala was one of the inhabitants of Gondal, and the fact that at the age of 21 Anne was on a fourth volume of her life story shows just how prodigious her Gondal output was. For Emily it was an obsession that she could never shake off. She would write tales of the kingdom until her last days, and for her the divides between Gondal and real life became irrevocably blurred. Anne, in adulthood, would occasionally return to tales of Gondal and Gaaldine, as much out of love for her sister Emily as anything else, but she would soon find a more compelling subject for her writing. Real life was about to intrude.

5

THE HAWORTH
THAT ANNE KNEW

We crossed the valley, and began to ascend the opposite hill.
As we were toiling up, I looked back again: there was the
village spire, and the old grey parsonage beyond it, basking in
a slanting beam of sunshine – it was but a sickly ray, but the
village and surrounding hills were all in sombre shade, and I
hailed the wandering beam as a propitious omen to my home.
With clasped hands, I fervently implored a blessing on its
inhabitants, and hastily turned away; for I saw the sunshine was
departing; and I carefully avoided another glance, lest I should
see it in gloomy shadow, like the rest of the landscape.

Agnes Grey

Haworth today is a beautiful village with a thriving tourist
industry, bringing visitors from all corners of the globe. The
attractions are centred around Main Street, the steep cobbled
road that rises up the hill. It is home to a number of inns, a selection of

guest houses, fine bistros bearing names like 'Villette' and small shops selling art and craft items alongside antique books. Main Street runs from Bridgehouse Lane at the bottom of the hill, with the imposing Haworth Old Hall on the opposite side of the road, to West Street at the top, and near to the summit itself is St Michael and All Angels' church, behind which lies the building that brings all the visitors to the village: the Brontë Parsonage, now a splendid museum run by the Brontë Society.

Being next to the moors, the village is a slave to the vagaries of northern English weather, but on a good sunny day it is an idyllic setting. For the throngs of tourists enjoying an ice cream in the bright Haworth sun it's easy to imagine that it was ever thus, but in fact the Haworth that Anne Brontë and her sisters knew was a very different place indeed. In fact, an official report of the time condemned Haworth as one of the unhealthiest places to live in the whole of England and comparable to the very worst slums of industrial London.

Even the name of the street itself has changed. At the time that the baby Anne was brought by her family to Haworth it was called Kirkgate, meaning the street that led to the church. The change in name to Main Street was a reflection of a change in Haworth itself: it was a village that was growing, that was becoming ever more industrialised. Streets were being created and dwellings were being built, running off Main Street like the becks that ran off the streams on the moors to the south and the west.

The driving factor behind the transformation of Haworth in the early decades of the nineteenth century was the Industrial Revolution. Textile mills surrounded the town, and many Haworth inhabitants found employment in the mills or as wool combers working in cramped houses. The moors, previously home to peat production and sheep farming, were now transformed by stone quarries based around the Penistone Crags.

Records show that the population grew from around 2,350 in 1838 to 2,629 in 1849, the year of Anne's death. This represents a rise of nearly 12 per cent in just over a decade, and the percentage increase is likely to have been just as sharp in the preceding decades of the century. This put an enormous strain on the village's resources and infrastructure, so that whilst some of the traditional families of the village, such as the farmers and landowners on the outskirts of Haworth, lived in comfort, others had to endure extreme poverty and deprivation.

The reason that we know so much about the Haworth of this time is an official report into the village carried out in April 1850 by Benjamin Herschel Babbage, a Superintending Inspector of the General Board of Health.[1] The government had sent Babbage to Haworth to answer petitions from the villagers, and leading these calls was Reverend Patrick Brontë himself.

By October 1849, Patrick had been the Church of England priest in Haworth for nearly thirty years, and in that time he could not fail to notice the astonishing death rate that the village had. Indeed he himself had had to bury his own wife and four of his six children there, with another, Anne, having recently died and been buried in Scarborough. Patrick, and many of his parishioners, believed that it was the unhealthy nature of the village itself that was leading to many deaths that could be prevented, and that's why on 9 October 1849 they sent their first petition to the General Board of Health's headquarters in London. Patrick organised and sent the petition, containing 220 signatures, but this was met with the reply that it could not be considered unless 10 per cent of the rate payers in the village signed it.

As in all things, when Patrick Brontë had set his mind to something he did not let it rest easily, and so he then began a correspondence with the General Board of Health and sent a second petition in October 1849 containing the required amount of signatures. The board wrote back that an inspector would be sent, but months went by without any sign of him. On 5 February 1850, Patrick wrote again:

Having long since petitioned for an authorised agent, to come and look into our situation, with regard to a sufficient supply of pure water, we are much disappointed at not having seen any such agent, nor having got any satisfactory answer to our petition: we would therefore request that you would be so kind as to inform us what we are to expect, or do; and we are the more anxious on this head, as spring and summer are drawing nigh, when the want of pure water would be extremely detrimental.[2]

At last the board were stirred into action and Mr Babbage arrived in Haworth on 4 April 1850. He spent three days in the school room next to the parsonage talking to the villagers, before inspecting conditions himself. His report makes shocking reading,[3] but it was to mark a turning point for Haworth that would save countless lives in the future.

Times were tough and lives were short across the north of England in the mid-nineteenth century, yet Haworth stood out even against this background. The average life expectancy in Haworth at the time that Babbage's report was compiled was 25.8 years,[4] although even that was an improvement on some of the years leading up to it. In 1848, the year of the publication of Anne's *The Tenant of Wildfell Hall*, the average age at death in the village was just 21.7 years. Ten years earlier, in 1838, it had been a mere 19.6 years. One reason that life expectancy was so low was the very real likelihood of infant mortality, with more than 40 per cent of children dying before they reached their 6th birthday.

Babbage calculated that the death rate for Haworth was 44.3 per cent worse than that of neighbouring villages such as Stanbury and Oxenhope. National health laws at this time stated that a mortality rate of 23 in every 1,000 indicated an unhealthy place requiring special remedies to be put in place. Haworth had an average death rate per 1,000 of 25.4, classing it officially as 'a very unhealthy place' and comparable with areas such as Whitechapel in the heart of the London slums.

Patrick Brontë could not help noticing this problem, as it was he who was burying many of these dead, but he had also recognised the source of the problem: sanitation and the village's water supply. At the time of the inspection, Haworth had eleven water pumps, but only nine were in working condition. There were less than seventy toilets for a population of around 2,500 people, and twenty-four houses shared just one toilet. Seven houses were found to have no access to a toilet at all.[5]

In these conditions, 'night soil', as it was called, was simply thrown out of the windows. There were no sewers in the village, so the human waste was left to slide down open gutters that ran along the steep street at the heart of Haworth. There was a slaughter house at the top of the village next to the King's Arms Inn, and some households had a pigsty or kept chickens, so animal waste and remains would mix with the human waste collecting in the gutters.

Even worse than this was the fact that in many cases it was the water itself that was killing the residents, once again owing to the unique situation the village found itself in. The water that collected in the wells, ready to be pumped out, would first run down the hills and across the graveyard next to Reverend Brontë's church. There are believed to be as many as 40,000 bodies buried in this cemetery, many in hidden mass graves. This graveyard had no trees around it at the time and was covered in flat stones. Babbage singled this out as a particular concern, claiming that it prevented air getting into the ground and aiding decomposition, and that the lack of trees and vegetation meant that there was nothing to prevent the disease ridden gases that rose up from the graves.

On particularly wet days, of the kind Haworth often enjoys, foul black liquid would pool on the flagstone floor of the church itself. This was one of the reasons that much of the church was demolished and rebuilt after the time of the Brontës. The water the villagers used on a daily basis would have crossed this vale of contamination on the way to the pumps, and this was a major reason why the death rate was so unusually high in Haworth.

After the report was completed, there was more silence from the General Board of Health, but after yet more prompting from Patrick, at last action was taken. The cemetery was extended and trees were planted all around it. Sanitation and water supply to the village was improved, and a purpose built reservoir was created to serve Haworth. The slaughtering of animals was forbidden in all but one specific area. The deadliest days were coming to an end, but too late for Anne and her siblings, and too late for countless others whose names history has forgotten.

The greatest area of deprivation in Haworth lay through a narrow entranceway opposite the church called Gauger's Croft, at the time spelled 'Guager's Croft'. This was an area of ramshackle, quickly built houses that was given the grand name of 'Piccadilly'. It quickly became notorious as the Pick, a place where people worked and died in appalling conditions. This was the area where the villagers worked as wool combers. It was hard, laborious, unremitting work, as Babbage found:

In order to obtain the proper temperatures for this operation, iron stoves are fixed in the rooms where it is carried on, which are kept alight day and night and the windows are seldom, if ever, opened. In some cases, I found that the business was carried on in bedrooms, which consequently became very close and unhealthy from the high temperature maintained by the stoves and the want of ventilation.[6]

Often a house would be shared, with large families living in just one room. Babbage found a cellar dwelling where one family of seven shared two beds in a room that also passed as a wool comber's shop. In circumstances such as these, it's little wonder that Haworth became a kingdom where disease and death held sway.

There were regular epidemics of typhus, cholera and whooping cough that swept through Haworth on an annual basis, and simply to live in the village was to be surrounded by people who had a collection of contagious and deadly diseases. The Brontës themselves were in a more privileged position than most, as the parsonage was one of only twenty-four dwellings that had its own privy, and it was also one of only two buildings that had access to its own water supply via a spring. Nevertheless, the threat of disease and infection was never far away.

Haworth was a bustling and ever growing village, with the expanding town of Keighley just 4 miles beyond it and Bradford beyond that. It would be a mistake, however, to think that this proximity of urban centres, and the industrial growth of Haworth itself, meant that the Brontë sisters did not live in a form of isolation compared to our modern way of living. Whilst Keighley was nearby, the 4 miles to it cannot be measured in modern terms. In the first half of the nineteenth century even such a short journey across the hilly, moor-clad surrounds of Haworth could be arduous and problematic.

There would, of course, have been many visitors to the parsonage, even though Patrick Brontë became more insular as he got older. That does not, however, mean that the Brontë children would have come into any meaningful contact with them, other than faces half glimpsed as they went by windows or doorways, or sitting nearby during church services.

Anne gives an indication of this in the first chapter of *Agnes Grey*:

> We never even went to school; and, as there was no society in the neigh-
> bourhood, our only intercourse with the world consisted in a stately
> tea-party, now and then, with the principle farmers and tradespeople of
> the vicinity (just to avoid being stigmatised as too proud to consort with
> our neighbours).[7]

As daughters of the parson, it may be that from time to time as they got older the daughters would have been called upon to carry out some of the social duties that would in other circumstances have been expected to fall on their mother. As the oldest daughter, it's likely that Charlotte would have been first choice for such duties, and whilst she, like her sisters, could be very shy, she would always strive to overcome it.

Emily would have been the next in line, but it was a task for which she was completely unsuited. Emily could be paralysed by timidity when in the company of people she did not know. It has been said that sometimes when people spoke to her she would stand in complete silence, unable to speak or move. Whenever Charlotte heard that Emily had been out in company, her first concerned questions would always be to ask how she had behaved.

In these circumstances Anne may have been preferred to carry out occasional duties as she got older, particularly when Charlotte was away at school. These may have included carrying messages to and from the parsonage or even visiting sick parishioners with her father. Whilst Anne too was painfully shy, she always put her sense of duty first, as her later actions show. In fact, out of all the Brontë children, Anne was to be the only one who would successfully hold on to a job for any length of time, even though she sometimes found it a dreadful ordeal to do so.

There were, however, certain members of Haworth society that Anne, Charlotte, Emily and Branwell would become acquainted with. Foremost among these was their servant Tabby Aykroyd. It is clear that between children and servant there developed a close bond. Unlike their strict aunt, Tabby would indulge their childish play and curiosity, and they found love and happiness in her company. Anne, Charlotte and

Emily would gather round her as she prepared meals or did the house-work, and she would relate tales that they listened to enthralled. Tabby's tales were not only the everyday gossip of Haworth and its surrounds but also the Yorkshire fairy stories and myths that had been passed on verbally for centuries.

At Tabby's feet, the children would hear about ghosts roaming the moors, about fairies, known as feys, who would snatch children away and replace them with goblins and sprites, and about strange creatures who had come straight from hell itself. She claimed to know people who had met feys and lived to tell the tale, but she said that increasing industriali-sation had driven many of the 'little folk' away. In the children's young writing, and in *Wuthering Heights* especially among their adult work, we can see what a profound and positive influence Tabby's storytelling had.

Tabby grew old in the parsonage surrounded by love and respect. This is demonstrated by an incident of December 1836. Haworth's Main Street could be treacherous in winter, and it was cobbled to give both human feet and horse hooves more grip in such conditions. Nevertheless, Tabby slipped on the ice and broke her leg. By this time she was 65 years old; Aunt Branwell insisted that they get rid of Tabby as she was a burden on the family and no longer able to do her work. The teenage Brontë children fiercely resisted this, insisting that they would look after her just as she had looked after them. They even refused to eat until the decision was reversed, and under these circumstances Tabby was allowed to stay.[8]

Tabby stayed in the employ of the parsonage for the rest of her life, outliving all the children except Charlotte, and she is now buried at the foot of the parsonage garden. As Tabby's leg would never fully heal and her movements were often restricted, Emily took on much of the day-to-day running of the house, including baking bread that the villagers said was the best they had ever tasted.

A new servant was brought in to help in 1839, Martha Brown. She was the 11-year-old daughter of John Brown, the sexton who had painted the tree that the Brontë children damaged during their play. John Brown had inherited the role of sexton from his father, and it was an essential job that was traditionally passed among the Brown family of Haworth. He lived in Sexton House, a short stroll from the parsonage itself.

John was a very hard-working man, as he had to be organising and preparing the huge number of burials that Haworth endured on a yearly basis. Like many working men of the time, he found solace in ale, and he was to become a regular drinking partner of Branwell. There was no shortage of places to enjoy their recreation. Right next to the church itself was the Black Bull Inn, while just as close to the parsonage on the other side was the White Lion Inn, run by William Garnett. Across from The White Lion Inn was the King's Arms, which at one point was run by Branwell's friend Enoch Thomas. It doubled as the site of the Manorial Courts, and its cellars held coffins waiting to be interred as well as kegs of ale, stout and porter. Just a short walk down Main Street was the Fleece Inn, and further hostelries could be found on West Street.

Spirits were also dispensed at shops along Main Street, which gave the streets making up the Pick their alternative name of 'Brandy Row'. Spirits and wine weren't only used as an inebriating drink, they were also considered to be a primary medicine. Adults and children alike were given wine or port to drink to ward off all manner of illnesses, so it's likely that Anne herself would often have been given it as treatment for her asthma and her regular attacks of cold and influenza.

People with illnesses of all kinds could also find cures at the apothecary shop on Main Street, near to the entrance to the Pick. Whilst medical knowledge and understanding was growing at this time, many of the treatments would amaze us today, especially the ubiquitous use of cocaine, morphine and opium, a forerunner of heroin. Laudanum, a mixture of opium and alcohol, was often used to help children sleep, as well as being used to treat everything from toothache to cholera. It's a highly addictive combination, and one that Branwell Brontë was to fight a losing battle against.

Away from the village of Haworth itself, the moors stretched out invitingly into the distance, in the summer months taking on a beautiful purple hue thanks to the predominant heather, while in other seasons being bare and brown or white with snow. Some of the locations found on the moors today have become particularly associated with the Brontës, including the abandoned farmhouse known as Top Withens, often spoken of as a possible inspiration for Wuthering Heights in the novel of the same name. Around a mile and a half across the moors from the parsonage is what is now known as the Brontë Falls. This waterfall can be a spectacular sight after heavy rain, and Emily and Anne loved to sit here and watch the water thundering by. The stone where they sat has been worn naturally into a chair-like appearance and is now known as the Brontë Seat. It is here that the two sisters would have discussed plots for their Gondal stories and their plans for the future. They would also gather plants and flowers, and as Anne revealed in her poem 'Memory' it was primroses, that 'source of strange delight', that she held a special love for.

It is primroses too that Anne's heroine Agnes Grey longs for as she walks through a beautiful countryside that, alas, is unlike the moors of home that she left behind:

> As my eyes wandered over the steep banks covered with young grass and green-leaved plants, and surmounted by budding hedges, I longed intensely for some familiar flower that might recall the woody dales or green hillsides of home: the brown moor-lands, of course, were out of the question. Such a discovery would make my eyes gush out with water, no doubt; but that was one of my greatest enjoyments now. At length I decried, high up between the twisted roots of an oak, three lovely primroses, peeping so sweetly from their hiding-place that the tears already started at the sight.[9]

Whilst Top Withens was already falling into disrepair at the time of the Brontës, there was another building on the moors that was anything but. It was the impressive and imposing Ponden Hall, seat of the grand Heaton family, and a place that Anne and Emily would often visit on their travels. The Heatons were at the very summit of society in the Haworth area, and although the Brontës could not match up to them socially, they were always welcome visitors owing to the father's position as head of the church.

The Heatons weren't just wealthy landowners, they were also entitled to be trustees and church wardens of St Michael & All Angels' church. They were a learned family, and their library held thousands of books, many of them rare. It's for this reason that Emily in particular spent time there, especially after Anne followed Charlotte to school. Ponden Hall shares many features given to Wildfell Hall in Anne's second novel, including its central portico beneath a date plaque and the tall latticed windows, making it the likely inspiration for the home of *The Tenant of Wildfell Hall*, although she moved the setting of Wildfell Hall to a coastal region reminiscent of Scarborough for the novel's purposes.

The Heaton family were firm followers of the Church of England in Haworth at the time of the Brontës, but you may be surprised to hear that they were in the minority. Haworth's church had gained great prominence and celebrity thanks to its incumbent priest from 1742 to 1763: William Grimshaw. Grimshaw was at the forefront of the evangelical movement that transformed the Church of England in the eighteenth century, alongside the famous brothers John and Charles Wesley. Grimshaw often preached on the moors outside Haworth to crowds of thousands, and his lasting fame meant that it was a very prestigious position to be given, even though it wasn't a lucrative one, as church statutes required that some of the income from the parish had to be paid as dues to the vicar of Bradford.

The movement founded by Grimshaw, George Whitefield and the Wesleys became known as Methodism. When Anne was young, Methodism was still ostensibly part of the Church of England, but it was becoming increasingly separate. New Methodist churches were built in Haworth, as were churches for the increasingly popular Baptist movement. An ecclesiastical survey of March 1851 found that only 15 per cent of the village's church goers went to the official Church of England church, St Michael's & All Angels', compared to 16 per cent who went to the Lower Town Wesleyan Methodists church and 35 per cent who went to the Hall Green Baptists church, with the remainder attending other Baptist and Methodist churches.[10]

Thus the traditional Church of England was in a tiny minority, yet all residents had by law to contribute to the church rates for St Michael's & All Angels'. This proved to be highly controversial, often bordering on inflammatory, and it was only Patrick's force of character, and respect within the community, that stopped the regular stand-offs erupting into violence.

As the attack on Rawfolds Mill in 1812 had demonstrated, the West Riding of Yorkshire was a tinderbox waiting for a spark. The Luddites were replaced in turn by Chartists seeking social and political reform. The threat of danger always hung in the air, and Patrick Brontë himself always kept two loaded pistols by his bedside. Once loaded, the pistols could not be unloaded again, and it was deemed unsafe to keep them primed and ready during the day, so every morning Patrick would discharge them by firing them out of his window at the church clock tower. It still bears shot marks today, and as well as providing a practical purpose it served as a reminder to the residents of Haworth that here was a priest and a family that wasn't to be messed with. In later years, with Branwell either unwilling or unfit to take on the mantle, Patrick taught Emily how to shoot pistols, and he was impressed by how expert she became.

The Haworth stationer John Greenwood, well known to the family, records how this went:

Patrick had such unbounded confidence in his daughter Emily that he resolved to learn her to shoot too. They used to practice with pistols. Let her be ever so busy in her domestic duties, whether in the kitchen baking bread at which she had such a dainty hand, or at her studies, rapt in a world of her own creating – it mattered not; if he called upon her to take a lesson, she would put all down. His tender and affectionate 'Now, my dear girl, let me see how well you can shoot today', was irresistible to her filial nature and her most winning and musical voice would be heard to ring through the house in response, 'Yes, papa' and away she would run with such a hearty good will taking the board from him, and tripping like a fairy to the bottom of the garden, putting it in its proper position, then returning to her dear revered parent, take the pistol which he had primed and loaded for her … She would take the weapon with as firm a hand, and as steady an eye as any veteran of the camp, and fire. Then she would run to fetch the board for him to see how she had succeeded. And she did get so proficient, that she was rarely far from the mark. His 'how cleverly you have done, my dear girl', was all she cared for. 'Oh!' He would exclaim, 'she is a brave and noble girl. She is my right-hand, nay the very apple of my eye!'[11]

Whilst Haworth today is very different to the Haworth that Anne Brontë knew, the parsonage itself is very similar in all but three aspects. John Wade, the priest who succeeded Patrick Brontë in 1861, added a new wing to the parsonage building, but the main part of the parsonage still contains many of the items that would have been there at the time of Anne, from the upright piano that she loved to play, to the dining table that the sisters wrote at, and upon which Emily has scratched her initial.

One thing it has today that it did not have during much of Anne's time there is curtains. Patrick had a phobia about house fires and thought that curtains were a major contributor to them. For this reason he insisted that all the windows remained bare, although Charlotte later persuaded him to allow curtains to be used. He had also had to bury many girls who had died after their dresses had caught fire, a common occurrence in days when cooking and heating were both provided by open flames. This is why Patrick always insisted, despite his financial constraints, that his daughters wore silk clothing that was less combustible than wool or linen.

In the time that Anne lived there, the house would also be filled with pets. Anne and Emily especially loved animals, and their keeping of pets was another victory they enjoyed over Aunt Branwell, who disapproved of having animals in their home. Together they raised a hawk, called Nero, which they had found injured on the moors, and they also had geese named Adelaide and Victoria after the royal princesses. Over the years they also had pheasants, rabbits, a canary called Little Dick, a cat called Tom and, of course, the most famous Brontë pets of them all, Emily's dogs Grasper and Keeper and Anne's dog, Flossy.

At four-yearly intervals Anne and Emily would write diary papers detailing a day in their lives. The first we have a record of was composed jointly by them on 24 November 1834, and although hastily written, and full of the spelling mistakes that characterised their early writing, it provides a glimpse of their domestic lives:

I fed Rainbow, Diamond, Snowflake, Jasper, Pheasent. Anne and I have been peeling apples for Charlotte to make an apple pudding ... Tabby said just now come Anne pilloputate (ie pill a potato) Aunt has come into the kitchen just now and said 'where are your feet Anne?' Anne answered 'On the floor Aunt'… The Gondals are discovering the interior of Gaaldine, Sally Mosley is washing in the back kitchin.

It is past twelve o'clock Anne and I have not tided ourselves, done our bed work done our lessons and we want to go out to play. We are going to have for dinner boiled beef, turnips, potato's and apple pudding, the kitchin is in a very untidy state. Anne and I have not done our music exercise which consists of b major. Tabby said on my putting a pen in her face 'Ya pitter pottering there instead of pilling a potate', I answered 'O Dear, O Dear, O Dear, I will directly'. With that I get up, take a knife and begin pilling.[12]

While death and disease was an everyday threat in Haworth itself, we see here that at the end of 1834 Anne and Emily still found a childish bliss in each other's company, safe within the four walls of the parsonage. That was to change within months, and to change forever, as Anne was sent to join her sister Charlotte at school.

6

A Purification Of Fire

And, O! there lives within my heart
A hope long nursed by me,
(And should its cheering ray depart
How dark my soul would be)
That as in Adam all have died
In Christ shall all men live
And ever round his throne abide
Eternal praise to give;
That even the wicked shall at last
Be fitted for the skies
And when their dreadful doom is past
To life and light arise.
I ask not how remote the day
Nor what the sinner's woe
Before their dross is purged away,
Enough for me to know
That when the cup of wrath is drained,
The metal purified,
They'll cling to what they once disdained,
And live by Him that died.

'A Word to the Calvinists'

The deaths of Maria and Elizabeth Brontë in 1825, as a result of the living conditions at their Cowan Bridge school, was a pivotal moment in the lives of the four remaining children. Their father, now grieving for his wife and two eldest daughters, was determined to hold on to the family that he had left. He became fiercely protective of Charlotte, Branwell, Emily and Anne, and one way it manifested itself was in their programme of home schooling.

Patrick was, by instinct, a man with a deep reverence for formal education, which is why he would always do all he could to encourage the education of the children within his parishes. He only had to look at his own history to see how schooling could take a child from an impoverished background and set them on course for a completely different life. Nevertheless, the fallout from Cowan Bridge shook him deeply and left him with a moral dilemma: he believed in education for his children, he wanted education for his children, yet he could not countenance, could not cope with, the possibility of the loss of any more of his children. There was only one decision he could make, his children would not be schooled with others, they would remain with him.

Charlotte and Emily at least had some experience of attending school, even if very inadequate and in Charlotte's case mentally scarring, but for Anne as the years at home passed by it seemed that there was no possibility of her ever gaining a formal education. Whilst attendance at school for the Brontë children had been ruled out, seemingly for good, they were still to receive an education that was as good, if not better, than they could have found elsewhere.

For young women of this time, the first half of the nineteenth century, there were few options available to them. As daughters of a Church of England priest, the Brontës were deemed respectable by society but solidly lower-middle class. Their future lives held only two possibilities: they would become governesses teaching the children of people who belonged to a higher social strata or they would marry somebody of a similar social background. In all likelihood, this meant marriage to a priest within the Church of England.

Life as a governess could be hard and unforgiving, with the governess being almost a pariah in the household in which they worked, too lowly to mix with the master and mistress of the house, yet too elevated to fit in with the other domestic servants. It was a life that Anne would systematically dissect in her first novel *Agnes Grey*, and it opened the eyes of many of its upper-class readers to what the existence of their own governesses must really be like. One such reader, Lady Amberley, noted in her diary, 'Read Agnes Grey, and should like to give it to every family with a governess and shall read it through again when I have a governess to remind me to be human.'[1]

Nevertheless, this was the only likely career open to the sisters, and so the home education that was designed by their father had this primarily in mind. The majority of their teaching was put in the hands of their aunt. An educated woman herself, she would teach them their reading, writing and arithmetic, as well as the essential skills of sewing and dressmaking. They would also learn about cooking and baking, and the everyday domestic management of a home, from Tabby Aykroyd.

Sewing was the skill that Aunt Branwell prized above all others. She would have them sewing for long hours at a time, a task that must have been onerous to all three daughters: Anne and Emily because they would long to be playing outdoors and Charlotte because she, like her father, was very short-sighted and the minute detail required would have tested her to the limit. These lessons, however, provided practical benefits for the present as well as the future. Money was always scarce in the parsonage at this time, and the girls would have to be able to make their own clothing as well as mend them until it became impossible to mend them anymore. They would often be reliant on clothing being sent to them by their godparents or from friends. We can see from some of Charlotte's letters on such occasions the pain it must have caused to the girls' pride, but they had little choice but to accept the charity being offered them.

One such example, of many, can be found on 4 July 1834, when she writes to Ellen Nussey:

I must thank you for your very handsome present. The bonnet is pretty, neat and simple, as like the giver as possible. It brought Ellen Nussey with her fair, quiet face, brown eyes, and dark hair full to my remembrance. I wish I could find some other way to thank you for your kindness than words. The load of obligation under which you lay me is positively over-whelming, and I make no return.[2]

As a young girl Anne was a keen and quick learner. Her character meant that she always wanted to please others, especially her father and her aunt. Although the youngest, she wanted to be seen as on a par with her sisters, and she would never allow herself to be indulged because of her lack of years. One of the crowning moments of a young girl's education at that time was the sampler. It is a piece of hand-stitched embroidery containing the letters of the alphabet, numbers and a piece of scripture accompanied by decorative flourishes. It was effectively a sewing gradu-ation piece, showing that a girl had mastered the craft and demonstrating what she could do.

Anne's sampler is now one of the treasures held at the Brontë Parsonage Museum in Haworth. It is intricate and delicately finished, and her two selections of scripture reveal a lot about Anne as a girl, and the woman she would grow up to be. The first is from Psalm 118: 'It is better to trust in the LORD than to put confidence in man.' Her second choice, from the book of Numbers, is moving and appropriate: 'Let me die the death of the righteous, and let my last end be like his.' Underneath this, Anne adds her embroidered signature, 'Anne Bronte: Finished this sampler Nov 28, 1828.'

Reading lessons would be centred upon the Bible, yet the children were fortunate in that their aunt, whilst often strict and unbending, was just as much a lover of literature as their father, so she would also encour-age them to develop more extensive reading habits.

Supplemental lessons to those given by their aunt would be provided by Patrick Brontë himself. It was he who taught them languages, history and their particular favourite, geography, sometimes allowing them to sit in on the lessons that were given to their brother Branwell. All in all, under the constrained circumstances that had fallen on them, it was as full and rounded an education as they could have had.

Patrick delighted in seeing his daughters happy, and he would indulge them as much as his money allowed. Proof of this can be found in the extra-curricular teaching that he arranged for them. Drawing and painting was a valuable skill for a future governess to have, and from an early age the children displayed a joy of painting and a real talent for it. Recognising this, Patrick arranged for all four of his children to receive tuition from John Bradley, an accomplished painter and art tutor based in Keighley. The results can be seen in some of the fine drawings and sketches that all three sisters left us, as well as in Branwell's future choice of portrait artist as his career.

The children would have been taught to copy popular paintings of the day, as well as drawing still life and from nature. Anne's drawings show a particular talent for capturing the personality of the subject, drawing the truth rather than the stylised ideal often portrayed at the time. Still other pictures take on a symbolic nature, showing that Anne was using her drawing to interpret her inner feelings rather than being purely representational.

The sisters also displayed an early appreciation of music. Their father would sometimes take them to listen to concerts put on by the Haworth Operatic Society, as well as to musical concerts in nearby Keighley. Anne and Emily especially had a love of music, and we can imagine their delight when, in late 1833 or during 1834, Patrick Brontë took delivery, much to their surprise, of an upright cabinet piano made by John Green of Soho Square, London. Again, as with many of the material acquisitions of the parsonage, it is likely that a kindly godparent or two helped with the cost of this purchase.

Branwell was already an accomplished player, being used as the organist at the parish church as well as being a keen flautist, and he would have been delighted to teach his sisters. The role of tutor appealed to his pride, and the compliments his sisters would have paid him as he showed off his skills would have been the greatest payment he could have asked for. Soon, however, both Anne and Emily were as proficient at the piano as he was.

Emily in particular was said to be a very accomplished pianist for one who was largely self-taught, although a tutor known to Patrick did provide them occasional music lessons in the parsonage. Ellen Nussey, always one who was moderate and precise in her judgements on people, was so impressed that she described Emily as playing 'with brilliance and precision'.[3] Ellen then described Anne: 'She also played, but preferred soft melodies and vocal music. She sang a little; her voice was weak, but very sweet in tone.'[4]

It's easy to imagine the happy times that the two sisters, who loved each other's company so much, must have spent playing the piano together, Emily playing the left side of the keyboard and Anne the right. When we read Ellen's assessment of both Emily and Anne's prowess, it's worth remembering that standards of piano playing among the public, or at least the portion of the public who could afford a piano, were much greater then than they are today. Therefore the ability of both girls would probably be viewed as exceptional to a modern listener. Charlotte, alas, was never to master the piano, as her poor eyesight made it difficult for her to read the music as she played, even when wearing the small circular glasses that she would adopt when not in company.

Whilst Emily was the better pianist, it was Anne who was the true music lover of the family. Throughout her later days as a governess, she would spend any money that she deemed spare on sheet music, so that she had an ever-expanding repertoire. She copied many of these scores by hand, and we still have her music books full of her notations. The music that she played, and her understanding and adaptation of it, shows that her skills were far above what could be called 'ordinary'. She had a particular love for light opera, which required skill and delicacy from both the pianist and the singer, and we can see that among her very favourite composers were Rossini, Weber and Mozart.

As Ellen has confirmed, Anne did not simply play, she sang along as well. Always a quiet speaker, as a result of the shyness that she fought so hard to overcome, she was a quiet singer too, so would have modulated the volume of her piano playing accordingly. Quiet though Anne was, she was also a beautifully melodic singer. Patrick in particular would love to listen to his youngest daughter sing, and he would often call for it at the end of hard and wearing days.

We see Anne's love for these activities, and the appreciation of her father, in *Agnes Grey* when she describes the heroine's melancholy preparation for leaving home: 'I had played my last tune on the old familiar piano, and sung my last song to papa.'[5]

By this time, the girls were in their teens and were adequate sewers and dressmakers, excellent at drawing, had well-developed musical talents, were avid readers and very keen writers, and had at least a basic knowledge of all the subjects they could be expected to know. Nonetheless, Patrick still worried that without at least some formal education they might struggle in their future pursuit of a life as a governess.

By 1831, six years had passed since the deaths of Maria and Elizabeth. The scars still ran deep, but time can be a great healer. When the Atkinsons suggested that they would like to pay for their goddaughter Charlotte to go to boarding school, he considered it seriously. He researched it thoroughly, and found that the suggested school, Roe Head, was very different to Cowan Bridge. The woman in charge of the school, Miss Margaret Wooler, was a caring and enlightened woman. The school itself was well maintained, with adequate provisions given to the pupils. Best of all it was situated in the hills above the village of Mirfield, a short walk from Hartshead where Patrick had once been priest and where his daughters Maria and Elizabeth had been born. Patrick knew the local clergy, and his good friends the Franks were also nearby and could be relied upon to keep a close eye on his daughter.

Thus it was that in July 1831 Charlotte made the journey to her second school, and she would find it very different to her first. It was a place where girls were encouraged to learn, free from the fear of physical punishment and, even more importantly, free from the physical hunger and risk of disease that always hung over Cowan Bridge.

Charlotte left the school in 1832 and returned to Haworth, but in her year at Roe Head she had studied diligently and learned a lot that she would later pass on to her sisters. There were only nine other pupils at the time Charlotte was in attendance, but two of them, Ellen Nussey of Birstall and Mary Taylor of Gomersal, would go on to be her lifelong friends.

Ellen Nussey would become a regular visitor to the Haworth Parsonage, and in time she would become a close confidante of Anne and Emily as well as Charlotte. Ellen herself had much in common with the Brontës: she was a thoughtful, intelligent woman from a large middle-class family whose fortune was rather less than outward appearances suggested. She had only one living parent, as her father had died when she was young.

She too had a brother who would suffer from alcohol and drug addiction, and he would spend long periods in a mental asylum. Although described as being pretty, she never married and seems to have had a pact with Charlotte that they would grow old together as 'old maids'. It is this in part that explains her fury when Charlotte later became engaged, an event that created a year-long hiatus in their communications, which had otherwise been conducted on an almost daily basis. She lived to the ripe old age of 80, and it is largely thanks to her collection of letters and loyalty to the Brontës that we know so much about them.

Ellen made her first visit to see Charlotte in Haworth in July 1833, and she would stay for three weeks. Her record of the event is detailed and illuminating. Here is her description of the parsonage itself, reflecting Patrick's distrust of curtains and drapery:

> There was not much carpet anywhere except in the sitting room, and on the centre of the study floor. The hall floors and stairs were done with sand stone, always beautifully clean as everything about the house was … Scant and bare indeed many will say, yet it was not a scantness that made itself felt. Mind and thought, I had almost said elegance, but certainly refinement, diffused themselves over all, and made nothing really wanting.[6]

Ellen also described the gardens, again noting how bare it was, except for a 'few currant bushes which Emily and Anne treasured as their own fruit garden'.[7]

She was a very clear and perceptive judge of character, and she noted how methodical Patrick could be. At eight every night he would gather the family for prayers. At nine he locked the front door and went to bed, always pausing to wind up the majestic grandfather clock on the middle of the stairs. His last call would be to his children, who stayed up later than him, telling them not to be late to bed. Ellen noted how cold and stern Reverend Brontë could appear, but she detected the warmth that he hid underneath this front. In Ellen's view it was a tragedy that Patrick had become a priest, when he would have been more suited as a soldier. She was less forgiving in her opinion of Aunt Branwell, although she did note that she treated her favourite niece Anne kindly.

Of Emily, then just turning 15, Ellen reveals:

> Emily had by this time acquired a lithesome, graceful figure. She was the
> tallest person in the house, except her father. Her hair, which was naturally
> as beautiful as Charlotte's, was in the same unbecoming tight curl and frizz,
> and there was the same want of complexion. She had very beautiful eyes,
> kind, kindling, liquid eyes; but she did not often look at you: she was too
> reserved. She talked very little.[8]

Ellen took an immediate liking to both Emily and Anne, sensing that
there was something out of the ordinary about them. Of Anne herself she
writes, 'Anne, dear, gentle Anne, was quite different in appearance from
the others. She was her aunt's favourite. Her hair was a very pretty, light
brown, and fell on her neck in graceful curls. She had lovely violet-blue
eyes, fine pencilled eyebrows, and clear, almost transparent complexion.'[9]
Following on from her observation of how Emily 'talked very little',
Ellen continued, 'She and Anne were like twins – inseparable companions,
and in the very closest sympathy, which never had any interruption.'[10]
Ellen also noted that whilst quiet in the parsonage, both Anne and
Emily would come to life when on their beloved moors. She would
remain a part of their lives, and become a true friend, until their very
last days.

Patrick was very impressed at the progress that Charlotte had made
in her year at Roe Head, and his fears of a second Cowan Bridge were
allayed, yet the funds were not there to allow Charlotte to continue her
education or to send her sisters after her. A new plan was hatched where
Charlotte became teacher to her younger siblings, passing on all the
knowledge she had learned.

Two years later, she would have the opportunity to put those teaching
skills to good use. The head of the school, Miss Wooler, remembered her
former pupil; she must have been very impressed with her abilities, for
in 1835 she invited Charlotte to return to Roe Head, this time in the
capacity of a teacher.

It was Charlotte who initiated this offer, having read that the school
had advertised for a teacher. Charlotte had been initially reluctant to seek

any position, she felt at home again among her family, and some of the demons within her were at rest while she could pursue her writings with Branwell, Emily and Anne. In opposition to this instinct, she realised that she needed to contribute somehow to the running of the parsonage, and the offer that came back from Miss Wooler was very appealing in this aspect. Not only would Charlotte receive a salary, although it was very small even for the time, but as part of the deal one of her sisters would receive free schooling. In this way, there would be two fewer mouths to feed and clothe at the parsonage.

As the eldest of the remaining sisters, it was naturally Emily who was awarded this scholarship. Branwell too was about to leave for pastures new, a helpful godparent having offered to pay for Branwell to train to be an artist at the Royal Academy Schools in London. By this time, however, the young man's behaviour was already becoming erratic, and although he left for London, he never entered the Royal Academy. The Brontë family unit was being broken up, and it would never again fit together in the same way.

Charlotte and Emily left on the near 20-mile winding coach journey to Mirfield on 29 July 1835. It was the day before Emily's 17th birthday, and the parting must have been hard to bear for both her and Anne. Their idyllic childhood days of playing together, writing together, playing music together and revelling in a silence together were finally ended.

Charlotte, as we shall see, was unsuited to the life of a teacher, but Emily was even more unsuited to the life of a pupil, even in a benign environment such as Roe Head. She missed the days spent baking bread with Tabby, she missed her pets, she missed the long walks on the moors and with that she also missed Anne, the sister who accompanied her on them.

To talk of Emily 'missing' these things or of being homesick is to seriously understate the condition she found herself in. She could think of nothing else but what had been left behind, and she quickly sank into a deep depression. She would talk to nobody and ate and drank very little. For a horrified Charlotte, the memories of Maria and Elizabeth were returning. After only three months at Roe Head, she knew that action needed to be taken, and wrote urgently to her father, as she later described:

Liberty was the breath of Emily's nostrils, without it, she perished. The change from her own home to a school, and from her own very noise-less, very secluded but unrestrained and inartificial mode of life, to one of disciplined routine (though under the kindest auspices) was what she failed in enduring ... Every morning when she woke the vision of home and the moors rushed on her, and darkened and saddened the day that lay before her. Nobody knew what ailed her but me – I knew only too well. In this struggle her health was quickly broken: her white face, attenuated form, and failing strength threatened rapid decline. I felt in my heart she would die, if she did not go home.[11]

The letter home must have been even more strongly worded, for Patrick was left in no doubt that Emily was in real danger of dying. The demise of Maria and Elizabeth was still seared in his mind, and so Emily was recalled immediately and in October returned to Haworth, where she made a full recovery.

Patrick, after talking to Emily and corresponding with Charlotte, soon realised that the breakdown was as a result of Emily's character rather than any failings of the school itself. The terms of Charlotte's employment still stood, and the benefit of schooling could now be passed on to Anne. Nevertheless, he paused before making the decision.

After Emily had departed for school, Patrick had written to Elizabeth Franks, née Firth, and told her, 'My dear little Anne I intend to keep at home for another year under her Aunt's tuition and my own.'[12] Could he now bring himself to go back on that pledge, and indeed could Anne, who had never been to a school, stand the regime of one better than Emily had? He knew that Anne was very like Emily in temperament, yet even weaker in health, whereas Emily had previously seemed to have a robust constitution.

This was to be one of the first moments when Anne, then 15, showed another side of her character: a willingness to assert herself when she felt she had to, allied to a stubborn unquenchable desire to do what she thought was best for others, whatever the cost to herself. She loved being united with Emily again, but she also accepted that the offer of free schooling, and with it one less person to look after, was not one that a family such as the Brontës could easily turn down. She forced her father's hand and begged him to let her take Emily's place at the school. Her father must have been happy to see this spark within her, and he knew that she certainly had the academic and intellectual ability to be a successful pupil. Perhaps she wasn't as frail and timid as he had thought after all? Convinced by her arguments, he sent Anne to Roe Head, where she arrived in late October 1835.

Roe Head was a large, imposing three-storey building, high in the hills above Mirfield itself. Nearby was the main route between Bradford and Huddersfield, and down below in the valley bottom were the mills and factories that had transformed this area, belching out black smoke that drifted across the fields and plains of the River Calder. Many of these factories were owned by the nouveau riche parents of the girls who attended the school.

As she stepped out of the carriage that had brought her, Anne must have known that she was entering a new world. Gone was the bare garden with her beloved currant bushes, and in its place were extensive grounds with a fountain in the middle. To the rear of the school, fields stretched away into the distance leading on to Robertown and Hartshead, the village that her father had told her about, and in which he and her mother had been so happy.

Roe Head had been built as a private residence by the Marriot family and had first opened as a school in 1830, the year before Charlotte arrived as a pupil. Its co-founder and head teacher, Margaret Wooler, always known as Miss Wooler, was an imposing yet kindly woman. She was the daughter of wealthy parents herself, and she founded the school to provide a first-class education for the daughters of the increasing number of wealthy merchants in the area.

It is said that Miss Wooler, at the time 43 years of age but appearing older, had a beautiful singing voice and was a great linguist, as well as possessing an ability to instil in her pupils a longing to learn.[13] On that first evening that Anne was brought into the school, however, she would have found Miss Wooler seated in an ornate chair, looking straight at her new pupil in an effort to gauge her character. Behind Miss Wooler would have been the other teachers, firstly Miss Wooler's younger sisters

Catherine and Eliza, and then Anne's own sister Charlotte. How Anne's heart must have leaped to see a friendly, well known and much loved face waiting for her, but her smile was met with a cold blank face and a hand outstretched as Anne curtsied before her.

When Emily had arrived as a pupil, Charlotte wrote that 'the idea of being together consoles us somewhat',[14] yet this had produced the opposite effect to that which she had intended, only making Emily more homesick until her health collapsed. Charlotte resolved not to make that mistake again, and from now she would keep propriety, always an asset she prized highly, to the fore. It wasn't simply that she would treat Anne just like any other pupil, she would be even less friendly with her than the others, so that nobody could accuse her of favouritism. As always, Charlotte thought that she was doing what was best, but by the time she realised her mistake it was almost too late.

Anne was heartbroken by this reception, but she vowed not to show it. Emily had failed, but she would not fail. She would show them that little Anne, the baby of the family, the girl who they thought was so fragile, could be stronger than any of them suspected. She even made efforts to make friends with her classmates, like Ann Cook and Ellen Lister, and through her obvious kindness and good nature she succeeded, even if she was never as boisterous as her fellow pupils.

Unlike the cramped accommodation that Cowan Bridge had offered, Roe Head was very spacious. The whole of the middle floor was used as accommodation, with the ground floor housing the school rooms and the upper floor unoccupied, although pupils often spoke of feeling an icy presence there and hearing the ghostly rustle of a dress sweeping by whenever they were on that floor. Every pupil had their own room, and it was the first time that Anne had enjoyed such a luxury, but it only served to increase her isolation and loneliness.

During the day she could focus her mind on the lessons, whether given by Charlotte or one of the Woolers made no difference. Anne was there to learn, and learn she would. She committed herself fully to the lessons of the day, whether Italian or geometry. The classroom itself was spacious and beautifully furnished, with decorative wooden panelling below the ceiling and three bay windows, two at the front and one at the right-hand side, looking out over the attractive gardens. If Anne had allowed herself to, she could have seen the nature that she so loved, but she kept her head lowered and her eyes on her books.

Her quick progress and natural ability was soon noted, and at the end of her first full year at Roe Head, Anne received a special prize from Miss Wooler. Her certificate read, 'A prize for good conduct presented to Miss A. Brontë with Miss Wooler's kind love, Roe Head, Dec. 14th 1836.' The prize was a copy of the book *The Improvement of the Mind* by Isaac Watts. It is an eighteenth-century book, containing guides on how to learn languages, overcome prejudices and use logic to improve the mind and memory, and much more, it was testimony to Anne's studious nature.

Despite Anne's scholarly success, she was hiding a dark secret. She was feeling increasingly alone and depressed, and in the dark moments of night-time, one thought above all others came constantly into her head: the dread moment of death and the judgement that was to come after it. All of Anne's childhood was spent listening to the hard-line beliefs on judgement and damnation from her aunt, but she soon found them at odds with what she believed in her heart. She knew that she had to listen to her aunt and respect her views, but although she dare not say it out loud she found difficulty in believing in a harsh, unforgiving God and a world where the beauty of nature was subservient to the rule of man.

At Roe Head she was introduced to an even more severe doctrine, that of Calvinism. All of the girls were required to attend Sunday services at Mirfield parish church, just over a mile from the school, although on other occasions they attended Hartshead church. The school was also visited by Reverend Edward Nicholl Carter and Reverend Thomas Allbutt, husbands of two further sisters of Miss Wooler who also taught at Roe Head from time to time. Many of these curates had Calvinist sympathies. This doctrine preached that some people were destined for heaven from birth. They were the elect. Others had no chance of ever attaining heaven and were doomed to damnation in the terrible fires of hell. Once a sin had been made, it could never be repaired and all hope was gone.

These thoughts went round and round in Anne's head. Blameless as others may see her, surely her hidden thoughts, even the questioning of the word of God as taught by the Calvinists, was enough to send her to eternal damnation? For Anne these fears were very real, all light and all joy in the world had been extinguished.

She poured out this anguish in her poems written while at Roe Head. When writing about Gondalian characters, she writes of people trapped in towers and dungeons, waiting for their inevitable, unavoidable fate. One such example of this comes from October 1837, in the starkly bleak poem we mentioned earlier, 'A Voice from the Dungeon'. It begins:

I'm buried now; I've done with life;
I've done with hate, revenge, and strife;
I've done with joy, and hope and love
And all the bustling world above.
Long have I dwelt forgotten here
In pining woe and dull despair;
This place of solitude and gloom
Must be my dungeon and my tomb.
No hope, no pleasure, can I find:
I am grown weary of my mind;
Often in balmy sleep I try
To gain a rest from misery,
And in one hour of calm repose
To find a respite from my woes,
But dreamless sleep is not for me
And I am still in misery. [15]

This was written under a Gondal pen name, but it masked an all too real cry for help. Unfortunately, the one person who could have heard it was undergoing a crisis of her own.

Charlotte quickly discovered that she hated life as a teacher. She had high standards for herself and despised others who failed to live up to them. The 'scribblemania' as she called her youthful Angrian writings had now become something much deeper and more meaningful to her. She felt her creative powers growing, and yet she also felt that the hours spent teaching were destroying the opportunity to indulge her talent as a writer. She longed to spend days around that table once more, writing with her sisters, yet instead she was in a noisy bustling classroom, with pupils constantly demanding her attention. Inevitably, memories of Cowan Bridge also returned. Depression grew within Charlotte, and this turned into a hatred of her pupils that she found hard to contain.

Its outlet was her 'Roe Head Journal', a visceral attack on her life as a teacher and on the pupils before her. She often wrote it secretly when she should have been teaching lessons, and it is fortunate that neither Miss Wooler nor her pupils ever saw it. One entry begins:

> I'm just going to write because I cannot help it … A. Cook on one side of me, E. Lister on the other and Miss W in the background. Stupidity the atmosphere, school-books the employment, asses the society, what in all this is there to remind me of the divine silent, unseen, land of thought, dim now and indefinite as the dream of a dream, the shadow of a shade?
>
> There is a voice, there is an impulse that wakens up that dormant power, which in its torpidity I sometimes think dead … O, it has wakened a feeling that I cannot satisfy! A thousand wishes rose at its call which must die with me for they will never be fulfilled.[16]

Elsewhere in the journal, Charlotte writes:

> The spirit of all Verdopolis … came crowding into my mind. If I had had time to indulge it, I felt that the vague sensations of that moment would have settled down into some narrative better at least than anything I ever produced before. But just then a dolt came up with a lesson. I thought I should have vomited.[17]

Her hatred of her pupils inevitably led to a hatred of herself, as she revealed in one of her many letters from the school to Ellen Nussey:

> Don't deceive yourself by imagining that I have a bit of real goodness about me … If you knew my thoughts; the dreams that absorb me; and the fiery imagination that at times eats me up and makes me feel society, as it is, wretchedly insipid, you would pity me and I daresay despise me.[18]

In another letter to Ellen, Charlotte too reveals the insidious influence of Calvinism upon her: 'I abhor myself – I despise myself – if the Doctrine of Calvin be true, I am already an outcast.'[19]

Thus it was that Charlotte, enveloped in her own self-hatred and grief, was blind to the sufferings of Anne in a way that she hadn't been to Emily's. She failed to notice that Anne's health was growing more delicate, that her attacks of asthma were becoming more frequent, that she was eating less and becoming more withdrawn. Anne's mental anguish was building to a physical collapse, and it would reach its head in late 1837.

Anne, with her resistance lowered, suffered a severe attack of breathlessness, at first thought to be another recurrence of her asthma. She became unable to keep any food or liquid down and suffered prolonged episodes of terrible pain. It was then diagnosed as gastric fever, what we today call typhoid. At last Charlotte saw what was happening to Anne and stayed by her side as doctors came and went. She had shunned the only person at Roe Head who was close to her, and now she too was on the brink of leaving her.

Medical assistance could only achieve so much, it was not only Anne's body that was under attack, but her mind as well, and what she cared for most of all, her soul. As she lay wide eyed in her bed, one thought above all else was in her mind: she was going to die a sinner, she was going to be sent to hell, her soul was doomed. Anne knew what she had to do, just as the young Jane Eyre knows what she must do when the cruel headmaster Mr Brocklehurst, Charlotte's depiction of Calvinist hypocrisy, tells her that the fires of hell await her and asks what she must do to avoid it. The young Jane replies, 'I must keep in good health and not die.'[20]

Anne knew that she too must not die, not with her soul and mind in the turmoil that it was. Her frail body struggled for survival, but she realised that hope must come from elsewhere. Whether she was to live or die, she had to find the truth about God, had to confront the dark despair that had being growing within her. Anne was going through a purification of fire, and she would never be the same.

7

GOING OUT
INTO THE WORLD

How delightful it would be to be a governess! To go out
into the world; to enter upon a new life; to act for myself; to
exercise my unused faculties; to try my unknown powers; to
earn my own maintenance, and something to comfort and help
my father, mother, and sister, besides exonerating them from
the provision of my food and clothing; to show papa what his
little Agnes could do; to convince mama and Mary that I was
not quite the helpless, thoughtless being they supposed.

Agnes Grey

Charlotte leaned in closer to Anne. She was so weak by this point
that she could barely be heard, but she had something important to say. Charlotte wiped away the tears, as her 17-year-old
sister asked to see a priest. Charlotte nodded and said that she would
fetch Reverend Carter, but Anne shook her head and whispered again.

There was one specific man she wanted to see, and the choice would have shocked her elder sister.

The young priest that Anne asked for, and who immediately answered her call, wasn't a member of the Church of England at all. He was James la Trobe, a member of the Moravian priesthood, and his views would have been an anathema to the Calvinist clergy around Mirfield.

The Moravian Church had been formed in what is now the Czech Republic in the fifteenth century, but after centuries of persecution the Church found itself exiled to Germany in 1722. From there they spread into Western Europe, and it was the Wesleys, among others, who invited the Moravian Church to come to England. They had a church in Mirfield itself and another at nearby Gomersal, where the Taylor family, including Charlotte's friend Mary, attended. It may have been from Mary herself or via the retelling of Charlotte that Anne first heard of this Moravian priest, or it could have been that she knew of him because of his occasional visits to Roe Head; however she heard of him, she liked the sound of his teachings.

The Moravian Church has elements of traditional Protestantism within it and elements of Methodism with which it was once thought it would combine, but it also has beliefs of its very own. It places a great value on having a personal relationship with God, an almost mystical belief. They also had no time at all for the hellfire and eternal damnation that the Calvinists preached, or for the idea of only an elect few being allowed into heaven.

When James la Trobe heard that a girl whose life was in the balance asked to see him, he answered the call with haste. It mattered little to him whether she was a member of his Church or not: when duty called for la Trobe he answered it. His reputation for kindness and compassion was well deserved, and he would later go on to be made a bishop within the Moravian Church. He found Anne very ill in bed, and he shooed out Charlotte and Miss Wooler so that he could have a private conversation with her.

He soon realised that Anne's primary concern wasn't the very real possibility of impending death but for her soul after the event. She opened up to him about the terrible dark fears that she had kept within her since she was a small child and which had spread throughout her like a slow and deadly poison. Holding her emaciated hand, la Trobe told her his view of God as a caring, loving being. He explained that no soul is doomed forever and that after a period of purgatory, everyone, however wicked they have been, can attain heaven. Sixty years later, in 1897, James la Trobe still recalled the event, as revealed in a letter to his friend William Scruton:

> She was suffering from a severe attack of gastric fever which brought her very low, and her voice was barely a whisper; her life hung on a slender thread. She soon got over the shyness natural on seeing a perfect stranger. The words of love, from Jesus, opened her ear to my words, and she was very grateful for my visits. I found her well acquainted with the main truths of the Bible respecting our salvation, but seeing them more through the law than the gospel, more as a requirement from God than His gift in His Son, but her heart opened to the sweet views of salvation, pardon, and peace in the blood of Christ, and, had she died then, I would have counted her His redeemed and ransomed child. It was not til I read Charlotte Brontë's 'Life' [he refers to the biography of Charlotte written by Elizabeth Gaskell] that I recognised my interesting patient at Roe Head.[1]

His words were exactly what Anne wanted to hear. They chimed perfectly with her own beliefs, and now at last she understood that they weren't heresy at all, they were held by many other people. Her spirit restored through a number of other visits from the Moravian priest, her health battled back as well, until she was well enough to return to Haworth with Charlotte.

Her battle with doubt, however, was one that would never be completely won, and she would struggle with it throughout her life. At the moments when she needed it most, however, this new-found belief in a loving and forgiving God would return and sustain her. From that moment on, the always-religious Anne would become even more devout, until her faith became the ultimate driving force in her life.

The Moravian Church would not forget Anne either. A poem of hers of 1848 entitled 'The Three Guides' looks at a trio of spirits that can guide people. The first two are the spirit of earth (which may have been intended as a reference to the nature-worshipping Emily) and the spirit of pride (in reference to Charlotte), but the third spirit, the spirit of faith, represents Anne herself, and this section is now a part of the official Moravian hymn book.

Anne implores the spirit of faith to clasp her hand and guide her through life. Night's terrors 'oft appal' her but the magical power of the spirit of faith will lead her through unharmed. She concludes:

Spirit of Faith! I'll go with thee;
Thou, if I hold thee fast,
Wilt guide, defend, and strengthen me,
And bring me home at last.
By thy help, all things I can do;
In thy strength all things bear.
Teach me, for thou art just and true,
Smile on me, – thou art fair![2]

Even though Charlotte was once more going through her own traumas, Anne's illness had at last awoken Charlotte to the neglect with which she had treated her own sister; the hacking cough and pallid skin that Anne had developed snapped Charlotte out of her self-absorption. It was the same symptoms that Charlotte, as a little girl, had seen strike Maria and Elizabeth: it bore all the hallmarks of the early stages of consumption.

Charlotte plunged head first into shock, grief and guilt. She wrestled with the conviction that she herself was to blame for the way she had ignored and ostracised Anne, but unable to cope with that accusation against herself she instead turned her fury on Miss Wooler. In a stormy meeting she accused the headmistress of ignoring Anne's illness and of causing the conditions that allowed it to develop. In a letter just after the event, Charlotte admits to Ellen that she had told Miss Wooler 'one or two rather plain truths – which set her a-crying' and later says that Miss Wooler was 'crying for two days and two nights together', but that she did not regret it because her 'warm temper quite got the better of me'.[3]

Charlotte's 'warm temper' when unchecked could reduce the strong-est person to tears, but on this occasion it had the desired effect. Miss Wooler wrote immediately to Reverend Brontë, explaining the situation, at which point he called them both back to Haworth. Back home, Anne recovered her strength again, so that in that same letter of 4 January 1838 Charlotte could conclude, 'Anne is now much better – though she still requires a great deal of care. However, I am relieved from my worst fears respecting her.'[4]

Anne would not return to the school after the Christmas break, yet despite her illnesses she had excelled in her lessons and had spent longer in a formal education than any of her siblings. Despite their recent alter-cation, Miss Wooler begged Charlotte to return to her teaching role, which she reluctantly acceded to.

At the turn of 1838 Miss Wooler had moved the school from Mirfield. She had realised that Roe Head was much too large for her needs and so had found new premises 2 miles away in Dewsbury Moor. The new school, known as Heald's House, was also on an exposed and hilly area, but the building itself was much less inviting. Charlotte hated this new location from the first moment. Her depression was growing worse, and she found herself imagining that she had a secret illness that nobody else could recognise.

Her mental torments were now becoming plain and could no longer be hidden from view. A doctor was called for and advised Charlotte to quit the school if 'she valued her life'. It was obvious to all parties now that Charlotte could no longer cope with the daily drudgery of the teaching life, and she left the school on 23 May. Perhaps surprisingly, it was not to be the end of her relationship with Miss Wooler. They con-tinued to correspond and eventually became firm friends, with the old headmistress and employer later giving Charlotte away at her wedding.

What had Anne achieved in her time at Roe Head? She had greatly enhanced her education, had proved that she could overcome her natural reserve and mix in company, and had found a new and stronger faith, along with a new love of life. It was also a place where she indulged her passion for poetry free of the influence of her sister Emily, and it was where she discovered how writing could be used to give vent to the secret feelings and emotions that she kept within her. She also produced some of her most beautiful sketches there, including one of Roe Head itself just weeks after her arrival. The school is still instantly recognisable from her sketch today. It is now called Holly Bank Trust and provides specialist education for people with severe disabilities, as well as full term of life care in its residential areas and hospices. Anne, and Miss Wooler, would be proud of it.

One thing above all else Anne gained from her school days: independence. No more would she unquestioningly accept what her aunt taught her on religious matters, and no more would she invariably fall under the influence of Emily, although she still loved them both dearly. She had proved to herself, in the most trying of circumstances, that she could survive in the wider world, and now she was determined to prove it to others too.

Emily had surprised everyone in September 1837 by taking a job as a teacher at Law Hill School near Halifax. Although Emily knew how alien the role was to her nature, she felt that she had let her family and herself down at Roe Head and wanted to give 'conventional' life one more try. The conditions were very harsh for a woman who loved freedom as much as Emily, with duties running from 6 a.m. until 11 p.m. every day. By March 1838 she was unable to take any more and returned to Haworth. She would never take a job again.

Thus it was that in 1838 the sisters found themselves reunited in Haworth once more, with the moorland walks and the communal 'scribbling' sessions that entailed. In each other's company they each regained their physical and mental vigour, but it was clear that things could not continue that way indefinitely.

Branwell had left at the start of the year for a job as a portrait painter in Bradford, a trade in which he showed much initial promise and which he had long planned to do. As a 16-year-old he had painted what is now infamous as the 'pillar portrait', the only painting of the three sisters together. Anne is on the left-hand side of the picture, with Emily, inevitably, by her side. Branwell was next in the painting, with Charlotte on the right-hand side. Unhappy with his own likeness, he later painted over himself with a white pillar.

Even with Branwell absent, there were too many mouths to feed at the parsonage: something had to be done. Emily had thrown herself into a new role as housekeeper, assisting the now infirm Tabby, and was proving to be a real asset. It may have been expected that Charlotte would soon try to find a new position, but she still bore the mental scars of her teaching experience.

Anne, however, had a very different point of view. She positively wanted to take a job. Her greatest dream was to see the world, do something useful in her life and provide a financial contribution for her family. She communicated this to them, but, mindful of her recent illnesses, they were reluctant to encourage her. Anne had more faith in herself than her family had; she felt in, what was for her, full health again and wanted to make the most of the knowledge and talents she had developed.

What was more, Anne was tired of being treated as the baby of the house. Her quiet personality and perceived physical frailty meant that she was often excused from the duties that her sisters carried out, even when she begged to be treated on equal terms. She puts this frustration into the voice of Agnes Grey when she too is looking to leave home to support her family:

> Though a woman in my own estimation, I was still a child in theirs ... Whenever I offered to assist her, I received such an answer as – 'No, love, you cannot indeed – there's nothing here you can do. Go and help your sister or get her to take a walk with you ... Go and practise your music, or play with the kitten'.[5]

Anne was persistent, insisting that she would make an excellent governess. When her father and aunt said that she was too young, being just 18 at the time, she insisted that was an advantage, as being not far removed from them in age she would have a better understanding of what the children in her charge were thinking.

Just as when Anne had asked to be allowed to attend school, Patrick saw that there was no dissuading her. She was becoming a forthright woman who knew her own mind, and, even if privately, he would have been proud of this. The plan was agreed, now all Anne had to do was find a suitable position, and she was to find it would take her back to a familiar location.

The schoolgirls at Roe Head, and their teachers, had their own pews at the imposing Mirfield Parish Church. The front pew, however, was reserved for one of the foremost and wealthiest families of the district, and major benefactors of the church, the Inghams. Anne must have often looked severely over at the young children in the family misbehaving during the service, little knowing that two years later she would be much better acquainted with them.

The Inghams lived at Blake Hall, an imposing manor house that dominated the town growing around it. The original hall was built, on the site of an even earlier building, in 1745 for a Maurice Avison, but it soon came into the hands of the Ingham family. The Inghams had for centuries been lords of the manor in all but name, and by the start of the nineteenth century they had great material wealth. The present master and mistress of the hall were Joshua and Mary Ingham, and with a growing family they decided that they needed a professional governess for their children.

We can safely assume that Anne received a helping hand in obtaining the position from Miss Wooler, who Anne would have contacted for assistance in finding a suitable post. Margaret was well known to the Inghams, and they also had close ties with two priests familiar to Anne, and who could vouch for her character, Reverend Edward Nicholl Carter and the Moravian James la Trobe, as well as with the Nussey family, who were by now so well known to the Brontës. With reassuring reports received on Anne's mature and serious nature and on her scholarly prowess, she commenced her employment at Blake Hall on 8 April 1839.

This was a time of great excitement for Anne. At last she was really starting out in life and doing something that would benefit herself, her family and the children in her care. She had supreme confidence in her own ability, but as she headed out into the world for the first time completely on her own, she must also have felt a little trepidation and a surfeit of emotions. As usual, she would have kept these emotions in check, only to reveal them in writing, as *Agnes Grey* recalls:

> I rose, washed, dressed, swallowed a hasty breakfast, received the fond
> embraces of my father, mother, and sister, kissed the cat – to the great
> scandal of Sally, the maid – shook hands with her, mounted the gig,
> drew my veil over my face, and then, but not till then, burst into a flood
> of tears.[6]

Whilst leaving her family was a wrench, she loved children and looked forward to meeting her new charges. As she approached the imposing gates of Blake Hall, she could not have known that these particular children would put her to the greatest test of her abilities, or that her experiences there would later form the initial part of her first novel.

Anne must have been impressed at first sight by Blake Hall itself. The fine and stately buildings she had known, such as Ponden Hall and Roe Head, paled in comparison. It was a three-storey building with a porticoed entrance and above it two sets of five windows. The hall was as deep as it was long, so that it held a cube-like appearance, although the eastern side had a grand bow window at its centre; it was surrounded by beautifully manicured grounds, where the Inghams would entertain their many visitors from all across Yorkshire.

The Ingham family had made their money in coal mines and wool factories, but they had held these concerns so long that by the 1830s they were well-established members of society, holding a loftier position than those who had more recently found riches. Mary also came from a well-established and respected family, and her father, Ellis Cunliffe Lister, was then Member of Parliament for Bradford representing the Whig Party.

The Inghams had five children at this point. Cunliffe was a boy of 6, and he had four younger sisters: Mary, 5; Martha, 3; Emily, 2; and an infant baby called Harriet. Charlotte was later to succinctly sum them up in a letter as 'desperate little dunces'.[7] She also reported back to Ellen after she had received a letter from Anne following her first week spent at Blake Hall. As would often be found with Charlotte, she seemed incredulous at her little sister's ability to do anything, so convinced was she by the reserved front that Anne often wore:

She expresses herself very well satisfied, and says that Mrs Ingham is extremely kind ... I hope she'll do, you would be astonished to see what a sensible, clever letter she writes; it is only the talking part that I fear – but I do seriously apprehend that Mrs Ingham will 'sometimes' conclude that she has a natural impediment in her speech.[8]

That Anne was 'very well satisfied' was far from the truth. She was determined to succeed at any cost in this, her first venture into the adult world, and she knew that any hint of disquiet or unhappiness would have caused misery and worry for her father. For this reason, Anne reverted to her default position of pretending that nothing was wrong; in fact, things were very wrong.

She had dreamed of finding children much like the ones she had known: Charlotte, Emily, Branwell, Maria and Elizabeth. All of them were bright and intelligent, and eager to learn; they were a little lively at times but at heart always well behaved. The Ingham children did not fit this image, and her dreams of domestic bliss and how delightful it would be to teach children were soon shattered.

The first problem that Anne encountered is that the elder children were very poorly educated, if at all. Charlotte revealed to Ellen how Anne found that neither Cunliffe nor Mary could read, and that they had little understanding of the alphabet. Whilst growing up with all the material advantages they could wish for, the children had been indulged to the point where it was almost impossible to get them to do anything they did not want, and they certainly did not want to learn.

Joshua and Mary Ingham were confident, successful people, used to giving orders and having them followed. The children, even at such a tender age, were already the same. They had no respect for the young timid governess who was supposedly in charge of them, and they resolved in their childish way to make things as difficult for her as possible.

We can see what problems Anne encountered through her portrayal of the Inghams as the Bloomfield family in *Agnes Grey*. The children within this book are a year older than the ones she taught at Blake Hall, but this was not only so that Anne could avoid any threat of legal action from the

Inghams but also because she felt people would not believe how savage children of that age could be.

Thus we read how the children would refuse to repeat the word she was teaching them, and how she would have to trick them into saying it. Cunliffe would strike out at Anne, and while she held his hands by his side he would encourage his sisters to take her bag and spit in it. At other times, Mary would fall to the floor and refuse to move all day long. They would scream high-pitched shrieks continually that would leave Anne having to cover her ears.

Cunliffe is represented in the book by the monstrous Tom, whose only pleasure in life is torturing birds and animals that he has caught in his traps. At one point, his uncaring uncle hands him a nest full of birds, which Tom announces he will torture by pulling off their wings and beaks. Agnes takes the nest from him, and to spare them their torment, crushes them instantly under a heavy stone.

If this, like much of the book, is taken from real life then we can imagine the pain that this must have caused the nature and animal-loving Anne:

> I got a large flat stone, that had been reared up for a mouse-trap by the gardener, then, having once more vainly endeavoured to persuade the little tyrant to let the birds be carried back, I asked what he intended to do with them. With fiendish glee he commenced a list of torments; and while he was busied in the relation, I dropped the stone upon his intended victims and crushed them flat beneath it.[9]

The Ingham girls, if anything, were even worse. Unwilling to learn, and impossible to rule, Anne found it a struggle even to clothe them and brush their hair in the morning. When in the classroom they would make a concerted effort to create as much chaos and noise as possible, but when Mr or Mrs Ingham came to see what the noise was for, it was Anne who received the blame. They had a wholly untrue picture of the goodness of their children, and they refused to let Anne take any action against the children in the form of punishment.

> I had no rewards to offer; and as for punishments, I was given to understand, the parents reserved that privilege to themselves; and yet they expected me to

keep my pupils in order … A good birch rod might have been serviceable; but as my powers were so limited, I must make the best use of what I had.[10]

The truth of the words that Anne puts into the mouth of Agnes are confirmed by Charlotte's letter to Ellen: 'The worst of it is that the little monkies [the Ingham children] are excessively indulged, and she is not empowered to inflict any punishment.'[11]

The troubles that Anne had to go to in her, often failed, attempts to keep some sort of order are not only related in *Agnes Grey*, they are also verified by a descendant of the family itself who later remembered, 'One day grandmother, Mary Ingham, went into the school room and found two of the children tied to opposite table legs whilst Anne wrote.'[12]

In the face of all this, and more, it is easy to ask why Anne stayed in the position rather than returning to the home comforts of Haworth? Agnes Grey gives us the answer:

Small as the salary was, I still was earning something, and with strict economy I could easily manage to have something to spare for them [her family], if they would favour me by taking it. Then it was by my own will that I had got the place: I had brought all this tribulation on myself, and I was determined to bear it; nay, more than that, I did not even regret the step I had taken. I longed to show my friends that, even now, I was competent to undertake the charge, and able to acquit myself honourably to the end.[13]

Anne, as always, was putting duty before everything else. In the face of evidence to the contrary, she refused to admit she was beaten. Charlotte and Emily may struggle to keep a job in the world outside of Haworth, she seemed to be saying, but I, little Anne, who people think incapable of even the simplest things, will succeed. There were three staunch friends that she turned to in her battle against the tyranny of the children: 'Patience, Firmness, and Perseverance, were my only weapons; and these I resolved to use to the utmost.'[14]

It is telling that Anne places patience at the head of the list, as it would be the first thing she would turn to throughout all her struggles. When she was in a job that she hated, when she could tell nobody that she was in love, when people misunderstood her writing, when she was ill, when she was dying, she would be patient, Anne would endure.

Come what may, Anne had resolved to remain at Blake Hall for as long as possible and to do all that she could to give a rudimentary education to the children and instil in them some sense of right and wrong. Before long, however, matters were taken out of her hands.

8

EXILED AND HARASSED

How brightly glistening in the sun
The woodland ivy plays!
While yonder beeches from their barks
Reflect his silver rays.
The sun surveys a lovely scene
From softly smiling skies;
And wildly through unnumbered trees
The wind of winter sighs:
Now loud, it thunders o'er my head,
And now in distance dies.
But give me back my barren hills
Where colder breezes rise;
Where scarce the scattered, stunted trees
Can yield an answering swell,
But where a wilderness of heath
Returns the sound as well.
For yonder garden, fair and wide,
With groves of evergreen,
Long winding walks, and borders trim,
And velvet lawns between;

Restore to me that little spot,
With grey walls compassed round,
Where knotted grass neglected lies,
And weeds usurp the ground.
Though all around this mansion high
Invites the foot to roam,
And though its halls are fair within –
Oh, give me back my HOME!

'Home'

The neglected garden, the grey stone walls, the bleak treeless landscape that was swept by wild and punishing winds, these were things of joy to Anne. During her time as governess to the Ingham family of Blake Hall she would see a different side to society, an elevated world where people with no financial or social barriers mixed, a world where anything was possible. At the regular garden parties that Joshua Ingham would arrange, Anne would be a figure lurking in the background, her sole job to keep the children out of the way of the adults, which was a difficult task in itself. But this silent woman would be watching, observing, judging, and she liked not what she saw.

As a girl, her aunt had taught her the importance of keeping the proper order of things. The most important order of all was that God was in charge of all, and in this Anne acquiesced, even if she did have a very different view of her maker. God's order, however, according to Aunt Branwell, spread down to the temporal world as well: he had ordained everything that happened, so that we must know our place in society and accept that it is God's will; we must serve lords, ladies and gentlemen, and look up to them with respect; animals are subservient to people; and women are subservient to men. In these matters, as she gained for herself a first-hand understanding of the way the world really was, Anne could not agree.

By June 1839 we receive another report of Anne at Blake Hall. Reverend Carter was no longer vicar of Mirfield but of Heckmondwike, but on 8 June he called in at Blake Hall and later passed on news of Anne to Reverend Brontë in Haworth. Charlotte reveals his report in a letter to Emily: 'Mr Carter was at Mirfield yesterday and saw Anne. He says she was looking uncommonly well. Poor girl, she must indeed wish to be at home.'[1]

If Charlotte had correctly guessed her sister's feelings, she had not as yet discerned that Anne's resolve was much greater than hers. Indeed, Charlotte had by this time taken on a governess's position of her own, but she would last just over two months in the role. Anne was made of sterner stuff, but in December 1839, just before she was due to return to Haworth for the Christmas holiday, she was summoned to Mrs Ingham's chamber. There Anne was told that she had been hired to improve the behaviour of the children, to round off their rough edges and improve their education, but as far as the parents could see, they had, if anything, gone backwards. In light of this, although Mrs Ingham admitted that she found no fault with Anne's character itself, her services would not be required in the new year.

Anne was devastated, and the conflicting emotions within her caused tears to stream down her face as soon as she was free of company. She was returning home to the family she loved, and she would be forever free of the unmanageable children who had made her life at Blake Hall a misery, yet she could not escape the feeling that she had failed. She had implored her family to have faith in her ability to govern children, but this position had lasted less than nine months. What was worse, she hadn't left it on her own terms as Emily and Charlotte had, she had been dismissed. It was with a heavy heart, a bruised spirit and an even quieter demeanour that she returned to the family parsonage.

In Anne's portraits of the Ingham children, we get a glimpse of how they would be as adults. Both Cunliffe and his sister Mary would become notorious for their tempers, although Cunliffe would put his to use by becoming an army officer, and he served in the Crimean War. Blake Hall itself, that huge imposing edifice that once dominated Mirfield, was sold off piece by piece in the 1950s and then demolished, like so many other stately homes that had become too costly to maintain and run.

There is an amusing, if rather unusual, postscript to this story. The grand staircase that ran from the entrance hall of Blake Hall was advertised at an antique furniture fair in Kensington, London, and was bought by a wealthy American called Allen Topping. At great expense he had it shipped over to, and rebuilt in, his Long Island mansion. In 1962 Mrs Topping, by then a widow, saw a ghostly figure descend the staircase. The figure was dressed in a long full skirt with a tri-cornered shawl, her hair was in a bun and she had a pensive look on her face. Mrs Topping's dog became agitated, and when Mrs Topping spoke to soothe the dog, the figure smiled and then disappeared. She called out to ask who had been there and says that she heard a voice in her head saying 'Anne Brontë'. She never saw the figure again, although she often heard footsteps going up and down the stairs.[2]

Blake Hall is gone, but the memories remain. The area where it stood is now home to Mirfield's Blake Hall housing estate, centred around Blake Hall Road and Blake Hall Drive. To the north of Blake Hall Road are the cul-de-sacs of Ingham Garth, Ingham Close and Ingham Croft, while branching off to the south are Brontë Way and Brontë Grove. In death, as in life, Anne and the Inghams are on opposite sides of the divide.

Anne found Haworth Parsonage quite changed upon her return. Tabby's leg had become infected after her fall, and her mobility was becoming increasingly impaired. In November 1839 she had been sent home to her family to recuperate, on the insistence of Charlotte and Emily that she could return when she recovered, which she later did. In Tabby's absence, her work was shared between Charlotte and Emily, with the young Martha Brown soon moving into the parsonage and helping where she could. It was a role that Emily was born to, proving an excellent cook and domestic organiser, but Charlotte found it a little more difficult, reporting how she managed to burn all the clothing on her first attempt at ironing.

Anne's father, too, was suffering from bouts of ill health, as well as failing eyesight. Patrick Brontë was by now 62, yet he was still dealing with an immense workload. To help him, a young curate arrived in Haworth in August 1839. His name was William Weightman, and his easy-going, flirtatious nature and handsome good looks made him a hit with the ladies of the parish, including, before long, all three Brontë sisters.

If Anne had been worried about the reception she would receive upon her return, her fears were soon allayed. Reticent to speak ill of anybody, let alone her recent employers, Anne laid the blame firmly on herself, but Charlotte would coax out of her the true character of the Inghams and their children, whilst stating her astonishment that Anne had lasted so long under the circumstances.

Aunt Branwell would have been most surprised. She had a natural deference for the upper classes, and it was she who had urged Anne to take the post when it became available, vouchsafing that she had heard of their excellent character. Nonetheless, she could not believe any ill of the young woman she had raised from a baby, and soon Anne found herself welcomed with open arms as a hero rather than a failure.

Anne had tried bravely to make her way in a world that was in many ways alien to her, and all things considered, she had done well to survive there for nearly nine months. She had satisfied her curiosity, and now she could return to life in the parsonage. She was always dedicated to whatever task was put before her, so with a little training from Emily, she would be able to help with the housework. She might be able to make a little money from providing needlework services or possibly music lessons. Patrick and Aunt Branwell even conjectured that their girls might be able to emulate their brother Branwell and sell some of their paintings. She was at home now, where she belonged, and would soon settle back into the Haworth routine, free of the longing for discovery and adventure that had led her to Blake Hall. That was what her family thought as 1839 turned into 1840, but Anne had other ideas.

She would stay in Haworth throughout early 1840, and it was a period in which she grew emotionally. She provided domestic help and recommenced walking on the moors with Emily. She also resumed her daily writing, both on matters of Gondal and matters that were much more personal, although she and Emily would often write independently of one another now. The two sisters' love for one another was undiminished, and, as Ellen Nussey said in her pen portraits of the girls she came to know well, ever would be, but they had both grown to love their private time alone as well. In these private hours, Anne could think of her writing, her beloved music and of new, strong emotions that were rising within her.

There were many reasons for Anne to remain at home, but she secretly yearned to try the life of a governess again. Her family may not have judged her as a failure, but this was still the opinion she kept within her own heart, and other than the final one which would one day come, this was the only judgement that would ever matter to her. As the months passed by since her departure from Blake Hall, she began to take a more dispassionate view of events there. Surely the monstrous children she had taught were one-offs? In another position, so she told herself, she was likely to find charges with a completely different nature.

Anne reveals this reasoning in the sixth chapter of *Agnes Grey*, entitled 'The Parsonage Again':

> I'm sure all children are not like theirs ... However, even if I should stumble on such a family again, which is quite unlikely, I have all this experience to begin with, and I should manage better another time; and the end and aim of this preamble is, let me try again.[3]

Her family were astonished at her decision, and her conviction, but they had already learned that their quiet little Anne could not easily be dissuaded once she had set her heart on something. And, indeed, as Agnes' father acknowledges, her skills were not commonly found in other parsons' daughters.

Anne now had concrete experience of looking after children, and she had departed from Mrs Ingham on good enough terms to ensure she could receive a fair character reference from her. Her academic ability was well above what would be expected of a governess, her knowledge of Latin especially was excellent and she spoke and read it better than either of her sisters. She was well versed in the scriptures. She had the necessary attainments at needlework and was a fine painter, and she could also play the piano and sing well. Out of all the children, much against initial expectations, it was Anne who was the one most equipped to succeed in the role of governess.

In *Jane Eyre*, Charlotte Brontë tells how the young Jane, who by then has graduated to being a teacher at Lowood School, decided that she would like to be a governess. To chase this dream she places an advertisement in a local paper. Similarly, when Jane announces that she must quit Rochester and Thornfield Hall, he asks her how she will find a position. She answers, 'I will advertise'. We don't have to look far to find where Charlotte got her inspiration from, as this was exactly what Anne did in early 1840.

Advertisements for situations wanted at the time were often placed under pseudonyms or, alternatively, respondents were asked to contact the newspaper directly, so it can be difficult to trace the existence or otherwise of a particular advertisement. One advertisement from *The Leeds Mercury*, a paper that we know the Brontës took, of 15 February 1840, however, catches the eye. Could this be the advertisement that Anne placed?

> A young lady, in her 21st year, is anxious to re-engage herself as GOVERNESS in a private family. She is competent to give instruction in French and Music, with the several branches of a solid and polite educa-tion. She has no objection to travel. Salary not so much considered as a comfortable home.[4]

The advert succinctly stated Anne's qualifications and merits, and it bore fruit. In the spring of 1840 she was contacted by the Robinson family of the North Riding of Yorkshire. They owned Thorp Green Hall, a mansion situated in Little Ouseburn, a dozen miles from the city of York itself. They had four girls and one boy aged between 9 and 15 years old, and a baby daughter, and they came from exalted stock, being related to the Marquis of Ripon. Mr Edmund Robinson himself was a reverend, having taken holy orders, although he wasn't a practising priest.

This position must have seemed very propitious to Anne. The fact that the master of the household was also a clergyman would have vouched for his good character, as far as Anne was concerned, and she would also have been pleased that the children were older than those she had encountered at Blake Hall. Surely by their ages they would already have a decent basic education and be more morally disciplined, and thus Anne could use her time constructively in furthering their achievements?

Thorp Green Hall was much further away from Haworth than Mirfield was, at a distance of around 40 miles, but this in itself would serve to strengthen her resolve to stay once she had arrived. There was also the attraction of nearby York and the beautiful York Minster that she had heard about from her father and which she longed to see for herself. One final advantage was that she was offered a wage of £50 per year, double what she had been paid by the Ingham family; this meant that she would be able to send money back to her family, as well as allowing herself the occasional luxury such as purchases of sheet music. She accepted the position and commenced her duties on 8 May 1840.

If the first part of *Agnes Grey* is inspired by Anne's memories of Blake Hall, the second part is inspired by Anne's time at Thorp Green Hall. We have to be careful not to take *Agnes Grey* as autobiographical in its entirety – Anne is a masterful creator of fiction after all – yet we do ourselves and Anne a disservice if we fail to discern the truth that is hidden within it. For Horton Lodge and its comings and goings within *Agnes Grey* we can read Thorp Green Hall, and for the Murray family of the novel, the Robinsons of the real world.

There are many aspects of the novel that are copied straight from the daily life that Anne encountered at Little Ouseburn and beyond: the location and setting of the hall, the number of children and their ages, the character and history of the master and mistress of the house, the sojourns to the seaside. There are also scattered clues as to Anne's life while a governess for the Robinson family, and it was a life of deep contrasts, from swooping highs to crashing lows.

Thorp Green Hall itself was a large and imposing building that had been through various guises since it was built in Tudor times. It had large and beautifully manicured gardens, and winding pathways that led past gently rolling water features. The grounds had once been home to a monastery, but all that remained of it by the time Anne arrived in May 1840 was a solitary building known as the Monk's Lodge. It should not be thought that this 'lodge' is a tiny, cloistered hut, as it is a fine and spacious property in its own right. It is all that is left of the buildings that Anne would have known during her five years of service with the Robinsons, and it was also to become very familiar to another of the Brontës, as we shall later see. On the site of the once grand hall itself now stands a newer building called Thorp Underwood Hall. It has long been claimed that a fire destroyed the original building, but recent research by architectural historian Helier Hibbs concludes that the hall was demolished by its then owner Mr Slingsby to make way for his new residence, the construction of which began in 1902.[5]

Whilst many may find the gentrified countryside around Little Ouseburn charming, it was utterly at odds with Anne's tastes. It is completely flat for miles around, offering uninterrupted views of grassy glades and pastures, but there are no hills to climb and no moors to explore. Running alongside Thorp Green Hall is Moss Hill Lane, and it would be harder to imagine a greater misnomer for any street.

Anne would have noticed the isolation of Thorp Green Hall as she approached it in the carriage carrying her and her meagre belongings of clothing, writing materials and perhaps her favourite music scores. The charming village of Whixley is passed and there then follows 2 miles of level nothingness, broken only by sporadic cottages belonging to agricultural labourers.

If the terrain did little to cheer Anne, she hoped that the company of Mr and Mrs Robinson themselves would be much more agreeable. These were people with aristocratic breeding, as opposed to the trade inspired riches of the Inghams. Anne was convinced that they would know how to treat a governess well, with respect and propriety, and with an acknowledgement that she was not to be treated like the other servants. On this count she was to be badly wrong.

Edmund Robinson was not a man who appreciated the subtleties of social distinctions. For him there was his family and those of a similar or higher social strata, and little else mattered. He loved the country pursuits of hunting, fishing and riding, and these he would in turn pass on to his children. Whilst he had obtained holy orders, he did nothing to exercise the duties that he was entitled to. The church records of Holy Trinity, Little Ouseburn show that he only officiated there on six occasions, five of which were for the christenings of his own children. In his absence, the incumbent of the church was a Reverend Edward Lascelles. Lascelles was a vain and uncompromising vicar, giving glory to himself as much as to God, and as such he was unpopular with the local churchgoers.

Edmund Robinson, a 41-year-old country squire, was the undoubted master of this little corner of the North Riding of Yorkshire. He was a loud, confident man who insisted on getting his own way, and as such he needed a wife that corresponded to a man of his stature. He thought he had found just the woman in Lydia Gisborne. Lydia was from a distinguished Lichfield family and had been a highly sought after bride. As she was later to impress on her daughters, she believed it was essential to pick a husband with your head, based upon his wealth and social standing, rather than your heart. In this sense at least, Mr and Mrs Robinson were perfectly matched.

Mrs Robinson was the daughter of the Reverend Thomas Gisborne, the Canon of Durham and a man who possessed significant personal wealth. She was praised for her beauty as a young woman, and her looks could still catch eyes and break hearts decades later. Anne describes the character Mrs Murray, without doubt based upon her, as a 'handsome, dashing, lady of forty, who certainly required neither rouge nor padding to add to her charms'.[6] The veracity of this description can be seen in a surviving portrait of Mrs Robinson. She looks coyly to the left, but a smile plays upon her lips and her averted eyes glimmer. Her neckline is daringly open, and diamond earrings hang on either side of her fine face. This is a woman who could be the hunter rather than the hunted, when she chose to be so.

Upon Anne's arrival at Thorp Green Hall they greeted her not with the bonhomie she had hoped for and expected, but with a cool reserve. Tired after a long journey Anne was shown up to her room, where she spent the night alone and in tears. The die had been cast, she must make the best she could of things, come what may.

In the morning, Anne descended the sweeping staircase and was introduced to the Robinson children. The eldest girl, Lydia, was nearly 15 and already full of the vanity and self-regard that possessed her mother. Next came Elizabeth, known as Bessie, aged 13. As Lydia took after her mother, Bessie took after her father. She loved to ride and to feel the wind blowing through her hair. There next came the daughter Mary, aged 12, who would spend most time as a pupil of Anne's during her time at Thorp Green, and then there was the only son, 8-year-old Edmund. Anne's duty would be to teach him Latin so that he could pass an entrance exam before entering formal schooling.

There was also a baby, the 2-year-old Georgiana Jane. Anne would have loved nothing more than to dote on such a young child, equating the innocence of the very young to the innocence of the animals she adored, but it was not to be. Tragedy struck within the first months of Anne's tenure, and little Georgiana died on 15 March 1841.

Anne had been right to assume that other children could not be like the Inghams. In their own way, the Robinson troupe, who had an ingrained sense of their own superiority, could be difficult, but they were not cruel and vicious as Cunliffe and Mary had been at Blake Hall. Nevertheless, Anne despaired of them from the first.

She had expected children of their ages to be much more advanced at their lessons than they actually were, but they possessed only rudimentary skills when it came to reading and writing, and they had little knowledge of the wider world around them. Rather than being engaged to tackle this ignorance, she was encouraged to preserve it. Mrs Robinson wanted her girls to learn perfect needlework, art, singing and music. These were all subjects that Anne could, and did, tutor them in, but she had hoped to teach them about history and geography, literature, languages and religion too. These were deemed superfluous skills in the hunt for a distinguished husband and so were made to play second fiddle to more superficial studies.

If Anne was disappointed at their educational accomplishments, she was even more disappointed at their moral accomplishments. She wanted young girls to be quiet, serious, thoughtful, caring and concerned with the world to come as much as the one they were living in. In short, she wanted them to be as she had been just a few years previously, but the Robinsons could hardly have been more different.

They loved the frivolous things in life, and serious things could be hanged. They thought nothing of flirting with men, and Lydia junior's primary concern was her appearance and Bessie's, doing whatever she pleased, whenever she pleased. These characteristics were anathema to Anne and were reproduced in the characters of Rosalie and Matilda in *Agnes Grey*.

Although not acting deliberately to make the life of their governess as difficult as possible, as her previous charges in Mirfield had, nevertheless they could not to be kept to a regular timetable. Lessons were held whenever the children felt they had nothing better to do. Anne was left in little doubt that it was the children who were in charge of the governess, rather than the governess in charge of the children. At times they would insist on being taught outside, where Anne would have to sit on the wet grass. This caused her to catch frequent colds, a condition she would always be susceptible to, which in turn exacerbated her asthma. With characteristic reserve and self-denial, Anne never complained about this treatment, but what hurt her most was that the children did not even realise they were being unfair or self-centred.

In these early days and months at Thorp Green, Anne felt the black clouds of despair descend once more. Although unfortunately the letters no longer remain, she must have written of these feelings to Charlotte and Emily, for we have letters from Charlotte to Ellen and others that talk of how Anne is being treated like a slave by the Robinsons and expressing her concerns for her health.

One direct correspondence we do have on this matter is Anne's diary paper of 30 July 1841. It was Emily's birthday, but the two sisters were apart and for the first time wrote separate diary papers to mark the occasion. Emily's piece is upbeat and talks of future plans being hatched for the sisters as a whole, as well as containing updates from Gondal. She closes by 'sending from far an exhortation of courage, boys, courage, to exiled and harassed Anne, wishing she was here'.[7]

Anne's diary paper is a very different matter. It is an epistle of despair, weighed down by the concerns of today and fears for tomorrow. Looking back to the last diary paper, written as their tradition dictated, four years earlier, Anne writes:

What will the next 4 years bring forth? Providence only knows. But we ourselves have sustained very little alteration since that time. I have the same faults that I had then, only I have more wisdom and experience, and a little more self-possession than I then enjoyed.[8]

She also notes that she has 'seen the sea and York Minster', these being the highlights of that four-year period. These indeed, were things that Anne loved greatly. York Minster is a vast cathedral that dates from the eleventh century, although frequently remodelled and expanded in the centuries that followed. It was home to the Archbishop of York, the second highest figure in the Church of England. At that time the archbishop was the aristocratic Edward Venables-Vernon-Harcourt, a man in his late eighties who had already been in the seat for thirty-four years and who had often been in correspondence with Patrick Brontë on religious and social matters.

York Minster is one of the largest cathedrals in Europe, and the exterior must have been staggering to a young woman who had never seen anything approaching such size before. The interior is even more awe inspiring, and it can be as breathtaking to tourists today as it was to Anne in 1841. She would sit quietly on a bench at the rear of the church, looking up to the lavishly embossed and decorated ceiling, and the stained glass windows depicting biblical scenes. This was an earthly depiction of heaven, and as Anne sat transfixed in silent wonder it would often bring tears to her eyes.

The summer of 1840 was the first time that Anne accompanied the Robinson family on their annual sojourn to Scarborough, and the first time she had seen the sea. It was to capture her mind and heart in the same way that the moors captured Emily's, and it was to remain a spiritual ideal for Anne right up until the very last moment.

In the year leading up to the 1841 diary paper, Anne had made significant progress at Thorp Green Hall. She had enough money to buy the music that she so loved, she had seen the wonders of York Minster and fallen in love with the sea at Scarborough. Edmund and Lydia Robinson, while still retaining the reserve they thought proper owing to the difference in class, were genuinely impressed with their new governess. This is evidenced by them agreeing to her later suggestion that Branwell could be brought in as a new tutor for their son, with all the dreadful consequences that would bring. She was even making headway with the girls, both in terms of their education and their behaviour, forging the moral backbone that Anne was so keen on establishing.

At the close of chapter seven of *Agnes Grey*, she says that the girls had become less insolent and had begun to show some signs of esteem. There then follows a section that is very telling, and very different to anything else in the writing of Anne or either of her sisters:

> Miss Grey was a queer creature. She never flattered, and did not praise them half enough; but whenever she did speak favourably of them, or anything belonging to them, they could be quite sure her approbation was sincere. She was very obliging, quiet, and peaceable in the main, but there were some things that put her out of temper: they did not care much for that, to be sure, but still it was better to keep her in tune; as when she was in a good humour she would talk to them, and be very agreeable and amusing sometimes, in her way; which was quite different to mamma's, but still very well for a change. She had her own opinions on every subject, and kept steadily to them – very tiresome opinions they often were; as she was always thinking of what was right and what was wrong, and had a strange reverence for matters connected with religion, and an unaccountable liking to good people.[9]

This section is contained within speech marks in the novel, yet there is no indication of who is saying it, and it has no place in the narrative around it. It is Anne giving us a report on herself at this time, perhaps using words that the Misses Robinson had said to her, and it is the greatest evidence of all that she is Miss Grey herself. She is the 'queer creature', again using the word that Charlotte had used to describe her when they received the wooden soldiers, and which she had undoubtedly used on many subsequent occasions.

She was rising in esteem among both her employers and pupils, and she had also made a friend among the staff in the shape of housemaid Anne Marshall. She had to face hardships, such as the frequent colds, long and irregular hours, and frustrations when people would not always do what she wanted or expected them to, yet these were inconveniences that she was very familiar with. On the face of it, Anne should have been very happy at this time, at last she was showing people that she could succeed as a governess, she could succeed on her own. Yet, she was far from happy. She sums up her situation succinctly in the diary paper we quoted from earlier: 'I am a governess in the family of Mr. Robinson. I dislike the situation and wish to change it for another.'[10]

What was it that made her want to leave this situation so soon, despite having pledged to make a success of it, when she had endured much worse with the Ingham family at Blake Hall? It was summer, and she was a long way from Haworth, the place that she wanted to be at that time more than anywhere else. The days were long, the nights were lonely and her mind kept telling her that she was 40 miles away from something that was waiting for her. Someone who was waiting for her.

9

THE BELOVED AND LAMENTED MR WEIGHTMAN

O! I am very weary
Though tears no longer flow;
My eyes are tired of weeping,
My heart is sick of woe.
My life is very lonely,
My days pass heavily;
I'm weary of repining,
Wilt thou not come to me?
Oh didst thou know my longings
For thee from day to day,
My hopes so often blighted,
Thou wouldst not thus delay.

'Lines Written at Thorp Green'

As the 1830s turned into the 1840s, the teenage Anne Brontë had already experienced a lot in life. She had seen her mother and two eldest sisters die. She had been to boarding school, where she herself fell gravely ill and descended into a religion-born depression. She had recently been dismissed from a job that she'd hoped would show her family how self-sufficient she really could be, and as the decades changed over she hadn't yet secured her new role with the Robinsons at Thorp Green.

Anne was quiet, downcast, serious and brooding, concerned chiefly with matters of religion and what was wrong and right in the world. This is the image that many people have of Anne to this day, and it was certainly an image she could project of herself even then. Yet, we must remember that she was also a 19-year-old woman, and one of a highly sentimental and susceptible nature. She loved walking the moors, stopping to pick a pretty primrose or bluebell as she thought about the imaginary land that she and Emily had created. It was a land full of intrigue and violence, yes, but it was also a land full of passion and long-ing. She adored reading the romance heavy novels of Walter Scott and would discuss the dashing heroes with her sisters when Aunt Branwell wasn't around to tut and shake her head.

Anne had the same feelings growing within her as grow within teen-agers today. She had a longing for romance: she wanted a love that she could experience for herself, not one that ended when the last page was turned over. When she raised her eyes upwards towards the looking glass she would see that, whatever Charlotte may say of her, she was passably pretty. She was bright and ambitious, and when the need arose she could even overcome her shyness. Why shouldn't she find a romantic engage-ment in her life? There was no reason why not, she assured herself; all that she had to do was to find the right man who was deserving of her love. In August 1839 that man arrived in Haworth, although she wasn't immediately to know it, in the fine shape of William Weightman.

Weightman was born in 1814 in Appleby, Westmorland, in what we now know as Cumbria. His father was a brewer and had elevated the family into a solidly middle-class situation. He enjoyed successful school days at Appleby Grammar School and was also later to enjoy academic success at Durham University, obtaining a Master of Arts degree in Classics and a licentiate in theology.

There has been a scarcity of records about Weightman's academic career, and the Brontë biographer Edward Chitham has previously claimed that Weightman never earned a master's degree at all, as this would have allowed him dispensation from his theology licentiate, meaning that he would have obtained it in one year rather than two.[1] Some have taken this as an indication of his general untrustworthiness, but in this, as with many of the other charges laid against him, he can be defended.

One very useful book on this period is *The Durham University Calendar* of 1842. It takes a look not just at the university in 1842 but at the history and achievements of the years leading up to it. Durham University was a very new establishment when Weightman was in attendance. Until 1832, Oxford and Cambridge had hung determinedly on to their academic monopoly, but as the industrial revolution led to a population explosion in the north of England, and with it a new class of wealthy northern industrialists, calls were growing for a new university to serve the needs of the North.

In 1832 plans for a university in Durham were approved, and it opened its doors in October 1833. The driving forces behind it were the Bishop of Durham, William Van Mildert, and his Archdeacon Charles Thorp. Through their perseverance and passion for the project, it was granted a royal charter by King William IV in 1837. This finally broke the stronghold of Oxford and Cambridge, and England now had three universities that could confer degrees. The first Durham graduates were honoured a week later, on 8 June 1837.[2]

The Durham University Calendar not only relates the history of the institution but the early students who had passed through it. William Weightman is mentioned in the book three times, including details of him sitting for his licentiate in theology in 1839. Careful study of the newspapers of the time are even more revealing and can at last lay to rest the mystery of his master's degree.

The *Leeds Intelligencer* newspaper took great pride in this new 'university of the north' and carried regular columns entitled 'Durham University Intelligence'. One such intelligence report of 23 June 1838 is particularly interesting. It details the 'Public Examinations, Easter Term, 1838', under the invigilation of Reverend C. T. Whitley M.A. It then provides a 'List of students who passed the examination for the degree of M.A.' Alongside details of seven other students, is the name of 'Weightman, William'. Below these eight new masters of the arts are the names of people who had passed the lesser degree of B.A.[3]

There can be no doubt, therefore, that William Weightman did gain an M.A. from Durham University and then extended his study further to take the licentiate in theology, a qualification that would be approaching a doctorate today. Now we can understand why Patrick Brontë, a keen classical scholar himself, praised Weightman as a classicist of the first order.

By 1839 Patrick Brontë's health was becoming less assured, his eyesight had been growing steadily worse and the growing demands for funerals, weddings and baptisms in Haworth, as well as his regular services, was putting him under considerable strain. In 1835 he had appointed an assistant curate called William Hodgson, but the two priests had never hit it off, and Hodgson left in 1837 to become vicar of Colne in Lancashire.

In the summer of 1839 he applied once more to the Bishop of Ripon for an assistant curate. Patrick did not have the funds to pay the assistant's wages himself, but he received a small grant for this expenditure from the Church Pastoral Aid Society. The bishop was charged with finding a young curate at the start of his career, who would therefore not be expecting much remuneration, and who was healthy and full of vigour. His mind turned to a young man who had just completed his studies at the new university in Durham. Weightman, yes, he would do.

When William Weightman arrived in Haworth in August 1839 as new assistant curate to Patrick Brontë, he could not have imagined the tight-rope he was walking. He was entering a parish where many of the locals resented the taxes they had to pay to the official church, and where others were not afraid of voicing their discontent in ministers who did not meet their expectations. He would be working for Patrick Brontë, a man who could be very hard to win over and who did not give praise and support lightly. Furthermore, he would have close connections to a parsonage which contained four young adults who were unused to strange faces and did not like people disturbing their usual daily routines. That Weightman made such an immediate and lasting success of his time in Haworth is perhaps the greatest testament to his true character of them all.

Anne would have heard about the new curate's arrival in letters sent to her in Mirfield from Charlotte and Emily. She would have learned that he had fitted into life in Haworth, and the parsonage, very quickly, and these early reports are sure to have piqued her curiosity. Although she returned to Haworth in December 1839 downcast and dispirited, following her exit from the Ingham household, one consolidating thought, alongside the prospect of seeing her family again, was that of seeing this much talked about Mr Weightman for herself. She was not to be disappointed.

William Weightman was, by all accounts, a very handsome, intelligent man, and he could talk to anyone. Anne would have been amazed to see how well he had integrated with the Brontë family. After only five months there, he was already as much a feature of parsonage life as Tabby, Aunt Branwell or the sisters themselves. We can imagine him stepping forward to greet Anne upon her arrival back at the parsonage, with his self-confidence, dazzling smile and an extended hand. Her sisters would have been watching on playfully to see how she accepted it, and Anne would have taken it briefly, before casting her eyes down and willing herself not to blush. This very first touch of hands, this formality, could have ignited the initial spark in her heart. It was to become an all-consuming conflagration.

In the following days, Anne would see him more and more, observing him silently as she often liked to do, blending into the background but missing nothing that was going on. She would have been astounded at his dealings with three of the people who were closest to her.

Patrick could be very stubborn when he wanted to be, and rather eccentric and idiosyncratic in his ways. His assistant curates often found him difficult to work with, but William Weightman had no such problems. Patrick took an instant liking to his new assistant. He was a hard worker, keen to learn and keen to take on new responsibilities. In the evenings, Patrick would spend time in his study with Weightman, usually a place where he valued solitude, and discuss classical works of literature, as well as biblical interpretation. Patrick was delighted to find that his new assistant was cut from the same cloth as himself, rather than having Calvinist leanings. He was a good preacher too, possessing a natural charm and eloquence, so that the parishioners of Haworth soon gave him their unreserved approval.

Weightman's arrival would also prove a blessing for Branwell. At last he had some male company of a similar age to himself, and they were to become firm friends. Together they would discuss the things that Branwell loved: war, art, poetry, girls. It is possible that he joined Branwell and his drinking companions such as John Brown in the Black Bull from time to time. However, Weightman never took this to the excesses that Branwell did, and that his own brother, Robert Weightman, was to do.

Perhaps his most surprising supporter of them all was Emily. By this time Emily could not usually bear to be in the company of strangers at all, and the only men she could spend any time with were her father and brother. Anne would have been amazed to see that Emily was relaxed and comfortable in Weightman's company, she did not hide from him and did not remain silent when he talked. If even Emily had regard for him, then surely he was a man who needed to be watched. Anne soon found that the more she watched him, the more she liked to watch him.

It is obvious that William Weightman had his charms, both physical and intellectual, yet some modern portraits of him are far from flattering. He is seen as a flighty man who played with women's hearts and then cast them aside, a man that could not really be trusted or relied upon.[4] This seems highly unfair when we have the testimony of Anne Brontë, her father and the parishioners in his favour, and just one dissenting voice against him. It is the powerful voice of Charlotte Brontë that is used to judge him harshly and unfairly, yet we can defend him by examining her motives.

When Weightman arrived in Haworth he implied that he was engaged to a woman called Agnes Walton from his home town of Appleby. Although it seems that he may have made an overture in that direction a year later, this is unlikely to have been true at the time – so why did he say it? The answer is that he was trying to put his new master, Patrick Brontë, and his daughters at their ease. Whilst the Brontë sisters were hardly bound by the conventions of their times, it would still have been judged strange for them to have spent so much time alone with a single man. By creating an engagement, he could put their minds at rest and prevent local tongues from wagging and damaging their reputations.

It has been said that he could never have hoped to be engaged to Agnes Walton, as the Waltons were on a different social level to the Weightmans; yet, William's father was a middle-class businessman, and by the time William arrived in Haworth, John Walton, the father of Agnes, had died. Would a newly qualified priest, with a glowing record at England's new university, and the potential to make a successful career in the Church, really be an unfit match for a fatherless young woman? It is certainly possible that in the loosest sense Weightman had been courting Agnes, and so, to meet the social niceties of the time, he embellished this into the tale of an engagement.

Weightman, with his good looks and pleasing manner, was certainly a hit with many ladies he met, yet that doesn't necessarily make him a philanderer. We hear that he had been wooing Caroline Dury, daughter of the Reverend Theodore Dury of Keighley, a friend of Patrick Brontë, as well as a young Keighley woman named Sarah Sugden.[5] We also hear that he had been refusing to answer letters from a woman in far away Swansea, yet the source for all these accusations is Charlotte, and on this matter she is a far from disinterested witness.

Through Charlotte's correspondence with Ellen Nussey at this time, we can witness her changing attitudes to the new assistant curate. Like most people who met him, she was instantly taken with his good looks. Charlotte could develop a crush on somebody very quickly, and she prized appearance above most other attributes. Day by day, she began to become more fixated upon Weightman.

By March 1840 she had developed a playful nickname for Weightman, 'Miss Celia Amelia', and praised him as an 'intelligent and interesting young person'. This nickname implies that his delicate features gave him an almost feminine appearance, and whilst in these early references it is used good humouredly, it is later used as a weapon against him.

In September 1840 Charlotte writes that he is still as 'handsome, cheery and good tempered as usual' but already she accuses him of having a 'whole, warm fickle soul'.[6] By March 1841 her tone and opinion has changed completely. She talks of the Valentine's Day card she has received from him, but unlike that of a year previously it, like he, is not appreciated:

I knew better how to treat it than I did those we received a year ago. I am up to the dodges and artifices of his Lordship's character, he knows I know him … for all the tricks, wiles and insincerities of love the gentleman has not his match for 20 miles round. He would fain persuade every woman under 30 whom he sees that he is desperately in love with her. I have a great deal more to say but I have not a moment's time to write it in.[7]

This is the image of Weightman that is readily believed, and yet they are the words of Charlotte in one of her warm tempers, and when she was quite possibly feeling bitter and as though she had been spurned. In this letter, she magnifies Weightman's faults to create character flaws that in reality weren't there, twisting his good deeds and kind character and imagining them to be built upon manipulation and artifice.

By February 1840, Weightman had been in Haworth for six months and was known, liked and respected by all the Brontë family. The sisters would let him into confidences that they would never tell anyone else, including the revelation that none of them had ever received a Valentine's card. With a smile on his face, Weightman resolved to do something about this. He walked 10 miles to Bradford so that he could post four cards anonymously, one each for Anne, Charlotte and Emily, and another for Ellen Nussey, who was at that time on one of her extended visits to Haworth.

Each card had a personalised verse inside it, and we can imagine the delight on the faces of the young women upon receiving them. It did not take them long, however, to work out who must have sent them, despite the misleading postmark, and they sent him a collective card in return. They too had composed a verse:

We cannot write or talk like you;
We're plain folks every one;
You've played a clever trick on us,
We thank you for the fun.
Believe us when we frankly say
(Our words though blunt are true),
At home, abroad, by night or day,
We all wish well to you.[8]

This demonstrates Weightman's character. He sent the cards not to mock the sisters but to brighten up their day. There was no malice intended, he could not begin to imagine they could be taken in that way, yet a year later when he repeated this act that was exactly how Charlotte reacted.

The card had served to increase Charlotte's growing infatuation. She painted his portrait, and Ellen mocked her friend for how many sittings she made him endure so that she could gaze upon his features. From the surviving sketch we see a handsome and young looking face, with wavy hair and long mutton chop sideburns. Charlotte hoped that Weightman would return her affections, indeed it seems that due simply to his usual kindnesses and ebullient character, she believed that he did.

Charlotte had by this time already rejected one proposal of marriage, from Ellen's brother Henry, because she could not countenance being married to a man she did not find attractive, yet she might not have not rejected Weightman if the proposal came. It never did, and Charlotte's love began to turn to anguish, then despair, and then anger.

Charlotte sought around for the reason that he had remained strangely immune to her charms. Agnes Walton would seem the most obvious suspect, and yet Charlotte betrays no jealousy towards her. She goes even further and paints a picture of Agnes for Weightman, just as Jane Eyre paints a portrait of St John Rivers' love in her famous novel. Could it be that an even worse betrayal had been carried out, that Weightman secretly harboured feelings for somebody that Charlotte, although she loved her, could never think of as an equal? It was a love that Charlotte could never quite bring herself to confront, preferring instead to think that Weightman was a faithless man who loved any and all women. As the months and years passed, she would look the other way: she could not accept that Weightman was turning his attention to her youngest sister, Anne.

Anne and William would come to know each other well in those first months of 1840. She was now at home in the parsonage, and he was a frequent visitor. We know that Weightman was a deeply devout man, and Patrick described him as a man who 'thought it better, and more scriptural, to make the love of God, rather than the fear of hell, the ruling motive for obedience'.[9]

Those views were the same as those held most deeply by Anne. His ebullience masked his kindness and thoughtfulness, as shown by the regular gifts of game that he sent to the parsonage when he was away; Anne's kindness and thoughtfulness were also hidden, but by quietness and reserve. They soon saw through each other's masks and recognised kindred spirits. We also know that Anne was the same age as the Agnes Walton he had left behind and that people thought of her as the prettiest of the sisters, despite Charlotte forever thinking of her as being 'queer looking'. There was no reason for Weightman not to develop feelings for her, and over time this seems to have happened.

We know the titles of three of the verses in the 1840 Valentine's cards that Weightman sent. They are 'Fair Ellen, Fair Ellen', 'Soul Divine', and 'Away Fond Love'.[10] We can say with certainty that the first was sent to Ellen Nussey of course, but could 'Away Fond Love' be for Anne, especially if she was at that point advertising for a new governess position, and had told him about her plans to move away?

We don't have to look very far for evidence of Anne's growing emotional attachment to William Weightman. From the moment of meeting him, her love poems leave Gondal far behind and take on a new and more realistic feel, and of course there is the character of Reverend Weston in *Agnes Grey*.

Edmund Weston is the assistant curate to the vain and self-centred Reverend Hatfield. He is a kind and spiritual man, much admired by the parishioners; gradually, he and Agnes fall in love. Their growing love is ruptured by a separation, but after a passage of time they meet again and embark upon a happy married life together.

There are many similarities between Weston and Weightman, yet one major difference. Whilst Weightman possessed good looks, Weston is described as being plain, and he is also described by Miss Murray as being brutish and ugly. Why would Anne have done this, if Weston were indeed intended to be a portrait of Weightman?

By downplaying his good looks, Anne was emphasising his spirituality and kindness, qualities that were infinitely more important to her. She would have been ashamed for people to think that she only loved a man because he was handsome, so she was careful through the depiction of

Edmund Weston to allay this charge of superficiality for both herself and her heroine.

It may also be asked why, if Anne loved Weightman and especially if she felt some reciprocation, she moved so far away? Again we must turn to Anne's principles of patience and endurance. To Anne's mind if something was worth having, it was worth waiting for. Put faith in God: if He willed it then it would happen. The proof of this belief is in both of Anne's novels. In *Agnes Grey*, Agnes has a long and lonely wait, thinking she will never see Weston again, until they are suddenly reunited. In the final section of *The Tenant of Wildfell Hall*, Gabriel and Helen endure a string of delays, misunderstandings and unfortunate incidents that stretch for years until they can finally marry. These delays are tests of love that Gabriel must overcome to prove his worth.

Anne would have turned to a favourite piece of scripture for sustenance and encouragement, St Paul's powerful 'hymn to love' in his first letter to the Corinthians. We are told that love 'suffereth long, and is kind', that it 'vaunteth not itself, is not puffed up', and that love 'beareth all things, believeth all things, hopeth all things, endureth all things'.

This then is Anne's perfect love. It will be kept quiet, rather than being vaunted and puffed up, and it will bear and endure all things. Like Anne, it will be patient, and testing love by moving away, making it endure even more, could only strengthen its eventual happy resolution.

Charlotte, unwittingly, is also responsible for an insight into Weightman's feelings for her sister. In her letter to Ellen of 20 January 1842 she writes of him: 'He sits opposite Anne at church sighing softly and looking out of the corners of his eyes to win her affection – and Anne is so quiet, her looks so downcast – they are a picture.'[11]

Overcome the hint of bitterness and jealousy in Charlotte's letter and what impression do we get of Anne and Weightman, two years after they first met? They are undoubtedly flirting with each other, hiding their love away, but still being observed by those who understand the true emotions within their hearts.

During those two years, their feelings had grown for each other. In the summer of 1841 especially, during Anne's month-long break from the Robinsons, they would have spent a lot of time in each other's company, as both Charlotte and Emily were abroad.[12] Could they have come to some sort of understanding during this time? They were both too poor to make a commitment to each other at that moment in their lives, but if they were patient and remained true then a bright future could be achieved. If Patrick saw anything of this, he would certainly have approved in a way that he steadfastly did not when a later curate asked for the hand of his daughter Charlotte. After all, Patrick admitted that he looked on Weightman as like a son to him[13] – high praise indeed considering his fractious relationships with other assistant curates.

For now, Anne would have to cling to her dreams of a future life with her William. She would have to make do with the exchanged glances in church, the brushing of hands when nobody was looking, the sighs and whispers. In the meantime she would delight in finding a man who she deemed worthy of her love. Even Charlotte now conceded that she might have judged him too harshly. She had once called him 'unclerical'[14] but had found evidence that he was anything but.

Charlotte saw Weightman returning to the parsonage late one evening looking sad and tired. Patrick asked him what was wrong. He replied that he was in low spirits because he had just been to see a poor young girl who was dying. The girl turned out to be Susan Bland, one of Charlotte's Sunday school pupils. She visited the house the next day and found that Susan was indeed dying, but also that Weightman had not only visited them but had taken them a bottle of wine and a jar of preserves. Mrs Bland added that 'he was always good-natured to poor folks, and seemed to have a deal of feeling and kind-heartedness about him'.[15] At last, Charlotte was forced to grudgingly concede to Ellen that 'he is not all selfishness and vanity'.[16]

This aspect of Weightman's character coincides exactly with that of Edmund Weston in *Agnes Grey*. We read of Weston taking a particular interest in poor people, visiting the sick, reading to them, rescuing their pets and delivering them uncalled for gifts and provisions, even though he had little himself. This is Anne's true tribute to the man she had loved, the man she still loved, after she had been mourning him for nearly five years.

In the summer of 1841, Weightman was called to Ripon to be ordained as a fully fledged priest in his own right.[17] The ordination took place in August 1840, and Anne believed that he would go from there to visit her at Thorp Green. It could be that they had already arranged this with each other through hushed conversations or secretly passed notes. Each day that passed without him made her more downcast, as shown in her 'Lines Written at Thorp Green' at the start of this chapter. Anne's wording in both her prose and poetry is always precise and carefully chosen, and in this case it is illuminating, 'Oh didst thou know my longings … thou wouldst not thus delay'.[18]

Anne does not write that she hopes he would not delay but that he definitely would not delay. Anne here is supremely confident of William Weightman's love for her. If she could only reveal it in its fullness, rather than the carefully shielded form, he would be hers.

It would even have been socially acceptable for Weightman to call upon Anne at Thorp Green, for he had connections with the family of her mistress, Mrs Lydia Robinson. Mrs Robinson's father, the Reverend Thomas Gisborne, was a leading name in the establishment of Durham University where Weightman had been an early scholar. This canon of Durham set up the university's natural history museum in 1835[19] and also provided the money for a Gisborne scholarship at the university.

Reverend Gisborne also arranged for his grandson Lionel Gisborne, the nephew of Lydia Robinson, to enter Durham University in 1839.[20] Further to these facts, the co-founder of the university, Archdeadon Charles Thorp,[21] was the first cousin once removed to Anne's other employer, Edmund Robinson. It is certain that Weightman would have seen and known both Thomas Gisborne and Charles Thorp in his time at university, looking up to them with the reverence they deserved, and it is also possible that he may have known Lionel Gisborne.

Under these circumstances, Weightman would have been a welcome guest of the Robinsons at Thorp Green. It could even be that Weightman knew that the Robinsons were looking for a new governess in early 1840 and had personally recommended Anne to them.

Anne waited, yet Weightman did not come. It is this that made her say that she 'disliked the situation and wished to change it for another'.

She longed to be with this man who, as her poems express, could bring about a feeling of bliss just by looking at her. She would endure further, she would wait longer, what else could she do? During Anne's winter and summer visits to Haworth over the year following the ordination, they grew closer still, yet time was not on their side.

We have seen how Weightman loved to visit the sick and dying, providing comfort at their time of greatest need, but in a town as infectious and disease ridden as Haworth this was a very dangerous game. He contracted cholera from one such patient and rapidly faded, dying two weeks later on 6 September 1842, aged 28, with a distraught Branwell weeping by his death bed.[22]

It was a noble end for a noble and honourable man, and the sense in which he was revered and loved by all who knew him was soon shown. Patrick Brontë delivered the funeral service for his erstwhile assistant, and for the first time at Haworth he read it rather than preaching extempore as usual. Patrick explained that this was because his parishioners had asked him to publish the funeral sermon afterwards, which he duly did.[23]

The sermon is a fine tribute to a man who was clearly loved by Patrick. Reverend Brontë was not a man who gave credit lightly, but on this occasion his praise was genuine and fulsome. He began the sermon, after discussing a reading from the first letter of St Paul to the Corinthians, by contrasting Weightman with others who make a good first impression that fails to stay the course:

> There are many, who for a short time can please, and even astonish – but, who soon retrograde and fall into dispute. His character wore well; the surest proof of real worth … But what he gained at first, he did not lose afterwards. He had those qualities which enabled him rather to gain ground.[24]

Patrick also praises him as a preacher, as well as an excellent teacher at the Sunday school. Weightman was 'himself a friend to many, and an enemy to none, so by a kind of reaction, he had, I think I might say, no enemies and many friends',[25] and he states that 'we were always like father and son'.[26] Perhaps the greatest praise that Patrick could give to William Weightman, however, was when he observed that he 'had classical attainments of the first order, and, above all, his religious principles were sound and orthodox'.[27]

The event was also reported by the *Leeds Intelligencer* of 29 October 1842:

He [Weightman] was admired and beloved for his sterling piety, his amiability, and cheerfulness, and the loss of so zealous and useful a Minister of Christ is deeply felt by those among whom he lived and laboured. This discourse [the funeral sermon], plain and touching in its language, simple yet expressive, pays a well deserved tribute to the memory of the preacher's beloved and lamented fellow labourer.[28]

This contemporary account of a man noted for his 'sterling piety' is a far cry from the image that some have of him today, or that Charlotte chose to portray in her letters. The parishioners would not hear a word said against him, and two years later they had raised enough money to have a tribute to Weightman placed on the wall of the church.[29]

One woman was not there to mourn him on that dark, damp October day. Anne had not even been told that William was ill. When she found out, probably through Branwell writing to her at Thorp Green, that her beloved William was dead, it would have felt as if the sky was falling and the ground shaking beneath her feet. She would spend the day weeping in her room, and even the Robinsons would know not to disturb her. How could it be that the world was carrying on just as it was yesterday and the day before, did it not know what had happened? Did it not know that something had changed, that it was less than before? Anne Brontë's world, and her writing, would never be the same again.

10

SEPARATIONS AND RETURNS

I will not mourn thee, lovely one,
Though thou art torn away.
'Tis said that if the morning sun
Arise with dazzling ray
And shed a bright and burning beam
Athwart the glittering main,
'Ere noon shall fall that laughing gleam
Engulfed in clouds and rain …
And yet I cannot check my sighs,
Thou wert so young and fair,
More bright than summer morning skies,
But stern death would not spare;
He would not pass our darling by
Nor grant one hour's delay,
But rudely closed his shining eye
And frowned his smile away.
That angel smile that late so much
Could my fond heart rejoice;

And he has silenced by his touch
The music of thy voice.
I'll weep no more thine early doom,
But O! I still must mourn
The pleasures buried in thy tomb,
For they will not return.

'To –'

Anne Brontë wrote this poem of mourning, of frustrated love, in December 1842, around three months after the death of William Weightman. She would not name the lost lover to whom she addressed the poem, simply giving it the enigmatic title of 'To –'. Her love for him would be something she would take to her grave, and yet it would never fade or diminish within Anne's heart.

This was the first of many poems that Anne would write about Weightman after his death, and although he is never named, there can be no doubt that he is the subject. To Anne, the brief love she had felt, and in some way received, was a gift from God, and she would nurture it and keep it fresh, in the hope and belief that one day it could be nurtured again and brought to fruition in a new celestial sphere. It was the only romantic love she would ever give or receive: Weightman was dead, but she would be forever faithful to his memory. To do anything else would, to Anne, be to cheapen the emotions that she'd felt.

As the years passed by she would write poems beginning with lines such as 'Oh they have robbed me of the hope, my spirit held so dear',[1] and 'Severed and gone so many years! And art thou still so dear to me'.[2] There would be no let up in the mourning expressed in these powerful poems, yet they were also a cathartic experience for Anne and part of the healing process. For Anne there were two ways to deal with the sorrows, challenges and torments that life presented. One was through the power of prayer, and she would value nothing higher than those moments when she could share her private thoughts and feelings with her Lord, and the other was through the power of poetry.

Anne's belief in an almost mystical healing power of poetic composition is detailed in the chapter entitled 'Confessions' within *Agnes Grey*, when the heroine reveals:

> When we are harassed by sorrows or anxieties, or long oppressed by any powerful feelings which we must keep to ourselves, for which we can obtain and seek no sympathy from any living creature, and which yet we cannot, or will not wholly crush, we often naturally seek relief in poetry – and often find it, too ... now I fly to it again, with greater avidity than ever, because I seemed to need it more.[3]

At this point in the novel Agnes is distraught because Weston is about to leave the parish, and she fears she will never see him again; this compares with the fact that Weightman had left and Anne would never see him on this earth again. Agnes then reveals one of her poems, one of her 'pillars of witness' as she refers to them, which is in fact Anne's poem 'Oh They Have Robbed Me of the Hope'. The lines that Agnes ends this poem with, within the novel, and her commentary on them are very revealing of Anne's thoughts in the days, months and years following Weightman's death:

> They will not let me see that face
> I so delight to see;
> And they have taken all thy smiles,
> And all thy love from me.
> Well, let them seize on all they can; –
> One treasure still is mine, –
> A heart that loves to think on thee,
> And feels the worth of thine.
>
> Yes, at least, they could not deprive me of that: I could think of him day and night; and I could feel that he was worthy to be thought of. Nobody knew him as I did; nobody could appreciate him as I did; nobody could love him as I – could, if I might.[4]

Once more in *Agnes Grey*, Anne is giving us a tantalising clue to her real life. This is, as she says, a pillar of witness, this is a 'confession' not of Agnes but of Anne herself.

In Anne's life sorrow often came in pairs, for example when her sisters Maria and Elizabeth died in quick succession, and later when the same occurred with Branwell and Emily, and so it proved to be in late 1842. She had not been able to attend William Weightman's funeral, but a month later she was back in Haworth from Thorp Green for the funeral of her Aunt Elizabeth Branwell.

Aunt Branwell was 66 years old, and for most of her time in Haworth had been in relatively robust health, but shortly after William Weightman's death, her own health sharply deteriorated. She had an obstruction of the bowel that caused her terrible agony, reminiscent of the agonies she had seen her own sister go through in the same parsonage twenty-one years earlier. She died on 29 October 1842, and again it was a distraught Branwell who was by the bedside.

Branwell had taken the death of his good friend William Weightman hard, but he was to feel the death of his aunt even more. She was much more than an aunt to him: in every way he looked up to her as a mother figure. She had shown him love, and he in return had loved her more than any other living thing. To some extent her sternness had also helped to curb some of Branwell's excesses, and now severed from this guiding adult, he would spend the next years accelerating his descent into drink and drug dependency.

Anne too would feel the death much more than Charlotte and Emily. Aunt Branwell was the only mother figure she could remember, and they had been very close when Anne was a child. Recognising this, the Robinsons allowed Anne to return home for the funeral on 3 November. During the service given by her father, Anne would join Branwell in an outpouring of grief as she mourned for two people.

Many previous Brontë biographies have emphasised the stern nature of Aunt Branwell, and her unflinching morality, yet she could also be very kind and held a genuine warmth of affection for her sister's children. She would buy them books, toys and clothing, and she would not forget them in her death either. Elizabeth Branwell left each of her nieces £300 in her will, a sum equivalent to around £30,000 in 2016 and equal to six years' wages for Anne.[5] Branwell, who his aunt had loved dearly but latterly despaired of, was disinherited. Their immediate money problems and worries about finding long-term situations for which they were suited subsided, and they could now turn their thoughts to another dream, one with which they had already been making progress.

Anne wasn't the only Brontë to return to Haworth for their aunt's funeral. Charlotte and Emily had also been away, and even further afield. In fact, they had been in Belgium, learning the skills they hoped would enable them to establish their own school.

In Anne's diary paper of July 1841, she writes, 'We are thinking of setting up a school of our own but nothing definite is settled about it yet and we do not know if we should be able to or not – I hope we shall.'[6]

Emily, in her corresponding diary paper, writes, 'A scheme is at present in agitation for setting us up in a school of our own, as yet nothing is determined but I hope and trust it may go on and prosper and answer our highest expectations.'[7]

The sisters had been discussing the idea of setting up their own school for some time, possibly even since Charlotte had left the employ of Miss Wooler at Heald's House. Since that date, Charlotte, Emily and Anne had all tried teaching and governess positions, but Anne was the only one who had the endurance and a temperament sanguine enough to make any sort of success at it. It was clear that they were not suited to working for others, yet they still thought they could be teachers, if only it were in their own establishment.

Setting up a school would take funds, of course, which none of the sisters had, and so in the summer of 1841 they decided to approach their aunt to see if she could help. Aunt Branwell knew that she was getting old, although she could not have known how close she was to her death, and wanted dearly to see her nephew and nieces make a success of their lives. She had brought a collection of jewellery of considerable value from Cornwall with her and had also a moderate personal wealth. The scheme put to her seemed sensible and measured, two of her favourite qualities, and so she agreed in principal to lending them £150 if they could form concrete plans.[8]

This prospect must have seemed delightful to Anne in 1841. She would be able to get away from the Robinsons and return closer to home, and to William Weightman. She would also be able to make fuller use of her not insubstantial learning. Every night, whether at Thorp Green or Scarborough, she would kneel by her bed and pray silently, 'Lord, let us find a suitable school that we can work in together'. In that summer of 1841, it seemed that her prayers were being answered.

Margaret Wooler had decided to give up her school at Dewsbury Moor and wrote to Charlotte Brontë offering it to her. If agreement could be reached, Miss Wooler would continue to reside in the building, and in return Charlotte could have free use of the furniture. This must have seemed a perfect opportunity, as the costs would be much lower than could otherwise be expected, and they would also have the experience of Miss Wooler to call upon for advice.

Aunt Branwell agreed to lend the girls £100 to take over the school, but to the despair of Anne and Emily, by the time this had been agreed Charlotte had already changed her mind. She had received a letter from her friend Mary Taylor, who was at that time living in Brussels with her sister Martha. She read of the wonderful architecture that could be found in Brussels, and she longed to see it herself. Charlotte, in stark contrast to her sisters, relished the idea of travelling abroad. The reports she had read in childhood of exploration in Africa, and the maps she pored over, had not only fired her creativity, they had also kindled the desire to travel herself. If she and her sisters took over the school in Heald's House now it would be a lifelong commitment, her dreams of seeing the world would be over. The plan would have to be modified; it would have to be delayed.

Charlotte now approached her aunt with a new suggestion. French and German were highly prized attainments, she explained, so if they could offer these skills, as well as sharpening up the learning they already had, then they would be able to attract a much better quality of pupil and would stand a much greater chance of lasting success. She therefore asked her aunt to pay for her and Emily to study in Belgium, after which they would be in a position to return and start their school with Anne.

It's hard to say how much of this Charlotte actually believed and how much was a ruse to get her aunt to pay for her to see the world, but Aunt

Branwell was eventually convinced and plans were made for Charlotte and Emily to travel to Belgium at the beginning of 1842. It was a body blow for Anne at the commencement of what was to be a year full of tragedy.

Charlotte, as always, had taken organisational duties upon herself, but it has to be asked why she chose Emily to accompany her rather than Anne, who would seem much more suited to the task. Emily had lasted just weeks at Roe Head with Charlotte before becoming so homesick that Charlotte thought she would die if not returned to Haworth, and yet now she was about to take her to a whole new country.

Charlotte herself offered an explanation of sorts in the letter she sent to her aunt on 29 September 1841, from a short-lived situation that she was currently holding with the White family of Rawdon:

> These are advantages which would turn to vast account, when we actually commenced a school – and, if Emily could share them with me, only for a single half-year, we could take a footing in the world afterwards which we could never do now. I say Emily instead of Anne; for Anne might take her turn at some future period, if our school answered.[9]

Here Charlotte is anticipating that her aunt may not have been so willing to fund the enterprise if she felt her favourite niece, Anne, was being excluded, yet as Anne watched the sisters preparing to travel at the end of 1841, excluded must have been just how she felt. Emily was simply taking the place because she was older, and that was only the right and natural order of things, Anne would have been told, but she may have suspected deeper and darker motives.

Was Charlotte remembering the way that she had snubbed her desperately ill youngest sister in the Roe Head days and fearful of something that could bring those guilty memories back? Could it even have been borne of jealousy? Charlotte and Emily were ostensibly travelling to learn language skills, yet Anne was already competent in French and Latin in a way that her sisters weren't. Whilst retaining her innate veneer of modesty, she was burning with indignation inside. Anne knew that it was she who possessed the finest intellect of all the sisters, had the finest educational attainments and was proving she could make a living for herself in the world, and yet once again she found herself being ignored and almost belittled by Charlotte.

As always in these circumstances, Anne swallowed her indignation beneath a veil of resigned acceptance. Pragmatism was needed now: if Emily was going to be away, somebody would have to take her place in the parsonage, and Anne wasted no time in suggesting herself for the role. Before returning to Haworth for Christmas 1841, she called for a meeting with her employers and there tendered her resignation, explaining that she would now be needed at home. To her dismay, Mr and Mrs Robinson countered that they were very pleased with the progress their daughters were making under Anne, that she had in fact become indispensable to them and that they could not possibly let her go. Thus it was that in January 1842 the sisters went their separate ways again. Charlotte and Emily were en route to the excitement of a new adventure, even if that excitement was being felt much more keenly by Charlotte than Emily, while Anne was returning to her lonely drudgery at Thorp Green Hall.

Patrick accompanied his daughters on their journey to Brussels; it was the first time that any of them had left the confines of Britain. He had initially been reluctant to agree with Charlotte's scheme, but his daughter had reminded him of the ambition he himself had shown as a young man when he left Ireland for England. 'I want us all to go on,' she said, 'I know we have talents, and I want them to be turned to account.'[10]

He was won round, and with a swell of pride he wrote to the Church of England chaplain in Brussels, Reverend Evan Jenkins, for advice on a suitable school. Whilst the Taylor sisters of Gomersal were at the city's exclusive Château de Koekelberg school, this was far too expensive an establishment to be considered. Reverend Jenkins suggested that an establishment called the Pensionnat Heger would be a suitable and respectable alternative, and it was here that the Brontës left for, with Mary Taylor and her brother Joe as travelling companions, on 2 February 1842.

After a brief stop in London, where they stayed at the Chapter Coffee House in the shadow of St Paul's, they made the crossing into mainland Europe. Patrick had prepared for the event by writing down French phrases in a notebook, along with the way in which they should be pronounced. One such example was 'Demain = de mang – tomorrow'.[11]

Patrick stayed in Brussels for a week before returning home. A new continental tomorrow was dawning for Charlotte and Emily, but Anne was waking up to the same North Yorkshire sunrise as before.

In these early months of 1842, Anne had three things to sustain her: her faith, the dream she clung to that when her sisters returned they could at last set up the school they'd talked of and her love for William Weightman, who she had left behind in Haworth. Little did she know that this third consolation was soon to be snatched from her.

Anne was indeed making good progress with her pupils now, and they were beginning to look up to her with respect and even something approaching love, yet Anne was far from happy. The landscape around Little Ouseburn was flat and lush, but it could never appeal to her in the way that the moors around Haworth did. She listened at night to the east winds rushing in and imagined how they had travelled across the moors on their way to Thorp Green, carrying messages that only she could hear and understand, carrying love.

As well as her consoling poetry, Anne had also by this time started to think of writing a prose work that would relate to the world she knew, not the world of Gondal. She also diverted her mind by painting sketches and portraits, including a drawing of 1840 entitled 'What You Please'. A young woman with long wavy hair is leaning against the bough of a tree, a cloak wrapped around her shoulders. It is an enigmatic picture. The woman seems to be deep in thought, is she walking away from something or towards something? The face of the young woman also bears some resemblance to a watercolour she painted at some time during her tenure as the Robinson's governess entitled 'Portrait of a Young Woman', as well as to a picture she created in June 1842, on which she has written 'A Very Bad Picture'. This picture too shows a young woman, with long curly hair, fine eyebrows and a straight nose. These two portraits are commonly thought to be of one of the Robinson girls, but could they, and the woman in 'What you Please', actually be self-portraits? Certainly they also bear some likeness to the Anne Brontë of Branwell's 'pillar portrait'. The main difference is that the young woman in Anne's portrait has a fuller, rounder face, but we have to remember that Anne was aged around 13 when she featured in Branwell's portrait, and in those painted around this time by Charlotte, so she could well have developed a rounder face into adulthood.

If, as seems almost certain, 'What you Please' is a self-portrait, there is another possible interpretation of its title. Could this attractive picture have been intended as a gift for someone, even if she never dared to present it, a special person who had entered her life months earlier and who Anne knew would appreciate it? Was she saying, '*This* woman is what *you* please'?

Just as she did in her writing, Anne was using art to express who she was, and who she wanted to be. Perhaps her most significant drawing of them all was crafted in November 1839, when she was coming towards the end of her time with the Ingham family. It is entitled 'Sunrise Over Sea', and in it we see a young woman in a long flowing dress looking out over a seascape. She has her right hand to her forehead, as if she is searching for something far out on the horizon. There is a boat on the sea and gulls in the air, and dominating the centre of the picture is a glorious sun, whose beams are cutting through a pre-dawn gloom. We then notice that the woman is standing precariously on the edge of a rocky precipice, but what does this mean?

Some commentators have speculated that this may be simply an art exercise, a copy of an earlier painting, but the facts don't support that. No 'original' for such a painting has been found, and art lessons for women at this time would have concentrated on painting nature and still life objects, rather than figurative work. This is an explosive picture, full of symbolism, which has come straight from Anne's mind. She is standing on the edge of something, but if she takes one wrong step she will be doomed. She is being called to something, or someone, but it seems impossible for her to reach it, or them. She has a white handkerchief in her left hand, but is it to wave goodbye or to signal that she is coming? Above all, the painting shows the beauty of the sea.

We only see the back of the woman, but the long wavy hair again signals that this is Anne drawing herself. At the time it was drawn, she had never seen the sea, but under the Robinsons all that changed. Every summer the Robinson family would decamp to Scarborough, on the east coast, for a month, and as governess Anne would have to accompany them. This part of her job, at least, was not a chore, and she fell in love at first glance with the sea and with Scarborough itself.

Scarborough at this time was a very chic and exclusive resort. The taking of 'seaside holidays' was a relatively new concept in the 1840s, and it had been embraced by the upper classes. The Robinson family would always stay at the prime location of 'Wood's Lodgings', which were on St Nicholas' Cliff, overlooking Scarborough's north bay.

The rather lacklustre name does not do justice to the luxury of the accommodation. Wood's Lodgings were centred upon a large, elegant and spacious regency house, with an uninterrupted view of the sea. The famous Grand Hotel of Scarborough now stands on the site. The great and good of Yorkshire society would go there in summer to see and be seen, and the local newspaper would report who was staying at the resort on a week-to-week basis. Thus we learn that in July 1842, as well as the Robinson family, Anne's previous employers, the Inghams, were in town. Anne would bow her head formally when she saw them, and give silent thanks that she no longer had to endure them or their children.

Scarborough had much to offer its wealthy visitors. There were regular concerts given at the town hall, which Anne would have been delighted to attend in the role as chaperone to the Robinson girls. An elegant bridge led from Wood's Lodgings to the new Scarborough Spa and the Pomona, where concerts, dances and balls were also held. These were attended by lords and ladies, ennobled gentry and recently enriched manufacturers. Anne would have delighted in being in the background at these events, observing how the upper classes dressed, behaved and talked, storing up details that she would later use in *The Tenant of Wildfell Hall*. She was the unseen watcher whose pen would later turn her into an anonymous assassin of their class.

The spa was also renowned for its health giving qualities, and Anne would hear tales of the seemingly miraculous recovery of people who had breathed the air and descended into the waters. On other occasions Anne would accompany the Robinson girls on walks along the beach, although she would have to admonish them for running ahead and leaving her behind. She took donkey rides in a carriage but insisted on taking the reins herself, as she did not like the way that the handlers would admonish and encourage the donkeys.

At night Anne listened to the sea roaring below her. Looking out of the window she could watch it crash against the rocks, throwing a white explosion of foam into the air. These were the nights that Anne liked best. There was something hypnotic about the sea, and the stormier and louder it was, the more she loved it. Men would come and go for millennia, as they always had, but this sea would still keep crashing against the rocks. It spoke of God's power, of hope and eternity. The sea would take on the same mysticism for Anne that the moors held for Emily, and she always longed to return to the coast when she was away from it, even in her very last days.

The summers in Scarborough would be the undisputed highlights of her time with the Robinson family, but this single month of happiness could not eradicate the growing displeasure she felt during the rest of the year at Thorp Green. I wonder how Charlotte and Emily are getting on, she would think as she lay in bed looking out at the stars that hung over them all; I wonder how our plans are progressing?

After Aunt Branwell's funeral she would get the chance to hear first hand how their Belgian adventure was going. Charlotte would enthuse about the wonderful country that Belgium was and how incredible the architecture of Brussels was. Typically, however, she could find little praise for her fellow pupils. The majority of her classmates were younger than she and Emily, and they were Catholics, a religion that Charlotte found idolatrous and intolerable. Nevertheless, she would put up with them, as she felt she was making great progress in her learning and her language skills.

Emily was less enthusiastic. She had been reserved as always at the Pensionnat Heger, but her added maturity had at least enabled her to overcome her homesickness. Whilst her teachers and fellow pupils would remember her as a shy and quiet student, they also praised her attitude and efforts in class.

The initial plan had been for Charlotte and Emily to spend half a year in Brussels and then return home, but at the end of this half a year the Hegers, who ran the school, approached them with an offer. They could continue their lessons for free if Charlotte would consent to teach English and if Emily would teach piano. Before Emily could raise any objection, Charlotte had accepted.

With their aunt now dead, however, it was obvious that plans would have to change again. Their ageing father needed a member of the family to look after his daily needs as he carried out his clerical work. Emily volunteered once more, and this time there could be no objections. She had done her duty this time, and she had even found some brief enjoyment in the change of scenery. Their fellow Brussels dweller Mary Taylor had written, 'Charlotte and Emily are well, not only in health, but in mind and hope. They are content in their present position and even gay.'[12]

When the opportunity presented itself, however, Emily was still keen to remain in Haworth. She was home at last, and she would never again leave it for any length of time.

When the formalities of the funeral were over, Charlotte kissed her family goodbye and returned to Brussels, but it was neither the architecture nor the lessons that she was keen on returning to: it was the professor in charge of the institute, Constantin Heger. He was a man in his early 30s, ostensibly employed like the other teachers by his wife, Claire, who owned the Pensionnat. He was tall, striking and an excellent speaker. He could be stern and demanding with his pupils, yet slowly but surely Charlotte fell in love with him.

She would remain in Brussels until the start of 1844, and after Charlotte's return to Haworth she sent the professor a string of letters professing her barely concealed passion.[13] Her declarations never received a reply, and indeed Heger ripped them to pieces, although for some reason his wife pieced them back together again. We can imagine the arguments they caused, as Constantin was forced to declare that he had never encouraged their erstwhile pupil.

Although Charlotte had returned to Brussels after her aunt's funeral, there was one other member of the family who had remained at home. Branwell had seen yet another job come to a premature end, after his failures as a portrait painter and tutor. He had lately been employed as a stationmaster on the newly formed railway at Luddendenfoot near Halifax. It was a position that paid well and offered opportunities for advancement, yet he spent much of his time drinking with new-found friends in local hostelries instead of at the station itself.

His greatest friend there was Francis Grundy, a railway engineer. Grundy later said that 'Had a position been chosen for this strange creature with the express purpose of driving him several steps to the bad, this must have been it.'[14]

Grundy explained how Branwell had little to do during the day except consort with 'wild, rollicking, hard-headed, half-educated manufacturers'.[15] This was an opportunity that Branwell did make the most of, to the extent that he failed to notice when a clerk began stealing from the station. Branwell was summarily dismissed for his 'constant carelessness' and failure to supervise his staff.

Branwell had failed yet again, and he bore it hard. His days would be spent carousing with friends at the Haworth hostelries or travelling to see them at his favourite haunts in Halifax, drinking away the money he had borrowed from his family and friends. This was further heartbreak for Anne. Although Branwell was sometimes cruel to her, at one point saying she was 'nothing, absolutely nothing'[16], she remembered the young man full of promise he had once been. She remembered the boy who had read to her and guided her on her early walks across the moors, the boy who had done sketches of fairy-tale castles to bring a smile to her face.

The possibility of redemption was at the centre of Anne's faith, and she believed it could transform Branwell's life too. If he could find a job and hold on to it, he would regain his self-respect and his control. He had been a close friend of her beloved Weightman, so surely he must have seen the good in Branwell as well? The idea had been sprung, and she immediately put it into action.

Anne explained to Mr and Mrs Robinson that she thought their son Edmund would fare better with a male tutor, and she knew just the person to fill the role. That they so readily agreed to Anne's suggestion is another indication of the esteem they held her in. When Anne returned to Thorp Green after the Christmas holiday of 1842, she had Branwell sitting in the carriage alongside her. Already he seemed to have regained some of his confidence and self-control, and as the miles towards York rolled by, she squeezed his hand and smiled. She would have a friend and confidante at Thorp Green at last, and now surely the future was looking brighter.

142

11

THE BIRTH
OF ACTON BELL

O God! if this indeed be all
That life can show to me;
If on my aching brow may fall,
No freshening dew from Thee …
Wandering and toiling without gain,
The slave of others' will,
With constant care, and frequent pain,
Despised, forgotten still …
If Life must be so full of care,
Then call me soon to Thee;
Or give me strength enough to bear
My load of misery.

'If This Be All'

Anne spent the journey to Thorp Green telling Branwell about the house and the family within it. She explained how he might find them aloof, or even condescending, but he must strive to keep his pride in check. She had put her own reputation on the line in securing her brother the position of tutor, and he would do well to remember that. Branwell felt the heat rise within him, how did it come to this, that his little sister was giving him orders, that he had to be beholden to her? Checking this impulse he smiled back at her, she would see how he could behave when he wanted to.

Branwell made a good first impression at the hall, much to Anne's relief. He had quelled his normal pride and exuberance when dealing with Mr Robinson, and Mrs Robinson seemed charmed by the diminutive, red-haired man with the Irish accent and a taste for the finer things in life. Things were progressing just as Anne had hoped. In this new environment, and aware for now of the opportunity he had been handed, he had kept the excesses of his Haworth days well under control. There was no drinking to excess, no shouting, no picking of fights. She had put the central tenet of her faith into practise and been rewarded for it. It was possible to reform someone; it was right to forgive people.

In March 1843 Anne and Branwell were visited at Thorp Green by their father. He had been in York as a witness in a fraud case, involving the will of one of his church trustees, John Beaver, and he took the opportunity to see how his children were progressing. He reported to Emily at home and Charlotte, via letter, that Branwell was already very settled and they both seemed highly valued by the Robinsons.[1] He was also impressed with the courtesy that the fine woman Mrs Robinson had shown to him, and to his son.

Branwell struck up a good bond with his young charge, Edmund Junior, regaling him with his favourite tales of war and adventure. Anne too was making great strides with her pupils. Lydia and Bessie were growing to maturity, and their schooling with Anne was becoming less frequent. Her teaching was now focused primarily on the youngest daughter, Mary, although she would still provide music and art lessons to the older daughters when they requested them. For the next two years the relationship between Anne and Lydia, Bessie and Mary Robinson began to change from purely one of governess and pupil to one of friendship. The girls valued Anne's common sense and straightforward honesty, and Anne would be pleased to dispense this advice, hoping that by doing so she might counter some of the artifice that they were learning from their mother.

In June 1843, Anne received a sign of their esteem, and she could have been given nothing better. The girls presented Anne with a young black and white cavalier spaniel, with a swishing tail, bright eyes and long floppy ears. She fell in love with the dog at once and named it Flossy. At last she had something she could hug and love, something she could whisper her secrets to and talk of the dreams she had.

Flossy would outlive Anne by five years, just as the other Brontë dog of this time, Keeper, the fierce mastiff that only Emily could control, would outlive his mistress. In a poignant letter written a month after Anne's death, Charlotte told W.S. Williams:

> The ecstasy of these poor animals [Flossy and Keeper] when I came in was something singular … I am certain they thought that, as I was returned, my sisters were not far behind – but here my sisters will come no more. Keeper may visit Emily's little bed-room, as he still does day by day, and Flossy may look wistfully round for Anne – they will never see them again – nor shall I.[2]

The happiness that Anne found in this first half of 1843 was to be short lived, as a problem developed that would test her faith and loyalty to the full, and Branwell was at the heart of it. By the time that she made her annual excursion to Scarborough, this time with her brother for company as well as the Robinson family, her suspicions were already growing. She had noticed the smiles that passed between Branwell and Mrs Robinson, and the fact that he would spend as much time in the company of the lady of the house as in the company of her son.

In Scarborough her suspicions deepened. Mrs Robinson would look for reasons to be apart from her husband, and at these times Branwell would often be absent too. It is unlikely that Branwell confessed everything to his sister at this time, but all the family commented on how much happier and healthier he seemed upon his return, with Anne, to Haworth for their summer holiday.

Anne kept a close eye on Branwell over the following months. She noticed the whispers that passed between Branwell and Mrs Robinson, saw their fingers touch as she passed a book to him for her son's lessons. As time passed it became obvious that the middle-aged woman and the young man she had hired as a tutor were having an affair, right under the nose of her husband.

Branwell was oblivious to the danger, but then he always was oblivious to danger, living in the moment and caring nothing for tomorrow. Anne, however, felt the danger sharply, and she felt shame too. Her brother's conduct had compromised her and turned her into a sinner along with him. Could she keep silent or even deny the truth if questioned, or should she do the right thing and in doing so betray her own brother? Would she be Peter or Cain?

Anne was not the only one who had noticed what was happening. The maid Anne Marshall, with whom Anne Brontë was on friendly terms, revealed that she had seen Branwell and his mistress in a more than compromising position.[3] By November 1843 he was writing to his friend in Haworth, John Brown, confessing that Miss Marshall 'saw him do enough to hang him'.[4] He also revealed the full extent of his relationship with Mrs Robinson. He first says that she, his 'little lady', is growing thinner by the day, but that she has the courage to bear anything except parting from him. With the letter he sends a lock of Mrs Robinson's hair that had lain on his chest that morning, but he laments that they could not lay with each other legally as husband and wife.

Here was the true dreadful situation that Anne had to face. The brother she had brought to Thorp Green in an effort to redeem his soul was now sleeping with her employer, and everybody seemed to know it except Mr Robinson himself. She remonstrated with her brother in private, but he mocked her and told her to keep quiet unless she wanted to be the cause of his ruin.

As the years 1843 and 1844 passed the affair continued, and now Branwell was becoming more confidant, careless and brazen. He would argue openly with Mr Robinson, who would complain that he was neglecting his duties with his son, and that he was drinking too much at the dinner table. On these occasions, Mrs Robinson would defend Branwell, and Anne would cast her eyes down, praying silently but fervently for the moment she could return to the solace of her room.

In January 1844, Charlotte returned to Haworth from Brussels. Anne's mind now turned to thoughts of escape. If the school plan could finally be put into place, she could leave Thorp Green and its scandalous scenes behind, yet Charlotte was too pre-occupied with thoughts of Monsieur Heger to do anything about their school. Charlotte was blissfully unaware of the situation that her sister and brother were in, and on 23 January 1844 she wrote to Ellen and reported that Anne and Branwell were thriving in their positions and were 'wondrously valued'.[5]

At the urging of Anne, who still had an ally in Emily, Charlotte at last put plans into motion. They would set up a small and exclusive school in the Haworth Parsonage itself. All three sisters had experience in teaching at the Haworth Sunday School, founded by their father and next door to the parsonage, to call upon and that may help to enhance their reputation in the area and attract pupils. One of the Sunday school pupils was later to recall that out of all the sisters who taught him, Anne 'looked the nicest and most serious like'.[6]

Modifications would be needed to the parsonage, but their first step would be to attract some initial pupils. This proved much harder than expected. They had cards printed that were entitled 'The Misses Brontës' Establishment for the Board and Education of a Limited Number of Young Ladies'.[7] These cards were sent to parents of potential pupils across the West Riding and listed the lessons they would give. For £35 per year pupils would be taught writing, arithmetic, history, grammar, geography and needlework. Optional lessons in French, German, Music, Drawing and Latin (which perforce would have to be taught by Anne), would cost an extra guinea each per term.

Anne's hopes were momentarily raised. At last there was some concrete form to their plans, if they could just find one or two pupils she could return to Haworth and commence what she dreamed of as her life's work, but to her dismay not one pupil was found. The attainments of the teachers were undoubtedly high, but so too was the cost.

The remoteness of Haworth also proved problematic, with parents also unwilling to send their children to board in a village that had a reputation for illness and disease.

There was one other problem facing the sisters' school plan, and that was Branwell himself. After Anne and Branwell returned to Haworth from Scarborough in the summer of 1844, it was the first time that all four Brontë children had been united again since the first days of 1842. Emily and Charlotte could not help but notice the change in their brother. His actions were becoming more unpredictable. One day he could be his old self, happy and full of life and hope, but the next he would be despondent and angry. On these days he would seek out his old drinking companions or spend the day in the Black Bull on his own before returning to the parsonage and railing against the injustice of the world.

It was clear that their plans for a school had reached an impasse. Nobody wanted to send their children to Haworth, and even if they did, could they rely on Branwell to behave respectably if he too was in residence? The sisters clung to their dream a little longer, but by November of 1844, when they had still to receive a single positive response, it was abandoned forever. For Anne this was a time of deep, dark despair, but within a year their situations would have changed again, and a new plan was born.

It was not just the ongoing affair between her brother and her employer that was grieving Anne but the way in which Mrs Robinson treated her children, the daughters Anne was increasingly fond of. Lydia and Bessie were reaching the ages where they would have to think about their future; for their mother that simply meant finding a wealthy and well-connected husband, and Anne despaired to find that although the children were not happy with that arrangement, they were nevertheless resigned to their fate.

Anne believed, unusually for her time, that marriage between man and woman was a contract between equals, and the only basis for marriage was a mutual love. The Robinson children, however, were taught that the sole function of marriage was to cement or improve one's position in society and that love was something to be avoided, even scorned.

In *Agnes Grey*, Anne talks about the unsuitable marriage that the mother of Rosalie, based upon young Lydia, is trying to foist upon her: 'I was amazed and horrified at Mrs Murray's heartlessness, or want of thought for the real good of her child; and, by my unheeded warnings and exhortations, I vainly strove to remedy the evil.'[8]

It is a strong word that Anne uses, and yet she really did think this was an evil act. The formalised courting that the girls were subjected to and the balls held in Thorp Green Hall with the sole purpose of finding suitably wealthy matches were, in Anne's eyes, contrary to the gift of love that came from God himself. She questioned the girls about their beliefs, and she tried to encourage them to find a match who they truly cared for, but at this point her entreaties met with little success. We can hear the echo of her pupil's words in those spoken by Rosalie: 'To think that I could be such a fool as to fall in *love*! It is quite beneath the dignity of a woman to do such a thing. Love! I detest the word! As applied to one of our sex, I think it a perfect insult.'[9]

Each day now seemed a mockery to Anne, with everyone in the hall behaving in what seemed to her a shameful manner. Branwell was sleeping with Mrs Robinson. The Misses Robinson were throwing away their chances of true happiness in the pursuit of material gain. Even Mr Robinson was becoming increasingly choleric as he attempted to avoid the truth that was flaunted under his nose, and he was drinking heavily as a coping mechanism.

Branwell was becoming more and more besotted with Mrs Robinson, and at the same time less concerned who knew about it. He knew, from his lover, that males in the Robinson line often died young, and Edmund Robinson's red face and increasingly vile temper gave him hope that his employer would not be long for this world. Branwell also harboured the belief that if Mrs Robinson were forced to choose between her ranting husband and her young lover, she would choose Branwell.

The more Anne tried to reason with her brother, the more he resisted. She was a fool, like she had always been. What did she know about love, about life? Once more she felt the cold shadows creeping into her soul, as she had done at Roe Head. She felt that every day longer she remained at Thorp Green she would be subjected to even greater indignities, and she could not take much more. As the school scheme had been abandoned, so too it was time to admit defeat in this venture.

In June she approached her master and mistress again, and explained that this time she really must resign her position. Lydia and Bessie were now young adults; the job she had been employed to perform had reached its natural end. This time she met with no opposition: Mrs Robinson would be glad to be rid of another witness, and she understood Anne's character well enough to know that her silence could be relied upon.

As the carriage waited to carry Anne back to Haworth, the children who had been in her care embraced her, with tears running down their cheeks. They had grown to love the governess that they had at first found strange and severe, and it was a love that would not be broken by their parting. For the rest of her life, Anne would receive letters from the Robinson children, seeking advice and help from her that they could not gain from their mother. Although she could not have known it at the time, she had not been unsuccessful in reforming and moulding their characters.

Both Bessie and Mary did marry wealthy husbands, although they had complained bitterly to Anne about the fates awaiting them, as Charlotte reveals in a letter to Ellen of 28 July 1848:

> Anne continues to hear constantly – almost daily, from her old pupils, the Robinsons. They are both now engaged to different gentlemen and if they do not change their minds, which they have already done two or three times, will probably be married in a few months. Not one spark of love does either of them profess for her future husband … Anne does her best to cheer and counsel her [Bessie Robinson] and she seems to cling to her quiet, former governess as her only true friend.[10]

Following Anne's guidance, Bessie Robinson broke off her engagement to a Mr Milner, although the case went to court and her mother had to pay over £90 in compensation. She was eventually to marry industrialist William Jessop of Butterley Hall, Ripley, in Derbyshire. As an adult she would follow Anne's example and demonstrate great kindness and compassion with the people around her. The *Sheffield Daily Telegraph* of 29 December

1881 reports on her 'annual treat to the poor of Ripley', where she and her husband invited over 200 people to tea and gave each a shilling.[11]

When they entered the room they were cheered by all present. On 17 January 1882 the *Sheffield Independent* reports the sad news of Bessie's death, saying the poor people of Ripley had lost a true friend. During her funeral the shops of the village closed and a Union Jack flew at half mast over the Butterley ironworks. If she could have known it, Anne would have been proud of the influence she had on her former pupil.

Anne cast one last look back at the grand hall she was leaving behind. The children were still waving, but Branwell stood arrogant and immobile in the doorway. Rotten interiors could lie behind grand façades; she was glad to be rid of the place once and for all. Her diary paper of July 1845, the last she would ever write, was very revealing when looking back at the paper of four years prior:

> I was then at Thorp Green, and now I am only just escaped from it. I was wishing to leave it then, and if I had known that I had four years longer to stay how wretched I should have been; but during my stay I have had some very unpleasant and undreamt-of experiences of human nature.[12]

Anne arrived back at Haworth after more than five years at Thorp Green Hall, by far the longest period of time that any of the Brontë children kept a job. She had been highly valued by her employer, and she had shown that despite her underlying shyness, she was strong enough to make her own way in the world. However, in the end she was not prepared to sacrifice the values she held so dear.

Emily was delighted to see her younger sister again, but she noted how Anne looked frail and tired. She suggested that they go away together, and Anne proposed that they visit Scarborough, the beloved town that she would never more visit in company with the Robinsons. The plans were made: they would first spend a few days in York before moving on to Scarborough. It was to be the first 'long journey' they had ever taken together, and Emily was enormously excited. On the train journey to York, Emily suggested to Anne that they act out the parts of their Gondal characters. To her it was as if the intervening years had never happened:

they were the closely bound sisters again, happiest when alone and yet together in their fantasy world.

Emily describes the adventure gleefully in her 1845 diary paper:

Anne and I went on our first long journey by ourselves together, leaving home on the 30th of June, Monday sleeping at York, returning to Keighley Tuesday evening, sleeping there and walking home on Wednesday morning. Though the weather was broken we enjoyed ourselves very much … and during our excursion we were Ronald Macelgin, Henry Angora, Juliet Angusteena, Rosabelle, Ella and Julian Egramont, Catherine Navarre and Cordelia Fitzaphnold escaping from the palaces of Instruction to join the Royalists who are hard driven at present by the victorious Republicans.[13]

Anne was delighted to see her sister so happy but could do little to raise her own spirits. Whilst she had been away Emily had regressed further into her childhood world until fantasy and reality were indistinguishable, but Anne had seen too much of the real aristocracy to be concerned with a fake nobility. She had escaped from a real palace of instruction, but her escape had taken all her strength from her.

The planned onward journey to Scarborough was cancelled. Anne was too weak and tired to make the journey, so Emily had to be content with a look around York Minster and the cobbled chaos of The Shambles before journeying home again. The walk home from Keighley would also have brought back memories for Anne, memories of an evening in 1840 when William Weightman had walked her home after taking the sisters to see him give a speech at the Keighley Mechanics' Institute. He was now a ghost that would forever walk this route, waiting to be joined; it was a memory that was strengthening, not diminishing.

Anne had still not told her family the truth about Branwell and her parting from Thorp Green, but just a month after her return she was spared the trouble. Branwell himself returned: he had been dismissed from his post in disgrace. He opened up his heart to his sisters, saying that Mr Robinson had discovered his relationship with Mrs Robinson; after a torrid scene, he had sent him packing, threatening that his very life would be in danger if he showed his face again.

Branwell's sisters rallied round him. Charlotte immediately blamed the wicked Lydia for leading on her tutor and using him for her own pleasure before casting him to one side, but Branwell would not hear a word said against her. It was true love, he insisted, becoming louder and more agitated with every sentence, and it was only a matter of time before she would divorce Edmund so that she and Branwell could be together lawfully at last. Anne kept her eyes fixed on the floor, her brother was consumed by fantasies of his own making, and she realised that he could never be free of them.

Branwell sought solace in drink more than ever before, and in laudanum as well. He would often become drunk to the point of insensibility, and at these times the sisters would refer to him euphemistically as being 'unwell'. Branwell had embarked upon a change from which he would never return, and in their own way his sisters were about to do the same.

Anne and Emily had resumed their youthful routine of writing Gondal poetry together, although for Anne it was more of a way to kill time and keep unwanted memories at bay than a labour of love. Emily wrote these poems down in a book, but one morning in September 1845 Charlotte discovered something else altogether. It was a book that she had not seen before, and when she opened it her breath was taken away. There before her, in Emily's handwriting, were poems that she had not known existed. They weren't about Gondal, they were about the very fabric of life and death, about love and loneliness, faith and despair. Charlotte describes this moment that changed literary history in her 1850 'Biographical Notice of Ellis and Acton Bell':

One day, in the autumn of 1845, I accidentally lighted on a manuscript volume of verse in my sister Emily's handwriting. Of course, I was not surprised, knowing that she could and did write verse: I looked it over, and something more than surprise seized me, – a deep conviction that these were not common effusions, nor at all like the poetry women generally write. I thought them condensed and terse, vigorous and genuine. To my ear, they also had a peculiar music – wild, melancholy, and elevating.[14]

Charlotte had discovered the secret that Emily had even kept from Anne. She had a second book of verse, and one that nobody else but her could ever see. These verses were the very heart and soul of Emily, this intensely private woman, so how did Charlotte 'accidentally' light upon them? Could it be that she had caught a glimpse one day of Emily hiding something away and had waited for the moment when she could uncover it?

The secret was out in the open, and Charlotte would not allow it to return to the dark. She confronted Emily, with the intention of asking her to send them to a publisher, but Emily's reaction was even worse than she had anticipated. She screamed and smashed crockery on to the floor, and had to be held back from physically confronting her sister. Charlotte locked herself away in the safety of her own room while Emily continued to rave almost incoherently. She had been betrayed by her own sister; in her mind she had been exposed, made a mockery of.

The initial rage subsided to be replaced by a grim silence. Charlotte, never easily deterred from doing what she thought was right, tried again to convince Emily that the poems had to be published. They were just too good to be kept to herself, but Emily remained resolute and angry. It was time for Anne to take sides, and for once she chose Charlotte over Emily. Once more, Charlotte described the scene in her 'biographical notice':

> My youngest sister quietly produced some of her own compositions, intimating that since Emily's had given me pleasure, I might like to look at hers. I could not but be a partial judge, yet I thought that these verses too had a sweet sincere pathos of their own.[15]

Emily was now caught in a dilemma. She had no desire to see her own poems published and held up for the world's approbation or disapproval, yet she would relish the opportunity of making Anne happy. Charlotte explained that she too could contribute some verses, and that they could try to have them published together. It would be like the school project again, with the three sisters working together for one common purpose.

Finally, after days of anguish, Emily consented, but on one condition: she would only allow her work to be published if it was done under a pseudonym. Her greatest fear was that people who knew her would read the poetry and by doing so gain an insight into the private feelings that she was always so careful to conceal.

The plan was now launched, and the sisters would spend evenings walking around the dining table, talking in hushed voices and considering the merits of one poem against another. Even Emily was excited now, and for Anne it was at last a relieving moment of happiness in what had been a dark succession of years. When deciding upon their pseudonym they chose to keep their own initials intact, that would be their secret joke on a world that could never penetrate it. They also decided to take on male names. Anne, more than any of them, had seen the different way that society treated men and women; if they wanted to be taken seriously, she told Charlotte and Emily, they would have to publish under men's names.

After running through various options, they decided on Currer Bell for Charlotte, Ellis Bell for Emily and Acton Bell for Anne. It was then time to collate their work. Each sister had a huge body of poems to select from, and in the end it was decided that Emily and Anne would contribute twenty-one poems each, and Charlotte, whose verse tended to be longer in length, would contribute nineteen. Anne's poetry was a mixture of Gondal compositions, with overtly Gondalian references removed, and her work that was inspired by Weightman, her battle for faith and life in the real world.

The poems were copied out by hand by the three Brontës, and each was then signed Acton, Currer or Ellis. The poems would alternate between the sisters, and Anne's first contribution to the collection is 'A Reminiscence'. The very first poem that Anne was placing before the world was one of her paeans to Weightman:

Yes! thou art gone! and never more
Thy sunny smile shall gladden me;
But I may pass the old church door.
And pace the floor that covers thee,
May stand upon the cold, damp stone,
And think that, frozen, lies below
The lightest heart that I have known
The kindest I shall ever know.

Yet, though I cannot see thee more,
'Tis still a comfort to have seen;
And though thy transient life is o'er.
'Tis sweet to think that thou hast been;
To think a soul so near divine,
Within a form, so angel fair,
United to a heart like thine,
Has gladdened once our humble sphere.[16]

Charlotte took charge of sending their work out into the world, from whence it rapidly returned bearing a string of terse rejection notes, until one publisher suggested that the brothers Bell send it to a specialist poetry press called Aylott & Jones. This the sisters did, and they were delighted with the reply that they would publish the work, but it would have to be at the sisters' expense.

With their aunt's legacy still in place, untouched by the abandoned plans for a school, they had no difficulty in finding the £31 and 10s that the publishers asked for, and no hesitation in sending it. Two months later, in May 1846, Anne proudly held a first copy of *Poems by Currer, Ellis, and Acton Bell* in her hands. Things would never be the same again for Anne, her sisters or English literature.

12

THE TRUE HISTORY OF AGNES GREY

All true histories contain instruction; though, in some, the treasure may be hard to find, and when found, so trivial in quantity, that the dry, shrivelled kernel scarcely compensates for the trouble of cracking the nut. Whether this be the case with my history or not, I am hardly competent to judge. I sometimes think it might prove useful to some, and entertaining to others; but the world may judge for itself.

Agnes Grey

Finally, with the publication of *Poems by Currer, Ellis, and Acton Bell*, the sisters had seen a collaborative plan reach fruition. This was the culmination of the past twenty-six years; it was what they had been born for. As with all families, they'd had their ups and downs, misunderstandings, moments of resentment and of jealousy, but their filial bounds were too strong to be broken. Yet there was still one family member who was not included in the venture: Branwell, who had himself been the first of the Brontë children to appear in print.

Branwell had been a keen poet in his youth, as well as a talented draughtsman and artist, and he had often sent poetry to local newspapers under the pen name of Northangerland, one of the characters from the tales of Angria. On 5 June 1841, the *Halifax Guardian* published Northangerland's 'Heaven And Earth'.[1] The choice of topic is surprising, as Branwell examines the illuminating power of heaven in contrast to the dreary earth. In truth, Branwell had long since abandoned his faith, suggesting that this poem had been composed many years previously. In total, the *Halifax Guardian* would publish twelve of his poems, and his work was also published in the *Leeds Intelligencer*, the *Bradford Herald* and the *Yorkshire Gazette*. This in itself was no mean feat, as these papers prided themselves on the quality of the poetry they published.

It says a lot, then, that despite his earlier proficiency in poetry, and despite his success in this field, he was not even consulted when it came to compiling a book of Brontë poetry. The sad truth was that by this time he had already entered into an unstoppable decline, where all he cared about was drink, laudanum and Mrs Lydia Robinson. He might still be living at the top of Main Street, but he was careering down the hill, and the brakes were off.

Branwell never knew that his sisters were creating a book of poetry, he was oblivious to the fact that it had been published, and he wasn't the only one. Their father's eyesight had grown steadily worse, and he was now suffering from cataracts that made him nearly blind. Tabby Aykroyd was back working in the parsonage again, but she was less than mobile and was there more as an act of kindness on the part of the sisters than anything else. In these circumstances it was easy for Charlotte to collect and sort the post without anyone other than Anne and Emily knowing anything about it.

It was a moment of intense pride for the Brontë girls as they saw the product of their own minds in print for the first time, but each of them had their own individual view of the finished product. Emily still felt a sense of intrusion and worried what others would think if they ever found out that she was Ellis Bell. Charlotte was racked by insecurity: from the days of her youth she had wanted to be a poet more than anything else, as she had confided in a teenage letter to the Poet Laureate of the time Robert Southey, but now that her poetry was in print she could not escape the fact that her verse was not as good or as mature as that produced by her two younger sisters. Anne kept her feelings to herself as she had always done, but inside she felt a sense of victory. Dear little Anne, the fragile girl who could not be trusted even to do the housework alone, had shown the world what she could do, and she saw it was good. She had disclosed some of her most private feelings, and yet nobody would ever penetrate her reserve or assign them to her.

This made her inner triumph even greater, and there was nothing that Anne valued higher than her ability to conceal her emotions from even those closest to her. Anne makes this clear in the ending to her penultimate contribution to the *Poems by Currer, Ellis, and Acton Bell*, 'Self Congratulation', where she talks about the ability to hide her feelings when her loved one walks by:

> But, thank God! You might gaze on mine
> For hours and never know
> The secret changes of my soul
> From joy to keenest woe.
> Last night, as we sat round the fire
> Conversing merrily,
> We heard, without, approaching steps
> Of one well known to me!
> There was no trembling in my voice,
> No blush upon my cheek,
> No lustrous sparkle in my eyes,
> Of hope, or joy, to speak;
> But, oh! my spirit burned within,
> My heart beat full and fast!
> He came not nigh – he went away –
> And then my joy was past.
> And yet my comrades marked it not:
> My voice was still the same;

They saw me smile, and o'er my face
No signs of sadness came.
They little knew my hidden thoughts;
And they will *never* know
The aching anguish of my heart,
The bitter burning woe![2]

On one occasion, however, we hear how Anne's emotions were betrayed by the merest hint of an upturned smile, and it was the visiting Ellen Nussey who caught her out. In December 1848 Ellen was visiting Haworth Parsonage to provide support and comfort for Charlotte and Anne at a time of mourning. Anne was sitting by the fireside reading a newspaper, when Ellen was surprised to see Anne's countenance change: 'I observed a slow smile spreading across Anne's face as she sat reading before the fire. I asked her why she was smiling, and she replied: "Only because I see they have inserted one of my poems."'[3]

The publication could have been either the *Leeds Intelligencer* or *Fraser's Magazine*, as both that month had published her poem 'The Narrow Way', a beautifully heartfelt hymn that preaches her familiar gospel of enduring all calumnies and holding on to faith. The prestigious *Fraser's Magazine* had even earlier published her long poem of religious reflection 'The Three Guides'. In fact, whilst Emily's undoubted mastery of verse often sees her hailed as the best Brontë poet, Anne was the only sister who had her poetry published independently, and without having to pay for it.

From Ellen's observation we see how even in December 1848, a time of personal despair for Anne, she could still find some delight in achieving recognition for her poetry. On that May day in 1846 when they held the first copies of their book, all three sisters harboured expectations of its success, yet they were to be disappointed.

They first had to make additional payments to their publisher to ensure that review copies could be sent to regional and national publications. Thrillingly for Anne and her sisters it gathered generally favourable reviews, including from influential magazines *The Critic* and *The Athenaeum*, yet still it failed to garner the sales they had hoped for.

'What you Please' by Anne Brontë, 1840. (Courtesy of the Brontë Society)

Portrait of Charlotte Brontë by J.H.
Thompson. (Courtesy of the Brontë Society)

Portrait of Ellen Nussey by Charlotte
Brontë. (Courtesy of the Brontë
Society)

Portrait of Anne Brontë by Charlotte Brontë, 1834. (Courtesy of the Brontë Society)

Portrait of William Weightman by Charlotte Brontë, 1840. (Courtesy of the Brontë Society)

Portrait of Anne Brontë by Charlotte Brontë, 1833. (Courtesy of the Brontë Society)

Photograph of Patrick Brontë in old age. (Courtesy of the Brontë Society)

Disputed photograph of (*left to right*) Charlotte, Emily and Anne Brontë. (© RPM collection)

Anne Brontë

November 13ᵗʰ 1839

'Sunrise Over the Sea' by Anne Brontë, 1839. (Courtesy of the Brontë Society)

'A Very Bad Picture' (a possible self-portrait) by Anne Brontë, 1842. (Courtesy of the Brontë Society)

Flossy, unfinished portrait by Anne Brontë. (Courtesy of the Brontë Society)

'The Brontë Sisters' (*left to right*: Anne, Emily and Charlotte), also known as the pillar portrait, by Branwell Brontë, around 1835. (© National Portrait Gallery, London)

Anne Brontë's grave at St Mary's churchyard, Scarborough.

Roe Head School, Mirfield, as it is today – now Hollybank Trust.

Thornton Parsonage, Anne Brontë's birthplace, as it is today – now 'Emily's' delicatessen.

'Brontë Moon', a collage by contemporary artist Amanda White. (© Amanda White)

Brontë Parsonage Museum, Haworth. (© Dave Zdanowicz)

The top of Main Street, Haworth, with St Michael and All Angels' church on the right. (© Dave Zdanowicz)

Haworth moors. (© Dave Zdanowicz)

It was Charlotte, reverting to her usual mother role, who took charge of the production of the book, and it was she who asked Aylott & Jones to produce a print run of 1,000 copies, double the amount that Matthew Arnold, as an example, had enjoyed for his early works. This was wildly ambitious, or naive, as poetry was in decline by the 1840s. The first decades of the century had seen a rapid increase in poetry sales, thanks to the likes of Wordsworth and Byron, but the bubble had burst. By 1846, even established greats like Elizabeth Barrett Browning and William Wordsworth himself were finding it hard to get their work into print and then on to bookshelves.

Anne and her sisters would have sat around their dining table at night, reading the reviews by candlelight, passing them eagerly from one pair of hands to another. It was a secret that they still kept from their family, but it also remained stubbornly a secret to the wider world. The £2 they had allocated for an advertising budget was not enough to bring it to the attention of the reading public, and although they considered spending a further £10 on advertising, it seems that this money was never actually committed.

A famous letter from Charlotte to Thomas de Quincey on 16 June 1847 reveals the fate of the book:

> My relatives, Ellis and Acton Bell and myself, heedless of the repeated warnings of various respectable publishers, have committed the rash act of publishing a volume of poems. The consequences predicted have, of course, overtaken us; our book is found to be a drug; no man needs it or heeds it; in the space of a year our publisher has disposed of but two copies, and by what painful efforts he succeeded in disposing of those two, himself only knows.[4]

Thomas de Quincey was not the only writer to receive a similar letter along with a copy of the book, an act that the sisters, via Charlotte, said was to prevent the books being transferred to 'trunk makers', the final fate of unsold books. What is less known, however, is that this was not the eventual fate of the *Poems by Currer, Ellis, and Acton Bell*, and that all copies of the book were eventually disposed of. In 1848, Charlotte's then publisher, Smith, Elder & Co., purchased the remaining 961 books from Aylott & Jones for the sum of 6*d* each. Thus it was that the sisters finally received the sum of over £24 from Aylott & Jones as return on their initial outlay. Over time, Smith, Elder & Co. managed to sell every last copy of the book.[5]

Charlotte's letter is written in a jocular tone, and this itself tells us all about the sisters' attitude at this time. They are not disheartened by the lack of sales of the book, indeed one of the purchasers, a Mr Enoch, loved the work so much that he wrote, via the publisher, asking for the autographs of the Bell brothers. These signatures were duly sent to Aylott & Jones, with the proviso that they were forwarded on from London so that nobody could find out their true location.

If the act of publishing poetry had failed to provide a financial return, it had provided a thrilling experience for Charlotte and Anne, and even Emily had been caught up in the excitement once she had assured herself that her anonymity would remain intact. The reviews, and the praise of Mr Enoch, showed them that it wasn't their writing that was at fault, but merely the medium they had chosen.

As soon as their poetry had been sent to Aylott & Jones, even before it had been published, their minds had turned to their next project. All three sisters had written both poetry and prose since their childhood, and Anne in particular had already been working on a prose treatment. In her 1845 diary paper, she writes, 'I have begun the third volume of passages in the life of an Individual. I wish I had finished it.'[6]

There is the possibility that this 'life of an Individual' is one of the Gondal stories that she wrote, but it was very unusual for her to write on purely Gondal themes when apart from Emily, and at this time she was still at Thorp Green Hall. It seems much more likely that the book she talks of is in fact an early version of *Agnes Grey*. Whilst the book as we know it now is one relatively slim volume, it does contain three distinct sections: life with the Bloomfields, life with the Murrays and life at the school her mother founds. Whilst the first two sections are based heavily on Anne's time with the Ingham and Robinson families, the final one is an intensely personal look into her dreams and wishes. It was for that reason she found it particularly hard to write, and wished that she had finished it.

Despite the heartache that writing this final section induced, writing in general was a sheer joy for Anne. It was something she had always done, firstly in conjunction with Emily and latterly on her own. She could never be completely lonely with a pen and paper to hand, and with characters and stories in her mind just waiting to be released. It is doubtful that she ever anticipated writing novels for public consumption, but this was just what Charlotte proposed one evening as they discussed the prospects for their poetry collection.

What was there to risk? They now had more experience of the publishing process, and determined that this time they would not pay for publication themselves, as they had with their poems. The atmosphere in their house was becoming increasingly dark and strained, thanks to the physical darkness their father found himself in and the mental darkness into which their brother had descended, but writing together gave the sisters moments of light and joy at the day's end. It was a return to their joyful days of childhood, even if one member of that creative quartet could no longer take part.

A new plan was quickly formed and agreed upon: the sisters would each write a novel, and the three novels would then be sent to publishers with a view to them being published together. In this way they hoped to make their novels more appealing to a prospective publisher. Books were an expensive item in the mid-nineteenth century and could cost around a month's salary for a domestic maid. The most common way for books to be read, and distributed, was through a circulating library. To maximise their revenue from this route, publishers would prefer to publish a book in three volumes rather than one, trebling the income they would receive from the libraries.

All that remained now, as the sisters still waited excitedly for their poetry to appear, was to write the books themselves. Anne's book was already practically finished, and Emily was also well advanced with her contribution, which would become known to the world as *Wuthering Heights*. It is the Brontë book that contains the least amount of biographical data, although it is possible to see some of Branwell's excesses reflected in both Heathcliffe and Linton, and the landscape itself was dearly familiar to the author. Emily had the least real world experience to draw upon of the sisters, but she had also become used to letting her imagination take full flight, unhindered by what society expected. It is this furious creativity that produced a book of such amazing strength and power from a woman who was on the surface shy and reserved.

Charlotte had an idea in mind for her contribution and, like Anne's novel, it was based upon an unfulfilled love, although one of a very different nature. Her volume was called *The Professor*, a novel set in a Belgian school where a young half-English girl falls in love with her stern professor. The professor himself, William Crimsworth, is the protagonist of the novel, and although his circumstances are very different from Constantin Heger – Crimsworth is a young man who travels to Belgium to escape problems in England – it is clear that Charlotte's real life unrequited love is the inspiration.

Anne's novel *Agnes Grey* takes a look at matters of the heart as well, but it also set out to provide instruction for its readers and society as a whole. She firmly believed that her prose could be used to educate and inform as well as entertain, and indeed that these were the most important aspects of writing. As a teacher or governess she could teach a handful of people at a time, but as a writer she could reach out to an unlimited number of people. She set out this personal manifesto in her preface to the second edition of *The Tenant of Wildfell Hall*:

> Be it understood, I shall not limit my ambition to this [giving innocent pleasure] – or even to producing 'a perfect work of art': time and talents so spent, I should consider wasted and misapplied. Such humble talents as God has given me I will endeavour to put to their greatest use, if I am able to amuse I will try to benefit too; and when I feel it my duty to speak an unpalatable truth, with the help of God, I *will* speak it, though it be to the detriment of my reader's immediate pleasure as well as my own.[7]

Whilst this famous defence of her writing and character was in direct response to criticism of her second novel, it is also relevant to *Agnes Grey*. Anne's début is a novel that isn't afraid to show both sides of life, from the sweet beauty of love to the cruelty that uncontrolled children can exert and the harsh way that high society can treat those they deem beneath them.

To ignore the autobiographical elements of *Agnes Grey* would be to do a disservice to Anne Brontë, especially as there are so many of them. At the very start of the novel she explains how she will lay bare her true history, shielded by her obscurity and the changing of some names. Readers of the time, unaware of the author, would take this to be a dramatic device where Agnes is saying she has changed the names of some of her characters, but in reality Anne is talking about the change of name from Brontë to Bell. It is this that makes her 'not fear to venture' into print.

Anne's preface to the second edition of *The Tenant of Wildfell Hall* also confirms how much real life events and people were used in *Agnes Grey*, when she writes, 'The story of "Agnes Grey" was accused of extravagant over-colouring in those very parts that were carefully copied from the life, with a most scrupulous avoidance of all exaggeration.'[8]

Some readers could not believe that children could be as cruel as those portrayed in the Bloomfield household, or that a mother could view the marriages of her daughters so cynically as that found in the Murray household. Anne here is defending the truth in these portrayals, and in her writing as in life, Anne was ever a seeker after truth.

The novel begins with Agnes at home in the parsonage that she shares with her sister, her mother and her father, a priest in the Church of England. He falls into money troubles, and Agnes resolves to try her hand as a governess because she wants to alleviate the financial strain on the family, as well as seeing something of the world. Her first position is with the unbearably cruel children of the Bloomfield family, modelled closely on the Inghams of Mirfield, and on trying her luck again, she becomes governess to the Murray family, who in many ways resemble the Robinsons that Anne was serving at the time she was working on the novel.

Whilst the first two sections of the novel are based closely on the life she knew, the third is based on the life that she never had the chance to know. Agnes' father has died and she sets up a school with her mother in a town only referred to as 'A', but which from the descriptions given is clearly identifiable as Scarborough. Her main concern when journeying to this town is that she will never more see Reverend Edmund Weston, the curate she has fallen in love with and who closely resembles William Weightman in character and deeds.

One day Agnes is walking along the Scarborough beachfront (still disguised as town 'A' of course) when a familiar terrier, her beloved Snap, runs up to her. Agnes is amazed, as she had left him behind when the Murray family had sold him to a rat catcher, but then she looks up and sees Weston with him. He has bought the dog, and he has also been trying to track Agnes down. She learns that he has now become vicar of his own parish just 2 miles from Scarborough, and he wastes no time in wooing her in the formal manner of the nineteenth century.

Weston visits Agnes one evening and asks her to accompany him on a walk. He seems agitated, and Agnes feels a state of dread growing within her, but then they reach the top of a hill and look down at the sunset over the Scarborough bay, a scene that cannot help but bring to mind Anne's portrait of 'Sunrise Over Sea'. What happens next is understated and yet effortlessly romantic:

> 'My house is desolate yet, Miss Grey', he smilingly observed, 'and I am now acquainted with all the ladies in my parish, and several in this town too; and many others I know by sight and report; but not one of them will suit me for a companion: in fact there is only one person in the world that will; and that is yourself and I want to know your decision?'[9]

Agnes is taken aback, although it is what she has hoped and prayed for. She tells Weston that she would need to ask permission of her mother, to which he replies that he has already asked for permission from her, and obtained it. He continues:

> 'And so now I have overruled your objections on her account. Have you any other?'
> 'No – none.'
> 'You love me then?' said he, fervently pressing my hand.
> 'Yes.'[10]

Here, at last, Anne could be bold: she has candidly put before the public what she could not reveal to her most intimate friend. She is declaring her love for William Weightman, and what's more she is giving herself the happy ending that she was never allowed in real life: the dream that she had carried around with her since receiving the Valentine's card in 1840, the dream that even Weightman's death could not take from her. Anne ends the scene at that point but then goes on to say that she, that is Agnes, and Weston marry and have children. He is not perfect, she is careful to point out, but he is well loved by his parish, and she defies anyone to blame him as a pastor, a husband or a father.

Agnes also talks of how they, like all couples, must prepare themselves for the final separation, which she deems 'the greatest of all afflictions to the survivor',[11] yet by looking ahead to their reunion in heaven, even that can be borne. We can imagine the racing of Anne's heart, the lump in the throat and the tears running down her cheeks as she wrote this. The book ends on another understated note:

> Our modest income is amply sufficient for our requirements: and by prac-tising the economy we learned in harder times, and never attempting to imitate our richer neighbours, we manage not only to enjoy comfort and contentment ourselves, but to have every year something to lay by for our children, and something to give to those who need it.
>
> And now I think I have said sufficient.[12]

A stunningly simple end, and simply beautiful. *Agnes Grey* did not, and still does not, garner the recognition it deserved, for reasons we will come to, and yet it is like no other Brontë novel. It is calm, quiet and yet leaves a powerful impression on you. It is a literary embodiment of the author herself, as Charlotte would later admit.

Not everyone has failed to recognise the brilliance of the book, and the acclaimed Irish novelist George Moore was especially fulsome in his praise. He declared that '*Agnes Grey* is the most perfect prose narrative in English literature … a narrative simple and beautiful as a muslin dress … We know that we are reading a masterpiece. Nothing short of genius could have set them before us so plainly and yet with restraint.'[13]

Moore also praises Anne herself: 'If Anne Brontë had lived ten years longer she would have taken a place beside Jane Austen, perhaps even a higher place.'[14]

This plain, simple and self-effacing genius would have experienced the thrill of anticipation when her novel was duly packaged up with *Wuthering Heights* and *The Professor*, and sent to the first publisher on a list that Charlotte had obtained from Aylott & Jones. The first terse rejection letter was not long in arriving, and it was to be the first of many.

Their attempts to gain a publisher were not helped by the fact that the same parcel was sent time after time, with the previous address crossed out and replaced by a new one. In Charlotte's biographical notice of her sisters, she explains, 'These manuscripts were perseveringly obtruded upon various publishers for the space of a year and a half; usually, their fate was an ignominious and abrupt dismissal.'[15]

Many people would have given up by this point, but Anne and her sisters realised that to end this dream would be an admission of ultimate failure. If this hope that had burned so brightly was extinguished, what did they have left? The package was sent on its weary way again and again, and it always seemed to find its way home to Haworth, but in July 1847 something magical happened.

A letter arrived at the parsonage addressed, as usual in these circumstances, to Mr C. Bell Esq., but this time it did not contain the standard terse rejection they had grown so familiar with. The publisher Thomas Cautley Newby of London had seen merit in the books that other publishers had missed, and he was prepared to make an offer. He would publish Anne and Emily's books, but they would have to pay £50 up front towards the cost of publishing. This would be reimbursed when and if the publisher recouped that sum in sales. The two sisters were elated, but for Charlotte it was another blow: the publisher declined to accept *The Professor*.

Anne clasped Emily's hands once more, just as she had done when they were children heading out to the moors. This was the moment they had dreamed of brought to reality. People had seen merit in their writing: their dream could now expand and reach out to new horizons. They would become successful authors to rank alongside Dickens and Thackeray, bringing out a stream of successful novels that would inform and educate as well as entertain. They would make enough money to look after their father in his old age and to fit themselves in the life of their choosing.

Such were Anne's thoughts as she stood reading the letter again and again, tears of happiness glistening in her blue eyes. Only then did she notice the pensive look on Charlotte's face, and at once she understood the emotions encompassing the older sister who had been eclipsed by those younger than herself. Anne took Charlotte's hands in hers and felt her sister's fingers squeeze hers appreciatively. 'Don't give up, Charlotte,' she urged. Charlotte was not to give up.

LIGHT FROM DARKNESS

I always lacked common sense when taken by surprise.

Agnes Grey

The line above is just one example of the humour that can be found in both *Agnes Grey* and *The Tenant of Wildfell Hall* to an extent not seen in either of her sisters' works. Despite her reputation for being stern and serious, Anne also had a well-developed, if self-deprecating, sense of humour. She certainly was taken by surprise with the offer from Thomas Newby, and the contract that she and Emily entered so readily into proved anything but sensible.

At the moment the sisters first sent their three novels out into the world they had vowed they would not pay to have them published, as they had done with their book of poetry. Whilst they still had a significant portion of their aunt's legacy intact, there was no telling how long the funds would have to last them. As time passed, this brave resolve began to weaken. When the offer from Thomas Newby arrived, Anne and Emily must have thought that this was the final chance to get their work published. The long list of publishers they had started with had now become a very short list; this was all or nothing. Could they really give up now, and write off the physical and mental effort they had invested in the project, for the sake of £50, especially when they had that sum to hand?

Charlotte felt instinctively that this was not a good deal for her sisters. For the £50 sum the publisher had offered to print 350 copies, yet they had already found how hard it was to sell just two copies of their poems. It was true that novels were much more fashionable than poems, and the market for them was consequentially much bigger, yet she saw that there was a great likelihood of her sisters never seeing their money again.

What was Charlotte to do? She saw how excited the letter had made her younger sisters: they looked healthy, happy and full of life in a way that she had not seen since their youth. She also knew how stubborn Emily could be. If you wanted Emily to follow a course of action, it was best to suggest the exact opposite. No, she must bite her tongue for once in her life. Anne and Emily were now adults; they could and must make their own decision, even if it was one that Charlotte strongly disagreed with.

In this instance Charlotte could not be accused of jealousy or insincerity. It had been a big blow when she opened that envelope, as she always did before handing the contents to her eager sisters, and read what was within it. Anne and Emily had written novels that were good enough to be published, and yet nobody was interested in what she had to offer. The product of her mind was not sufficiently illuminating; she had been found to be distinctly average. A stinging resentment and battered pride held mastery of Charlotte for a few seconds, the letter trembling within her hands, but these emotions were quickly superseded by the glow of filial love.

The judgement on *The Professor* was to be a lasting one, and Charlotte would not find a publisher for it in her lifetime, although she never gave up trying; yet the judgement of the book is actually an unjustly harsh one. Whilst not matching the brilliance of other Brontë novels, it is still a well-structured and well-written book, and an entertaining read. Much of it would be recycled, modified and improved for her later novel *Villette*.

Over the previous year and a half Charlotte had become used to rejection, but she had also taken steps to defend herself against it. If they did not like *The Professor*, and she had more than enough proof that they assuredly did not, she would write something different and see if that suited their tastes better. The writing bug now had Charlotte firmly in its grip; it was one that she could not and would not shake off.

This second novel was conceived and started during the time that her début work was doing the rounds of the remaining publishing houses. Thanks to Elizabeth Gaskell, in her trailblazing biography of her friend Charlotte Brontë, we know exactly when this work was begun, and it came at a moment when a particular darkness was gripping the family.

It was August 1846, and Patrick Brontë was by this time in his 70th year. He had always suffered from extreme short-sightedness, as did Charlotte, and both would be reliant upon their slim pairs of eyeglasses. As Patrick got older his eyesight began to diminish rapidly, to the extent that he could no longer read or go out for walks, as he once loved to do. His daughters would take turns reading for him, but the darkness continued to encroach upon the light.

A specialist doctor was sought, and he diagnosed that Patrick was suffering from cataracts. These not only made it hard for him to live his usual life, he was also finding it hard to carry out his ecclesiastical duties, relying more and more upon his new curate, Arthur Bell Nicholls. It was intimated that a specialist surgeon in Manchester might be able to perform an operation known as couching, which could produce successful results. This involved depressing the lens of the eyes to restore or at least improve vision. Charlotte made the journey by rail to Manchester in the company of Emily to question the surgeon directly.

Once again Anne had been left at home whilst Charlotte chose her other sister as a travelling companion. With her usual stoicism, she complained not and set about being nursemaid to both her 69-year-old father and her 29-year-old brother, who was now suffering increasingly from bouts of 'illness' and whose behaviour was becoming even more unpredictable.

In Manchester, Charlotte and Emily spoke to a Dr Wilson, one of the leading eye surgeons of the time. He agreed to perform the operation and an appointment was made for the following week. The operation took place on 25 August, and rather than the couching, the lenses were cut away completely. All this was done without anaesthetic, and

Charlotte, who had accompanied Patrick, was amazed at how controlled and uncomplaining her father was under this trial, a trait that was passed down to his youngest daughter, Anne.

Charlotte and Patrick had taken lodgings at Mount Pleasant, Boundary Street, Manchester, just off Oxford Road. Patrick would have to stay there in darkness and peace for weeks until the bandages could come off and they could return together to Haworth. On the day the operation was due to take place, Charlotte received a letter that had been forwarded from the parsonage. It was yet another rejection for her unloved and unwelcome book. She was in a strange city, looking after an ageing and temporarily blinded father, yet even then she refused to despair, instead taking up her pen once more. Mrs Gaskell writes of this event:

> She had the heart of Robert Bruce within her, and failure upon failure daunted her no more than him. Not only did 'The Professor' return again to try his chance among the London publishers, but she began, in this time of care and depressing inquietude – in those grey, weary, uniform streets, where all faces, save that of her kind doctor, were strange and untouched with sunlight to her, – there and then, did the genius begin 'Jane Eyre'. [1]

A nurse was also present in the house, and she twice had to administer leeches to reduce inflammation, eight on one occasion and six on the other. In notes that he later wrote in the margins of a medical textbook, Patrick explained that in these cases the leeches must be applied to the temple rather than the eyelids. He also stated that the operation had not been as painful as he had expected, and he had felt merely a burning sensation in his eyes. They were to remain at 83 Mount Pleasant for over a month, with Charlotte's primary concern at that time being, as she confessed in a letter, how to prepare and cook meals, tasks that she was used to Emily performing. She made the most of her time in the Manchester sick room and made swift progress on her second novel. It was soon to be called upon.

Back in Haworth, Anne was understandably concerned about her father. Would the operation cure him or leave him blinded permanently? If he did indeed become blind, she would be ready and willing to do her duty. She would take his arm and walk him across the moor, she would guide him to church and read the scriptures to him. That was the duty of a daughter, and it was the duty of Anne, as she saw it, to serve people whenever and wherever she could.

To the delight of Anne and Emily, but hardly acknowledged by Branwell, who in his moments of sobriety hated not being the centre of attention himself, in September 1846 they saw their father walk through the parsonage door unaided, with a smiling Charlotte behind him. The operation had been a complete success, and Patrick could now see and read clearly again. This relief would carry the sisters through the winter and spring, and by the following summer Anne and Emily were correcting the proofs of their now accepted books.

Thomas Newby had arranged that the books should be published in a three-volume format, with Emily's *Wuthering Heights* occupying the first two volumes, and Anne's *Agnes Grey* being published as the third volume. They received the proof copies eagerly but were disheartened to find that they contained a number of printing errors. These errors were diligently corrected and the proofs were returned; now they had only to wait for the completed volumes themselves to arrive.

Anne waited with her usual patient resignation on the surface, which as always belied a maelstrom of emotions underneath. If this was the moment she had been waiting for would it bring affirmation or disappointment? For her sister the wait was even worse. Emily did not know whether she wanted to see the first edition of *Wuthering Heights* or not, she was still in turmoil over the decision to go public with her work and in dread lest local people such as the book-loving Heatons of Ponden Hall should recognise the local landmarks contained within it. They would be made to wait yet longer and were to find that Newby's could never be relied upon to do things in a timely or appropriate fashion. While they were waiting, something entirely unexpected happened.

Charlotte had nearly exhausted her list of publishing contacts, when in late July the manuscript of *The Professor* landed back at the parsonage again. It had been sent by Smith, Elder & Co. of Cornhill, London, but this time there was not the one line note that she was used to, but an actual letter. Once more the book was declined, but this time the publisher went to some length to give Charlotte some feedback. They explained that the main factor mitigating against the publication of *The Professor* was its brevity, and they intimated that if she had a longer novel, one that would be suited to a three-volume treatment, they would look upon it with some interest.

The fires that had nearly been extinguished were ignited again: if they wanted a 'three-decker' novel, she would give them a three-decker novel. *Jane Eyre*, begun in such unpromising circumstances in Manchester, was now almost completed, and she duly dispatched it to Smith, Elder & Co. on 24 August.

Anne was delighted to see her sister invigorated again: she could, after all, never feel joyous in her own good fortunes if those who were closest to her were suffering bad fortunes. It was Charlotte's turn now to be in turmoil. The dreamer in her, the remnants of the young girl who had, in her own words, 'very early cherished the dream of one day becoming author',[2] read hidden depths into the letter from Cornhill until it became almost a promissory note. The pragmatist within her took a different view. Why should *Jane Eyre* escape the fate that had befallen *The Professor*? If they read it all, it would soon be back with the familiar rejection note.

Charlotte did not have to wait very long to find out which side of her character was right. Just two weeks later she received a reply from Smith, Elder & Co. Charlotte ripped open the package, and her eyes registered instantly that there was a letter of some substance waiting for her, rather than just one line. She dared not read it at once but scanned quickly through it until she was finally convinced that it was a letter of acceptance. Emily and Anne led her back to the familiar sofa and sat her down before her legs could give way beneath her. Charlotte continued to gaze at the page before her; it was a letter to be savoured slowly, not devoured.

Her book's first port of call had been the publisher's chief reader, William S. Williams. It was he who had read *The Professor* and had since had a further letter from Charlotte asking him if he would reconsider that book, to which he again asked her to submit a three-volume work. As he opened the package that had come all the way from Keighley station in far away Yorkshire, he gained his first surprise. The sender, a Mr Currer Bell, had not been able to pay the postage but asked him to kindly confirm how much it had cost them to take delivery of the package, and he would send them postage stamps to that value by return. He laughed inwardly: this was surely no ordinary author. As he commenced reading the work, he was soon convinced that he also had no ordinary novel.

George Smith, the young and wealthy head of the company, mocked another of the reading team who said he had been enchanted by the book, but at the behest of Williams, who praised its merits to the hilt, he decided to read *Jane Eyre* himself. It was now Sunday morning, and Smith decided that he would start reading Currer Bell's manuscript in the hours leading up to a dinner appointment at twelve o' clock. When twelve came he found that he could not put the book down and instead sent a note to his friend asking to be forgiven for his absence. Later that day a servant came to tell him that lunch was ready, but again he would not leave the book and asked for sandwiches and a glass of wine instead. By that evening, he had completed the book and was in no doubt that he held a work of rare genius in his hands.

The letter sent from London to Mr Currer Bell left Charlotte in no doubt of the high esteem they held the novel in. There was no payment asked for in advance, and they offered the author £100 for the copyright to the book, on condition that they also had first option on her next two novels as well. Charlotte, of course, was quick to agree the deal with Smith, Elder & Co., although she did write to them saying that £100 seemed small remuneration for a year's work. With royalties, she was to earn around £500 a year from her books, around twenty times what she could have expected to receive as a teacher.

The Cornhill publishers were quick to act. Charlotte had sent the novel to them from Keighley railway station on 24 August 1847, and by 16 October 1847 it was published and in the hands of the public. This rapidity had been completely unexpected, and she was at Ellen Nussey's house Brookroyd when the first proofs were forwarded to her by Anne. This caused a dilemma for Charlotte, to work on the proofs now, as she wanted to, would be impossible to achieve under Ellen's nose, yet she had made a promise to her sisters that their life as novelists would be revealed to nobody. In compromise, Charlotte swore Ellen to secrecy and asked her never to let Anne and Emily realise that she knew their secret. Ellen Nussey was the first woman outside of the sisters themselves to discover the identity of the Bell brothers, but she kept her word and held her tongue.

Jane Eyre received almost uniformly rapturous reviews and enjoyed unprecedented sales for a first novel set before the public. Charlotte, safely hidden, even from her publishers, behind her male pseudonym, had become an overnight success. *Jane Eyre* is a novel that lingers long in the memory, and it shows the huge strides the author had made in the year since writing *The Professor*. Some of the scenes in the book are drawn from her personal experience, so that in the strong, strict, yet secretly kind-hearted man that is Mr Rochester, we see a reflection of Constantin Heger. As Jane leads the now blinded Rochester by the arm and feeds him, we see a reflection of what Charlotte was doing for her father at the time of the book's genesis. Other aspects of the book, however, owe a clear debt to Anne's *Agnes Grey*.

The three distinct sections of *Jane Eyre*, Lowood, Thornfield Hall and then post-Thornfield Hall, mirror the three sections of *Agnes Grey*. *Jane Eyre*, like Anne's novel written a year earlier, is the story of a simple governess who falls in love with a man she meets during her work. The heroines of both novels advertise for a position. Both lose their father, Jane before the novel commences and Agnes during the novel. They are both separated from the man they love, seemingly forever, until fate somehow throws them back together again. Both books end with the heroine marrying their true love and raising a family.

In some aspects the character of Jane Eyre herself bears resemblance to Anne. She is described as being small and plain, in effect 'queer looking', which is how Charlotte still thought of Anne, even if others did not agree. Jane leaves her post at Thornfield Hall because she is unable to live any longer in what she perceives to be a nest of sin, just as Anne had done at Thorp Green Hall. Jane's advertising for a governess's position, determined to make her own way in the world, mirrors what Anne herself did. Jane keeps her feelings locked within her, and her still, thoughtful, reserved nature matches Charlotte's description of Anne to W.S. Williams. Jane plays piano 'a little' and paints wild and unconventional seascapes. It cannot be said that Jane and Anne are an exact match, but it isn't hard to imagine Charlotte's thoughts turning to her sister when in need of inspiration for her main character.

The instant success of *Jane Eyre* brought real joy into the lives of the sisters, and after a discussion they agreed to, at last, let their father into their secret. Charlotte knocked on the door to Patrick's study and then, at his bidding, entered; Anne and Emily remained in the doorway, looking in to see what his reaction would be. In one hand Charlotte held her book and in the other a selection of reviews, including the rare critical ones. Pragmatic as always, she did not want herself or anyone else to get carried away. Elizabeth Gaskell recalled how Charlotte related the event to her:

'Papa I've been writing a book.'

'Have you my dear?'

'Yes, and I want you to read it.'

'I am afraid it will try my eyes too much.'

'But it is not in manuscript: it is printed.'

'My dear! You've never thought of the expense it will be! It will be almost sure to be a loss, for how can you get a book sold? No one knows you or your name.'

'But, papa, I don't think it will be a loss; no more will you, if you will just let me read you a review or two, and tell you more about it.'

So she sat down and read some of the reviews to her father; and then, giving him the copy of *Jane Eyre* that she intended for him, she left him to read it. When he came into tea, he said, 'Girls, do you know Charlotte has been writing a book, and it is much better than likely?'[3]

This statement is full of the restraint and self-effacement that Patrick would share with all his daughters, if not his son. Behind the cold and studied words, Patrick was extremely proud of his daughter's achievements and would continue to be so for the rest of his life. Whilst Charlotte's secret was out, those of Anne and Emily remained concealed. The end of the year grew closer, and despite them signing a publishing deal with Thomas Cautley Newby two months before Charlotte did likewise with Smith, Elder & Co., there was still no sign of *Agnes Grey* or *Wuthering Heights* in print.

Anne's earlier joy was becoming tinged with doubt and concern, could she really be sure that the publisher hadn't simply taken her money? At the bidding of her sisters, Charlotte wrote to her publisher to ask if they knew of Thomas Cautley Newby and whether they were reputable and could be trusted.[4]

In this aspect at least, Thomas Newby could be trusted. He had been in no hurry to unveil the two new novels, but the publication of *Jane Eyre* changed all that. Newby was a man who always had an eye on profit, and his eyes lit up when he realised that he had books by the brothers of Currer Bell, the now esteemed author of *Jane Eyre*. He waited a further two months until public demand for Currer Bell was at its height, and then he finally published *Wuthering Heights* and *Agnes Grey*. Anne and Emily received six copies each, and they launched eagerly into them. Their elation was tempered somewhat by the fact that many of the errors they had corrected in the proofs were still present in the final printed copy, but this was a fleeting concern when they considered that they had done it at last: they were published novelists. It was December 1847, and now all three sisters' works were before the public.

14

THE SCANDALOUS TENANT OF WILDFELL HALL

My object in writing the following pages, was not simply to amuse the Reader, neither was it to gratify my own taste, nor yet to ingratiate myself with the Press and the Public: I wished to tell the truth, for truth always conveys its own moral to those who are able to receive it … Let it not be imagined, however, that I consider myself competent to reform the errors and abuses of society, but only that I would fain contribute my humble quota towards so good an aim, and if I can gain the public ear at all, I would rather whisper a few wholesome truths therein than much soft nonsense.

Preface to the second edition of *The Tenant of Wildfell Hall*

The print run of the three-volume edition of *Wuthering Heights* and *Agnes Grey* was 250 copies, rather than the 350 that Thomas Cautley Newby had promised, but despite Newby's limited advertising spend, it garnered considerable interest in the press. Word soon spread that the brothers of Currer Bell, Messrs Ellis and Acton, had also produced novels, but what the public and critics found was not at all what they had expected, despite the advert placed by their publisher.

The adverts appearing in national newspapers such as *The Examiner* suggested that the books were the work of one man and linked the three volumes repeatedly to *Jane Eyre*. They read, 'Mr Bell's Successful Novel, In 3 Vols. Wuthering Heights And Agnes Grey', going on to include quotes such as *The Athenaeum*'s, 'Here are two tales so nearly related to "Jane Eyre" in cast of thought, incident, and language, as to excite curiosity', and *The Spectator*'s, 'It bears affinity to "Jane Eyre"'.

Wuthering Heights made up the first two volumes of the triple-decker, and following on from that contrasting novel did *Agnes Grey* few favours. The wonderful delicacy and elegant charms of *Agnes Grey* are indeed things to savour when on their own, like a beautiful consommé that is all the tastier for its simplicity and clarity, but if such a consommé is produced after a large, highly spiced meal it will go unnoticed. The sheer unstoppable ferocity of *Wuthering Heights* attracted critical attention, while the perfectly crafted *Agnes Grey*, with not a phrase or word out of place, was paid mere lip service.

The Star was especially fulsome in its praise of Ellis Bell's debut novel, saying, 'It is not often that two such novels as "Jane Eyre" and "Wuthering Heights" are published in the same season.'[2]

Whilst critics generally admired *Wuthering Heights*, many found it to be a flawed work of genius, too brutal and ill mannered to be acceptable to all readers. That was not a charge they could lay against *Agnes Grey*, but it was instead damned by faint praise. The *Atlas* was typical when it proclaimed that '"Agnes Grey" is more level and more sunny', but then went on to call it a 'somewhat coarse imitation of one of Miss Austin's [*sic*] charming stories' and concluded that 'It leaves no painful impression on the mind – some may think it leaves no impression at all.'[3]

A more favourable impression was left on the critic from *Douglas Jerrolds' Weekly*, who stated that *Agnes Grey* was a tale 'well worth the writing and the reading'.[4] Nevertheless, it continued to be the wildness of *Wuthering Heights* that drove the success that the three volumes enjoyed.

Emily's indignation was fired up by the scathing reviews of *Wuthering Heights*. She would throw the papers to the floor, unuttered curses seething away within her. Anne took reviews both indifferent and bad with her usual stoicism. Let the readers decide, she would say, not the critics; a good author never writes for the critics but from the courage of their own convictions.

There was one accusation, however, that did wound Anne, and it would be used against her again with her forthcoming novel. She could not countenance people saying that elements of her story that were based upon incidents she had seen at first hand were too fantastical, too monstrous to be true. People could accuse Anne of many things and she would bear the charges without complaint and unflinchingly, but she would never allow her honesty to be called into question. It is for this reason that she used the introduction to her second novel to also defend her first novel. She had not invented or embellished the incidents that some people found distasteful in *Agnes Grey*; that was something she would never do, as they were about to find out.

The *Atlas* review that had been so dismissive of *Agnes Grey* finished with a prediction: 'We are not quite sure that the next novel will not efface it.'[5] This was exactly what Anne intended, for by the time the review appeared she had already completed its successor, *The Tenant of Wildfell Hall*.

Just as her sister Charlotte had finished *The Professor* and then quickly commenced writing *Jane Eyre*, so Anne refused to rest on her laurels. In July 1847, the very month that she received an offer of publication from Thomas Cautley Newby for *Agnes Grey*, she began to work on her next offering, and her two novels were to be as different as they could be.

With *Agnes Grey*, Anne had written on a very personal theme. She opened up the heart that was usually locked so firmly shut and revealed her personal dreams of love and marriage, as well as exposing some of the harsh conditions that governesses of the time were having to endure. Anne's attitude to marriage is also a theme of *The Tenant of Wildfell Hall*, but this longer book, perfectly tailored to the prevailing three volume format, takes a much broader look at the problems affecting society as a whole.

To Anne, being a novelist was an extension of her duties as a governess and teacher. Just because the people reading her book would be in cities she would never see, leading lives she would never know about, did not mean that they would escape a lesson or two from her. This earned her great censure from some quarters of society, and some of those who were closest to her, but she refused to apologise if she had upset a proportion of her readers and clung courageously to her doctrine of pure and unadulterated truth, as she again espoused in her preface to the novel's second edition:

> When we have to do with vice and vicious characters, I maintain it is better to depict them as they really are than as they would wish to appear. To represent a bad thing in its least offensive light, is doubtless the most agreeable course for a writer of fiction to pursue; but is it the most honest, or the safest? Is it better to reveal the snares and pitfalls of life to the young and thoughtless traveller, or to cover them with branches and flowers? O Reader! if there were less of this delicate concealment of facts – this whispering of 'Peace, peace' when there is no peace, there would be less of sin and misery to the young of both sexes who are left to wring their bitter knowledge from experience.[6]

Some people have discerned in this preface, and in the book as a whole, an attack upon, or response to, Emily's *Wuthering Heights*, but this is a false interpretation. Yes, the dangers of alcoholism, gambling and cruelty are exposed to the light in a much more honest and judgemental fashion by Anne's book than by Emily's, but could she really be referring to *Wuthering Heights* when she talks of books that have a 'delicate concealment of facts' or contain 'much soft nonsense'? *Wuthering Heights* could surely never be described as 'soft' or as a book that conceals the harshness and brutality existing in the world.

Whilst the Anne and Emily of 1847 were not in the close twin-like accord that they had been as children, due in large part to Emily's increasing retreat into her own isolationism, they were still full of love and respect for each other. Their relationship had not broken down but had merely evolved, just as relationships between sisters must always evolve as they grow older. Anne had been fully aware of the content of Emily's book and would not have allowed her own *Agnes Grey* to be published alongside it if she had felt it immoral or damaging to its readers.

Anne saw *Wuthering Heights* for what it was: a brilliant piece of fiction. A fairy story, similar to those that Tabby Aykroyd had told them as young children or those that she and Emily had woven into their Gondal tales and poems. Emily did not share Anne's religious fervour for teaching and improving her readers, all that she cared about was creating a great novel that was thrilling to read, much in the way that her literary hero Sir Walter Scott had done. Anne appreciated this and accepted that she and her sister were writing with different aims in mind, but she was determined that her second novel would be a work of fiction that held a mirror up to reality.

Although Anne's novel is not a direct response to *Wuthering Heights*, and especially not an implicit criticism of it, there are some points of similarity that showed the influence Emily's book had on her, just as Anne's first book had influenced *Jane Eyre*. Both novels feature a large and imposing hall in a solitary moorland setting (revealing the use of Ponden Hall as a model for both buildings) and both centre on a mysterious newcomer with a hidden past. There is also, of course, the fact that both houses share the same initials, WH, and the superficial similarity between the names Heathcliff and Huntingdon. Even so, there are more points of difference than congruity between the two novels.

The Tenant of Wildfell Hall is a book that is centred upon big themes: the importance of love in marriage, how addiction can destroy both the addict and their family, society's attitude to class, belief in a loving and redeeming God and equality of the sexes. On all these issues, Anne was often to find herself at variance with the prevailing thoughts of her day, and she was castigated for it. This would take its toll on Anne's reputation and her health, but in the early period of writing the novel, at least, she was happy.

It is from this period that we have the first of five Anne Brontë letters that are currently known to survive. Charlotte had recently returned from Brookroyd at Birstall, and Ellen Nussey had sent back presents for all the family, even including a cap for Tabitha Aykroyd. For Anne she sent a jar of medicinal crab cheese, an object that may sound less than appetising today but one that shows how thoughtful Ellen could be and reveals the increasing closeness between the two. Ellen was aware that Anne had suffered a particularly severe asthma attack in late 1846 and that in October 1847 her health was still weakened as a result. Nevertheless, Anne's letter by return to Ellen is cheery in its nature and begins by affirming that the recent spell of windy weather had not brought her the usual coughs and colds that she dreaded more than anything else. She also thanks Ellen for her gift, saying, 'the crab cheese is excellent, and likely to be very useful, but I don't intend to need it'.[7] Anne later alludes to a wedding that Ellen was planning to attend and writes that 'when the wedding fever reaches you I hope it will be to some good purpose and give you no cause to regret its advent'.[8] This cheery and compact epistle finishes by passing on the best wishes of the Major, Emily's nickname, and a profession that Anne is Ellen's affectionate friend.

Writing the letter would have been the precursor to the evening's work on her new novel. She would have licked a taster of crab cheese from the end of her finger and then pulled the sheet of paper closer to her, before continuing her work by candle light. She was finding the writing of the first section of *The Tenant of Wildfell Hall* to be no onerous task as the ending of *Agnes Grey* had been. Indeed her cheery disposition at the time is evident in this portion of the work itself, which is full of flashes of a vivacious humour, to an extent not seen in any other Brontë book.

The male hero of the novel, and narrator for large parts of it, is the gentleman farmer Gilbert Markham, and he is a beautifully rounded character. We see the serious, love struck side of him, but Anne is also unafraid to show the self-aggrandising, narcissistic, almost buffoonish side to him. This family trait is also carried down to Gilbert's younger brother, Fergus, whose sole intention it is to annoy his family so much that they allow him to leave them and join the army. Fergus is sarcastic and sneering, and yet he often ends up the object of the humour, as in the first chapter of the novel, when he attempts to mock his sister Rose for wanting to know more about the new tenant who has arrived at Wildfell Hall:

> 'Pray, be quick about it; and mind you bring me word how much sugar she puts in her tea, and what sort of caps and aprons she wears, and all about it; for I don't know how I can live till I know', said Fergus, very gravely.
>
> But if he intended the speech to be hailed as a master-stroke of wit, he signally failed, for nobody laughed. However, he was not much disconcerted at that; for when he had taken a mouthful of bread and butter, and was about to swallow a gulp of tea, the humour of the thing burst upon him with such irresistible force, that he was obliged to jump up from the table, and rush snorting and choking from the room; and a minute after, was heard screaming in fearful agony in the garden.[9]

The Tenant of Wildfell Hall can be divided into three distinct parts. The first is narrated by Markham as he gets ever closer to the mysterious tenant herself, a woman known to the villagers of nearby Linden-Car as Helen Graham. The second section takes the form of a diary narrated by Helen herself, where we finally learn the truth about her past. Section three looks at the aftermath of Markham reading Helen's diary, as he narrates the story of how they eventually come to be married.

The initial section of the book is conventionally nineteenth century, although as always with Anne, it is superbly written, full of little details and yet never bogged down by extraneous words. We learn that a woman has taken residence in a house that has long been abandoned, the Wildfell Hall of the title. We, and the villagers, soon learn that she is a widow with a young son and that she also lives with an ageing maid. She likes to paint, and indeed makes a living of sorts out of the sales of her paintings.

Anne has created a suspense-filled opening that will have her readers guessing: will this be a romance, a mystery novel or even a gothic horror? In fact it is none of the above: it is a revolutionary novel, completely different from anything that had preceded it. Before long we learn that Helen Graham isn't a widow at all, and that Graham is an assumed name. The truth that Anne reveals about Helen would shock and delight her readers by equal measure, and scandalise the refined society it so scathingly depicted.

Markham has an arrangement of sorts with the vicar's daughter Eliza Millward, although they have little real affection for each other. He has dismissed all the talk about the mysterious new neighbour until he happens to be walking past Wildfell Hall with his dog Sancho. A small boy, who we learn is called Arthur, tries to climb a wall to reach the dog but becomes fastened upon a tree branch. Markham catches the boy just as his mother, Mrs Graham, runs from the hall. On this first meeting he finds the woman intriguing yet aloof to the point of ingratitude. Later he sees her again in church, and once more finds her cold and distant, yet almost hypnotically beautiful.

Over the course of this first section, Markham sees more and more of Helen, and he falls inescapably in love with her, to the point where he desists in his regular visits to Eliza Millward. As his ardour is growing, however, Helen's reputation with the villagers is plummeting.

We first see this when Helen and Arthur accept an invitation to visit the Markhams. Gilbert's mother is scandalised by the way that Helen treats her son, and especially by the fact that she won't let him touch alcohol. To society at this time it was not shocking that a child of around 5 years of age should drink wine but that he should be forbidden from doing so. Helen reveals that she has purposely made alcohol repugnant to her son, and she is laughed at by the assembled company, who then upbraid her for turning him into a 'milksop'.

Rumours continue to circulate that Helen Graham is not all she should be. There is even talk that she has not been married at all and that she is having an affair with Mr Lawrence, the squire of the village, one of Gilbert's friends. These vicious barbs are brought to a height at a party where Eliza points out the physical similarity between Arthur and Mr Lawrence. Markham is roused into a fury, and refuses to believe anything against the woman, but his faith is soon to be put to the test.

One evening Markham hears how the vicar has been to visit Mrs Graham to point out what he sees as reprehensible in her conduct. Markham rides quickly to Wildfell Hall and finds Helen in tears of anguish. They hold hands, and Helen explains that she has a dreadful secret and has wronged him, but if he meets her on the moors at midday on the morrow, she will reveal the truth to him. Markham agrees reluctantly to leave her, but then returns to the hall to ensure she is okay. Whilst approaching a window, he hears a voice and hides behind a holly bush. To his horror, he sees Mr Lawrence with his arm around Helen.

We have now reached a point where Markham's indifference has turned to love and now to hate. He meets Lawrence on his horse and attacks him with a whip, nearly killing him in the process. The planned meeting doesn't happen, yet although he attempts to avoid Helen at every opportunity, she eventually finds him and asks him to come to Wildfell Hall one last time. He does so, and Helen presents him with a diary, asking him to read it and then return it to her.

The first section of the novel is now completed. It had started with humour, a comedy of manners almost, but has ended with violence, hatred and anguish. These are themes that will be continued in the second section, the part of the novel that would become infamous in its day.

We now pass into Helen's diary, beginning with her as an 18-year-old living with her aunt and uncle. Her mother is dead, and although her father and brother are still alive she lives apart from them. Her aunt begins by warning her against the perils of marrying unwisely. Love and looks should be discounted in a wise marriage she contends, and Helen is in agreement. It is not what is on the outside that matters she asserts but on the inside.

This resolution is put to the test when she meets a handsome young man at a ball. He is Arthur Huntingdon, and he soon asks for her hand in marriage. Helen's aunt is strongly against the union: the man has already squandered much of the fortune he inherited through gambling and intemperate living. Helen, however, insists that she can change his behaviour and redeem him from any past sins: 'If I hate the sins I love the sinner, and would do much for his salvation.'[10]

They are soon married, and Helen becomes Mrs Huntingdon of the grand Grassdale Manor. At first she is happy, although she finds fault in her husband's self-conceit and in the control he exerts over her. She can never do anything without his permission and he calls upon her constantly as if he were her child rather than her husband.

The marriage rapidly worsens. Huntingdon travels to London for a week but is gone for months, returning dissipated and with a wild look in his eye. Every year his friends spend long periods at Grassdale, where Helen is forced to witness their orgiastic and drunken behaviour. Each character in the party is sketched impeccably by Anne. We have Lord Lowborough, the man who has gambled away his fortune. He has given up drink only to become hooked on laudanum, yet soon his friends hold him down and force him to drink again. Mr Hattersley is a violent, loud, drunken man, who abuses his friends and his wife, Helen's friend Millicent, in the company of others. Mr Hargrave behaves more respectably than the others, but it becomes apparent that this is merely part of his scheme to attract Helen into having an adulterous relationship with him. Grimsby is a rank misogynist, always looking for ways to turn Huntingdon even further against his wife.

These are the characters that the virtuous Helen has to spend time with, and Anne does not flinch from revealing the depths of depravity they sink into. We see men unable to speak and walk, laughing helplessly on the floor. Others fight drunkenly with each other, until candles are held to their hands, and there is sexual depravity and infidelity too. Helen, by means of hiding in the shrubbery just as Gilbert had done in the book's first section, finds that her husband has been having an affair with his friend's wife, Lady Lowborough.

A crisis has been reached. Helen asks her husband if he will let her leave and take the young son that they now have with her. Huntingdon refuses, although he has said that he has no love for the son as Helen spends too much time doting upon it instead of him. To have a wife walk out on him would be too shocking for him to contemplate, and a slight on his reputation. An agreement is then reached whereupon they will live under the same roof as man and wife in name only, an act of keeping up appearances.

The next few years pass in this manner, with Huntingdon's drunken debauches getting worse and Hargrave's attempts to steal Helen for himself becoming more persistent, yet now the final betrayal is committed. Huntingdon is trying to corrupt their son as well, encouraging him to drink, swear and curse his mother. This Helen cannot abide, and she hatches a plan to escape Grassdale with her son, assume a new name and make a living through her painting.

This scheme is discovered, and Huntingdon destroys her painting equipment before confiscating her money and jewellery. He then brings a new governess for his son, but Helen soon realises that this is simply another of Huntingdon's conquests. She makes a new plan to escape and writes in secret to her brother, asking him if he will prepare a wing of the house that they were born in, now abandoned, for her to live in. The brother is Frederick Lawrence, and the house is Wildfell Hall. The flight is successful, and the diary ends with her living under the assumed name of Helen Graham, which had been her mother's maiden name.

Finishing the diary, Markham is shocked that he has judged Helen so wrongly. He rushes to her and they finally declare a love of sorts for each other. Markham insists that Huntingdon no longer has any right to expect loyalty from his wife, but Helen is repulsed that he is resorting to the same arguments that Hargrave had tried to use. She insists that she must leave forever and that Markham cannot know her new address, although after six months have passed he may write to her courtesy of her brother. By that time, she reasons, their ardour will have cooled to an extent that will allow them to indulge in a friendly correspondence.

Before that six months is up, Markham is shocked to hear, via the ever venomous Eliza, that Mrs Graham has left Wildfell Hall and returned to the husband that she had apparently run away from. Through letters that Mr Lawrence, now reconciled with Markham, has received, we learn that she has been notified that Huntingdon is very ill after a fall and has returned to nurse him.

Helen has extracted, with some difficulty, a written promise that she can leave Wildfell Hall with their son at any time, if his behaviour necessitates it. At first, Huntingdon responds to Helen's nursing and seems to get better morally and physically, but he soon begins to drink to excess again, and this brings on his death, which is accompanied by a terrible physical and spiritual torment.

A period of sixteen months passes before Markham and the now wealthy Helen are reunited, but this separation has only strengthened their love. Anne creates a tender scene at this meeting, in stark contrast to the debauchery and misery that has preceded it. Helen opens a window, and Markham wonders whether it is to cool her feelings or to pluck a solitary Christmas rose growing outside:

> Pluck it, however, she did, and having gently dashed the glittering powder from its leaves, approached it to her lips and said –
>
> 'This rose is not so fragrant as a summer flower, but it has stood through hardships none of *them* could bear: the cold rain of winter has sufficed to nourish it, and its faint sun to warm it; the bleak winds have not blanched it, or broken its stem, and the keen frost has not blighted it. Look, Gilbert, it is still fresh and blooming as a flower can be, with the cold snow even now on its petals – Will you have it?'[11]

The Tenant of Wildfell Hall ends on a happy note. Helen is now Mrs Markham, and her son, Arthur, is living at Grassdale Manor with his wife, the daughter of Millicent and Hattersley, who was himself reformed by a lecture from Helen. It is a powerful book, an undoubted masterpiece, and it deserves to be ranked alongside *Wuthering Heights* and *Jane Eyre*. Like Anne Brontë herself, the book is unflinching in its honesty, but it is this honesty that would adversely affect the novel's reputation, and hers, for over a century after it was published.

There are two subjects within the novel that were seen by contemporary readers as both revolutionary and shocking. The first of these is the treatment of religion within the novel. Anne had mentioned the doctrine of divine redemption in *Agnes Grey*, through the words and actions of Edmund Weston, but it forms a central part of her second novel. She unequivocally dismisses the Calvinist doctrine that was widely held in the Church of England and which is represented in the novel by the views of her aunt.

When Helen is first contemplating marriage to Huntingdon, her aunt asks how she can marry a wicked man when they will be separated eternally at the final judgement, where he will be cast into 'the lake that burneth with unquenchable fire' forever. 'Not for ever', Helen exclaims and uses scripture to support her belief that all people, whatever sins they may have committed, will attain eventual salvation:

He that 'is able to subdue all things to Himself, will have all men to be saved', and 'will in the fullness of time, gather together in one all things in Christ Jesus, who tasted death for every man, and in whom God will reconcile all things to Himself.'[12]

The aunt is scandalised, just as Aunt Branwell had been when she heard Anne say the same words, and asks where she had learned all this. 'In the Bible, aunt. I have searched it through, and found nearly thirty passages, all tending to support the same theory.'[13]

Helen then goes on to explain that doctrines that people such as the Calvinists espouse to the contrary have come about because of an incorrect translation of the scriptures. What is translated as 'everlasting' or 'eternal' from the original Greek of the New Testament actually means for a long time, or enduring, it does not mean never ending. Here in print was Anne's faith in a nutshell, and she had the scriptural and linguistic knowledge, and the intellectual capacity, to defend it to the full. This doctrine of eventual forgiveness is also repeated by Helen to Huntingdon on his deathbed, although he cannot bring himself to believe it.

This in itself was enough for many critics to decry the novel as ungodly and scandalous, but worse still to them was Anne's depiction of marriage and women's place in society. Anne, encouraged by her father, as all her sisters had been, was a deep-thinking woman who made up her own mind about things. At the time she was writing there were clear delineations between a man and a woman, and it was accepted in law, and by society in general, that men were superior to women. Anne could not honestly accept that she was in any way inferior to a man, and she would use *The Tenant of Wildfell Hall* to develop this theme.

In Anne's time the wife became the property of her husband upon marriage, and any possessions, money, land or inheritance she had also became his to do with as he pleased. Divorces were very difficult to obtain, even if the husband had physically abused his wife or cheated on her, as in the case of Huntingdon and Helen. The terms of divorce were also vastly more favourable to men. Until the 1857 Divorce and Matrimonial Causes Act, husbands were still entitled to keep the earnings of the woman he had divorced. Children over 7 were always placed into the custody of the husband, whatever the circumstances behind the divorce, until the Infants Custody Act came into place in 1886. Wives remained the legal property of their husband until 1891, and prior to this time a husband could legally keep his wife imprisoned if she refused to have sex with him.

This was the world that Anne and her sisters grew up in, yet there were still some enlightened men, and their father provided a shining example. In 1841 he was visited at the Haworth Parsonage by a Mrs Collins. She was married to John Collins, the assistant curate to Reverend Busfield of Keighley. In tears, Mrs Collins explained her problem. Her husband, despite being a man of the cloth like Patrick, was a gambler and a drinker, who beat both his wife and his children. He had run up debts that could never be paid, and Mrs Collins saw no way out of the problem she was in.

It says a lot that she had chosen to come to Haworth to speak to Patrick rather than speaking to Reverend Busfield himself. Patrick's opinion on these matters must have been known to her, and others, although it certainly did not comply with the perceived wisdom of the time. Patrick told Mrs Collins that she should leave her husband, and take her children with her. Acting on his advice, this is just what she did, and just at the time that Anne was thinking of writing *The Tenant of Wildfell Hall*, the Brontës found out the results of that action.

In a letter to Ellen Nussey dated 4 April 1847, Charlotte reminds her friend of the story of Mrs Collins, who had been abandoned 'to disease and destitution in Manchester, with two children and without a farthing in a strange lodging house'.[14] A day earlier Martha Brown had told Charlotte that a ladylike woman wished to speak to her in the kitchen. To her amazement, it was Mrs Collins, who stood there 'cleanly and neatly dressed as was her little girl who was with her'. In a conversation, Charlotte learned that Mrs Collins had made a new and respectable life for herself and now ran a boarding house in Manchester. In Charlotte's words, she had 'triumphed over the hideous disease'[15] of staying with a man who did not love her and who mistreated her.

In the tale of Mrs Collins we see more than a reminder of Mrs Huntingdon, and it was a story that chimed particularly with Anne because it was so attuned with her own opinions on this subject. The great crime against God wasn't in leaving a husband but in forcing or encouraging a woman to marry against her will. We see this in the way that the Robinson girls wrote to her for advice on the matter after she had left Thorp Green Hall, and we even hear Anne giving Ellen a warning on this subject in her letter of October 1847.

Towards the close of the novel, Helen tries to counsel the young Esther Hargrave against marrying against her wishes to please the persistent demands of her mother. In this we see a reflection of Anne's relationship with the young Robinsons, as well as recognising a portrayal of Mrs Lydia Robinson in Mrs Hargrave herself:

> I have seen Esther Hargrave twice. She is a charming creature, but her blithe spirit is almost broken, and her sweet temper almost spoiled, by the still unremitting persecutions of her mother, in behalf of her rejected suitor – not violent, but wearisome and unremitting like a continual dropping. The unnatural parent seems determine to make her daughter's life a burden if she will not yield to her desires.[16]

There was one character even closer to home that would have a huge influence on Anne's novel. We see elements of Branwell in both Huntingdon and in Lord Lowborough. By this time, Anne's brother was a hopeless addict to both drink and laudanum. Debt collectors would knock on the parish door,[17] Branwell would be dragged home from the inns, threats would be made against himself and his family.

At a time when she should have been celebrating the fulfilment of her writing dream, all hope and happiness for Anne was gone. She found the completion of *The Tenant of Wildfell Hall* to be even more difficult than *Agnes Grey*, and yet she could not turn away from her promise to reveal the truth, come what may. She would often sit crying at the table, as she realised that in writing about the death of Huntingdon she was really writing about the death of Branwell that was surely to come.

Anne's sisters would try to comfort her and even to dissuade her from continuing the book, but she would shrug away the arm around the shoulder, and with a stern look she would silence any words on this matter. The decline in her health was plain for all to see, it was as if the act of writing the book was draining away her very life.

Charlotte reveals her own thoughts on this in her 'biographical notice' of Anne:

> Hers was naturally a sensitive, reserved, and dejected nature; what she saw sank very deeply into her mind; it did her harm. She brooded over it till she believed it to be a duty to reproduce every detail (of course with fictitious characters, incidents, and situations) as a warning to others. She hated her work, but would pursue it. When reasoned with on the subject, she regarded such reasonings as a temptation to self-indulgence. She must be honest; she must not varnish, soften or conceal.[18]

Charlotte knew well how sensitive and reserved Anne could be, and yet she again failed to credit her sister's courage and inner strength. Anne was not dejected, because she would always have the hope that her faith brought to her, and although reserved she refused to be silent when she had something to say. At last, the novel was completed, yet still she would not rest. Charlotte encouraged Anne to contact her own publisher, Smith, Elder & Co., rather than using Thomas Cautley Newby, but Anne would not hear of it. It was as if she could sense the failing of her own powers and hear time's winged chariot approaching. No, there could be no delays. *The Tenant of Wildfell Hall* was despatched to Newby in May 1848, and by June 1848 it was already published. What happened next was a shock to Anne, and her sisters.

THE BRONTË SISTERS MAKE THEIR ENTRANCE

Respecting the author's identity, I would have it be distinctly understood that Acton Bell is neither Currer nor Ellis Bell, and therefore, let not his faults be attributed to them. As to whether the name be real or fictitious, it cannot greatly signify to those who know him only by his works. As little, I should think, can it matter whether the writer so designated is a man, or a woman as one or two of my critics profess to have discovered… I make no effort to refute it, because, in my own mind, I am satisfied that if a book is a good one, it is so whatever the sex of the author may be. All novels are or should be written for both men and women to read, and I am at a loss to conceive how a man should permit himself to write anything that would be really disgraceful to a woman, or why a woman should be censured for writing anything that would be proper and becoming for a man.

Preface to the second edition of *The Tenant of Wildfell Hall*

Thomas Cautley Newby had hardly proved to be an ideal publisher for Anne Brontë. They had delayed the publication of *Agnes Grey* until they thought they could make capital out of the appearance of *Jane Eyre*, and the published copy itself had contained errors that Anne had earlier corrected. They also failed to provide any remuneration for Anne and Emily. It was little wonder that Charlotte tried to persuade Anne to turn aside from publishers she saw as charlatans, but Anne would not hear of it. She was fatigued mentally and physically from writing the novel, and was giving it up to the world to do with as they pleased.

Thomas Newby had been expecting a second novel from Acton Bell, and encouraged both Anne and Emily, still known to him as Ellis Bell, to return to their writing endeavours. Their first books had been moderately successful and had created some interest in the authors themselves, primarily through their association with Currer Bell. A second novel from either author would be likely to build on this initial success and generate profits for the publisher, if not for the authors themselves.

As Newby unwrapped *The Tenant of Wildfell Hall*, he could not have been prepared for what he read. This was a different book to *Agnes Grey* altogether, a book that would make an impact on the circulating libraries and in the reading rooms of country houses. Newby may not have been a lover of literature, but he was a keen lover of money, and as he turned the pages it was as if he were turning the bank notes in his hand. There would be no delay in publishing this novel, nor any requirement for a payment towards the cost of publication. Anne was paid £25 up front, with another £25 to come once it sold 250 copies. *The Tenant of Wildfell Hall* was published with as much publicity as Newby could muster, and it soon captured the imagination of the critics and the public.

If the reviews of *Agnes Grey* had been half-hearted in their praise, or even faintly damning, there were to be no half measures in the reviews of *The Tenant of Wildfell Hall*. It was a coarse and brutal book, designed to shock, a book that had no place in the hands of a person of proper character. One reviewer lamented Acton Bell's 'scandalous insistence on presenting scenes which public decency usually forbids'.[1] *The Spectator* railed against the author's 'morbid love of the coarse, not to say of the brutal',[2] and the critic in *The Rambler* was even more damning, saying,

'the scenes which the heroine relates in her diary are of the most disgusting and revolting species'[3] and pronounced disgust at the way it portrayed
people as animals, less than human.

The *Morning Post* was confused by the difference between the sections
narrated by Markham and Helen: 'There are *two* portions in the book
so distinct in their style that we have not any doubt they were originally separate works, if not by different hands.'[4] They found the end of
the novel to be 'peculiarly pleasant, from a species of arch and piquant
simplicity which is not often found in such stories',[5] but this contrasted
with the section containing Helen's diary, which was 'not so interesting
or pleasing as the rest'.[6]

The reviewer for *The Examiner* cast a critical eye over the Bell brothers
themselves:

> The Bells are of a hardy race. They do not lounge in drawing rooms or
> boudoirs. The air they breathe is not that of the hot-house, or perfumed
> apartments; but it whistles through the rugged thorns that shoot out their
> prickly arms on barren moors, or it ruffles the moss on the mountain tops.
> Rough characters, untamed by contact with towns or cities; wilful men,
> with the true stamp of passions upon them; plain vigorous Saxon words,
> not spoiled nor weakened by bad French or school-boy Latin; rude habits;
> ancient residences – with Nature in her great loneliness all around: these
> are the elements of their stories.[7]

If the aim of the critics was to prevent people purchasing this scandalous
book by expressing a moral outrage, they were to be greatly disappointed.
Word of this new novel from the Bell brothers was spread by whispers
and winks. It was scandalous, it was dangerous, it was out of control; it
was, in short, a must read.

The Tenant of Wildfell Hall became the fastest selling Brontë novel of
them all, a fact often forgotten today. Within six weeks it had sold every
copy of its initial run of 2,000 and a second edition was being prepared.
It was one of the most requested books in the all-important circulating
libraries, and Acton Bell was the name on the lips of people in salons
across the land. The critics had been scathing, and yet the public had

silenced them, but there was one critic closer to home that could not be silenced.

Anne was distraught at the reviews the book had received, throwing newspapers aside after reading them, yet keeping her secret anger and heartbreak locked deep within as usual. She had written the book to teach people how to live better lives; it was at heart a deeply moral book, and yet she saw it denigrated as an immoral, and even irreligious, book. This was the worst possible form of criticism for Anne, and it cut her to the quick. If the critics had known that the author was a quiet, unworldly woman, they would have been even more outraged and even more vehement in their attacks, yet the most hurtful criticism of all would come from her sister Charlotte.

We get a glimpse of Charlotte's distaste for the book not only from the fact that she suppressed its publication after Anne's death, but also from Charlotte's assessment of it in the biographical notice of Ellis and Acton Bell:

> The Tenant of Wildfell Hall by Acton Bell, had likewise an unfavourable reception. At this I cannot wonder. The choice of subject was an entire mistake. Nothing less congruous with the writer's nature could be conceived. The motives which dictated this were pure, but, I think, slightly morbid.[8]

Whilst this was written a year after Anne's death, there can be little doubt that Charlotte would have made Anne very aware of her views. Charlotte was a forthright and plain-speaking woman, even with those closest to her, and would not have been deterred from saying what she thought was right, but just why did she take such a disliking to her youngest sister's work? There are three possible reasons, and the truth is likely to be a combination of all three.

It could be that Charlotte was jealous of Anne. This in no way denigrates the genius that Charlotte was, but simply shows that she was prey to the natural emotions and frailties that siblings across the world, and throughout the ages, have suffered from, even in an otherwise loving and respectful relationship. Whilst Charlotte held Emily in awe, she had long thought of Anne as the weakest, least significant member of the family, even though she had been disproving this ever since she had joined Charlotte at Roe Head School. We have seen how Charlotte reacted when William Weightman spurned her advances and instead preferred Anne. Charlotte had rightly taken pride in the spectacular success of *Jane Eyre*, and Currer Bell had been the talk of the town, but now she was finding herself usurped by the person she had rocked as a baby on her knee.

The second reason is that Charlotte and Anne had very different world views. Charlotte stuck to her high Tory principles, and whilst she also believed that women could be just as successful as men in literature and work, she still supported the strict delineations between what was acceptable for a man and what was acceptable for a woman. She found Anne's story of a woman leaving her husband and making her own way in life truly shocking, an 'entire mistake' as she put it, and she was not shy of voicing this opinion. Literature could challenge conventions, as *Jane Eyre* itself had done, but it must never set itself up in opposition to them.

Finally, and perhaps most critically, Charlotte was mortified by the character of Arthur Huntingdon. She could not fail to read the tale of the hard drinking, gambling, cursing, boastful man who turns away from God and puts the fulfilment of his own desires above all else and see a reflection of Branwell. By this time Branwell's behaviour was becoming increasingly violent and unpredictable, and yet instead of finding relief from these everyday horrors in a book, here was one that was reminding Charlotte of the awful reality within her own family.

Tensions between Anne and Charlotte were growing, but within weeks of the publication of *The Tenant of Wildfell Hall* an incident was to occur that would bring them together like never before. Thomas Newby was delighted with the early sales figures for Anne's new novel, and with the controversy it had generated. He believed that there was no such thing as bad publicity, yet he soon discovered that it was easy to overstep the mark when dealing with the Bell brothers.

Newby had already sold rights to *Agnes Grey* and *Wuthering Heights* in the United States, and encouraged by the excellent sales of *Jane Eyre* in that country, he was soon offering *The Tenant of Wildfell Hall* to American publishers. He had previously told a New York publisher that *Wuthering Heights* was the work of Acton Bell, and now he tried the same trick again. Newby declared that to the best of his knowledge *The Tenant of Wildfell Hall* was the new work by the celebrated Currer Bell and that in fact all of the supposed brothers were actually one man, who for unknown reasons liked to publish under alternative names. He also contended that *The Tenant of Wildfell Hall* was the finest book that the mysterious Mr Bell had yet produced.

The American publisher was duly excited by this prospect, snapped up the rights and began to advertise their new purchase. This was where Thomas Newby's deceit began to unravel. Charlotte's publisher Smith, Elder & Co. already had a deal in place with Harper & Brothers of the United States under which they would be offered the first rights to any new work by Currer Bell. They were angry to have been deceived, as they thought, in this way and wrote to Smith, Elder & Co. in London to let them know of their anger.[9]

Smith, Elder & Co. were equally bemused. They thought they had a good relationship with their new author Currer Bell, but could he really have deceived them and played one publisher off against the other? The only way to solve this conundrum was to write to Currer Bell for an explanation, and this they duly did.[10] Their letter arrived in Haworth on the morning of 7 July 1848. It was curt and to the point, unlike the long and friendly letters Charlotte had become accustomed to receiving from Cornhill. Whilst not directly accusing Currer of deception, they asked for permission to contradict Mr Newby's statement, which they were quite sure was untrue.

Charlotte pushed the letter on to the table with a thud and slipped it across to Anne, too angry to trust herself to speak. She had told Anne not to trust that charlatan Newby and now look where it had landed them. It was easy to read between the lines, she was being accused of being a liar. Almost as bad, in Charlotte's eyes, was that people now thought that she, or rather Currer, was responsible for a work that she found wholly distasteful and immoral. This could not be allowed to go unchallenged.

Whilst Charlotte sank silently into a chair, Anne paced the room, tears running from the eyes that often produced them in moments of joy, sadness or anxiety. The letter was next passed to Emily, who had sat impassively watching it all. Charlotte broke the spell. 'Something has to be done,' she opined, and in that moment the sisters were united once more by a common goal, to restore their good name.

Sitting around the table, a plan was quickly formed. There was only one way that they could prove the falsehood of Newby's assertion, but at first it seemed almost too dreadful to contemplate. A letter would be no proof of any kind, the only possible option would be to present themselves in person and abandon their mask of anonymity. Anne, for whom nothing could be worse than the accusation of dishonesty, agreed with this plan, but could Emily be persuaded to agree to it? She could not put aside her anonymity, it would be the death of her to do this, but she would not object to Charlotte and Anne doing so. It was they, after all, who were concerned in this matter. A compromise reached, the sisters hugged each other and then entered their father's study to explain the news to him.

It says much about the indignation that Charlotte and Anne felt, as well as their naivety in worldly matters, that they could brook no delay in this venture. Their minds had been made up, a plan formulated and they must put it into action immediately. The letter had arrived at the parsonage after breakfast, and by evening Anne and her sister were on the train to London.

They had packed a trunk with some meagre belongings and a change of clothing and sent it on with a cart boy to the railway station at Keighley. After tea they set off together to walk the 4 miles to Keighley, but the black clouds were already gathering overhead. A storm broke with the typical ferocity of the Yorkshire moors, and by the time they reached the station they were tired, weary and thoroughly bedraggled. From there they took the train to Keighley, and while a porter was transferring their trunk on to the overnight express to London, Anne and Charlotte enjoyed a drink of tea, warming their hands on the sides of the china cups.

Charlotte had arranged for them to have first-class accommodation on the train, costing them £2 5s 6d each, which was by their standards a highly extravagant purchase. Nevertheless, it meant that they had a carriage to themselves and could finally change out of their sodden clothing.

It was nearly 8 p.m. when the train pulled out of Leeds station; a new adventure was beginning.

Although Anne had travelled by train with Emily to and from York three years earlier, this was the first time she had journeyed anywhere with Charlotte since she had entered Roe Head School nearly thirteen years previously. Both sisters had changed since then, they had developed their own characters, one proud and fiery, one quiet yet strong. There had been misunderstandings, arguments and accusations, but at the heart of everything they still loved each other in a way that only sisters who were raised without a mother can.

The train passed through Sheffield and then rolled between the limestone crags of the Peak District. Charlotte pointed out the landscape she knew from visits to Ellen Nussey during her occasional sojourns with her brother at Hathersage. Anne instantly thought of the Robinson girls, who were still writing to her from Derbyshire, and their treacherous mother, who was now ensconced in the nearby Allestree Hall. They were in a new county and still heading southwards; it was the first time that Anne had ever left the confines of Yorkshire.

Anne still felt anger, rage even, at the way that her publisher had deceived them all, but as the miles wore steadily on a new feeling began to grow: excitement. It was an adventure such as she had never experienced before, she was about to see London itself, home to Queen Victoria and her young family, and St Paul's Cathedral. She was travelling to the capital of the nineteenth-century world, and when she got there she would finally have to reveal herself to it.

The sisters were so excited that they found sleep impossible, even though their seating had been designed for this purpose. They passed time by talking about the sights of London and the authors and poets who lived there. The hours passed with relentless speed, and as the summer morning dawned, the train pulled into Euston station. At last Anne and Charlotte, exhausted by both the journey and the thought of what must be the ordeal to come, could enjoy a brief sleep, and they were allowed to stay on the train until 7.30 a.m. The hustle and bustle of Euston greeted them as they stepped out of their carriage, and for Anne it was like stepping into a new, chaotic world.

Plans had been formalised on the journey. They would see both publishers that day and then return to Haworth on the following morning, after the Sunday morning service. As they walked through the station, Charlotte striding along in front, Anne would have gazed about her at the iron girders and the throng of life. It was warmer than she had expected, there was no icy wind to cool the July mornings as she was used to in Haworth. A cab was hailed, but where would they go? Charlotte asked the driver to take them to the Chapter Coffee House on Paternoster Row. It was where she and Emily had stayed with their father en route to Brussels, and as she later admitted in a letter to Mary Taylor, she did not know anywhere else to go.

The Chapter Coffee House is no longer standing; the area now houses banking offices and upmarket eateries. It was already an old building by the time that Anne and Charlotte arrived there. The ceilings of the rooms were low, which was no impediment to the short Anne and her even more diminutive sister, and heavy oak beams ran across them. By chance, the sisters had found a perfect dwelling place. The area around Paternoster Row was full of stationers and bookshops. At the end of the eighteenth century, the coffee house itself was famous for being the meeting place of the most celebrated writers of the time, and the doomed young Chatterton writes of meeting Oliver Goldsmith there. Now, unknown to the establishment, it was playing host to two writers of even greater stature.

For Anne, the coffee house had an even stronger advantage, as it was in the shadow of Wren's mighty St Paul's Cathedral. As soon as the new guests were shown to their room, Anne threw the window open, breathed in the London air and gazed in awe at the cathedral before her. A porter, apparently charmed by the young provincial women, brought them breakfast, but they had no time to waste. They must call upon Smith, Elder & Co. immediately, every hour that passed without them doing so was another hour that their character was stained and besmirched.

After quickly refreshing their appearance, the determined sisters set out to walk to 65 Cornhill. It was a very easy walk of just over half a mile from the Chapter Coffee House to the headquarters of Smith, Elder & Co. Anne and Charlotte had simply to walk past St Pauls' Cathedral and turn right on to Cheapside, which then quickly transforms into Cornhill. Unfortunately, there was no way the sisters could have known this, and they were too timid to ask for directions or hail a cab. The streets were becoming busier and noisier, and Anne and Charlotte simply pushed on against the crowd, hoping that they were going in the right direction. They weren't, and a walk that should have taken ten minutes took them over an hour before, by chance, they found the building they were looking for.

The entrance to the address was a large bookshop, with the publishing office above it. They paused on the threshold, even now wondering if they had the courage to do what had to be done. Anne, who had been content to follow Charlotte's prolonged meanderings, and who had gazed wide-eyed at the architectural delights that seemed to be on every corner, squeezed her sister's hand in encouragement. They must be, like the character in Emily's poem that they knew so well, no coward souls, no tremblers in the world's storm-troubled sphere. A deep breath taken, they stepped into the premises.

It was early Saturday morning, and already the shop was busy with both customers and the young men and women who worked there. There was no going back now, and Charlotte approached the nearest member of staff and asked to be introduced to Mr Smith. The man paused, it was not a question he had ever heard a customer ask before, but Charlotte repeated it with more urgency, and the man departed.

While they waited for him to return, they took a book each from the counter and seated themselves in comfort. It had not occurred to the sisters that the publisher himself might not be in his office on a Saturday morning, but as luck would have it, on this occasion he was. He was also busy and did not particularly appreciate being disturbed at his work. George Smith had only recently taken over the business upon the death of his father. He was 26 years old, a handsome and well-connected man about town, hard working and fiercely ambitious for his publishing company. Smith asked the man to return and find the name of the person who was asking for him, and he was amazed when he returned to announce that it was two women who would not give their names but said they had come on important business and must be seen immediately.

He had important work to complete – it felt like he always had important work to complete – yet something about this story intrigued him. After making them wait a few minutes longer, he asked for them to be called up. Anne and Charlotte were admitted to his office, both stood nervously before him as he looked at them in silence, appraising their characters. This wasn't what he had expected at all, two small women who were obviously not from London by way of their dress and their timidity.

Smith asked them what business they had that could not wait and that had to disturb him from his work on a Saturday morning, and that's when he got an even bigger shock. Charlotte produced the letter to Currer Bell she had received in Haworth a day earlier and placed it on his desk. 'Where did you get this letter from?', George Smith asked, still blinded to the truth. 'From the post office. It's addressed to me,' said Charlotte, 'I'm Currer Bell, and this is Acton Bell.' Smith's mouth fell open; for once he was lost for words as he surveyed the women who now met his gaze with a strange look of pride.[11]

He quickly ushered the sisters to sit down, and there followed another silence as he tried to understand what had been said. The Bell brothers weren't one man, they weren't men at all, so what then was the truth? More proof was needed. Smith made Charlotte sign a piece of paper as 'Currer Bell' and compared the signatures with correspondence he had. He questioned both women firmly yet politely, and he was astounded to hear how they were in fact sisters by the name of Brontë, who lived in a remote parsonage, and who had wished to keep their identities secret, and still wished to do so.

Papers were locked in a drawer; the business of the day could wait. Here sitting opposite him was the genius who had written *Jane Eyre*, in whom he had such high hopes for the future, and in company with the controversial author who had written the literary cause célèbre of that season. He looked again at the demure women in their unfashionable clothing: it was impossible for them to have been more different to how he had imagined.

It was a moment that George Smith would always remember, and he recalled the appearance of the sisters on that day: 'I must confess that my first impression of Charlotte Brontë's appearance was that it was interesting rather than attractive. There was but little feminine charm about her and of this fact she was herself unusually and perpetually conscious.'[12]

Of Anne he was more complimentary: 'She was a gentle, quiet, rather subdued person, by no means pretty, yet of a pleasing appearance. Her manner was curiously expressive of a wish for protection and encouragement, a kind of constant appeal, which invited sympathy.'[13]

In these assessments we must consider that the Brontës were not at all the sort of women that George Smith was used to meeting. They were shorn of the adornments borne by the society women he usually saw, and he was never one to praise unduly, yet he still found Anne's appearance to be pleasing. What he saw as a wish for protection was merely a result of Anne's usual shyness when first in the company of someone she did not know, the eyes cast downwards and the hesitant speech.

Another man must be admitted into this fascinating secret. Smith called his chief reader to his office. A quiet, mild-looking man in his 50s was admitted. It was Mr W. S. Williams, with whom Charlotte, as Currer, had been corresponding and who had first discerned the brilliance of *Jane Eyre*.

Williams looked around in confusion, a faint smile playing on the faces of the sisters, but when Smith explained the situation to him, it was all he could do to stop himself snatching Charlotte's hand and pressing it to his lips. He was fulsome in his praise, expressing what an honour it was to be in the company of the two Bells, or rather the two Brontës. Here at last was the affirmation the sisters never expected to receive. They were not now the quiet girls of the parsonage, they were not the teachers and governesses to be spoken down to. They were women who successful businessmen, learned men of letters, were honoured to meet, and they had effected this change with nothing more nor less than the power of their own minds.

With a surge of pride, which she would do her utmost to quell, Anne also felt her confidence returning. She spoke alongside Charlotte as they explained that they would now visit Thomas Cautley Newby before returning to Haworth the next day. Despite protestations from Smith, they insisted on retaining their pen names for their books, and they also refused to discuss the identity of Ellis Bell. On one matter, however, George Smith would not be defeated. He would not hear of

Anne and Charlotte returning to Haworth on the next day; he insisted that they stay in London for a few days and let him and Mr Williams show them the sights of the capital. It was suggested that they stay with George Smith and his mother, but of course the sisters would not dream of such an imposition, preferring to remain at the Chapter Coffee House.

Anne and her sister had planned to go straight from Smith, Elder & Co. to Thomas Cautley Newby, but it seems likely that this visit was postponed until the Monday, now that they would be staying in London until Tuesday. The long journey without sleep, the downpour near Keighley and the nervous excitement of their visit to the publisher had all taken their toll. Anne could feel the beginnings of a cold coming on, with the difficulty in breathing that always accompanied it, while Charlotte suffered from a terrible headache. Nevertheless, before they retired to their room for rest they found time to do a little shopping, in which they bought a parasol each and presents for the people at home, including a Walter Scott novel for Emily.[14]

While the visit to the unworthy Newby could wait, there was another publisher the sisters may have taken an interest in, and they were located on the very road that they were staying on. Aylott & Jones, who had published *Poems by Currer, Ellis and Acton Bell*, were also to be found on Paternoster Row. We have no concrete evidence that they visited this publisher, but it seems likely, as it was shortly after this time that the rights to the collection of poetry were transferred from Aylott & Jones to Smith, Elder & Co.[15]

At last the sisters had an hour to themselves, and Anne lay down upon her bed, letting the memories of the day wash over her. It was not over yet, and for Anne the best was yet to come. The dashing George Smith had arranged a very special treat for the celebrated, if unknown, authors, and it was one that could not have been better suited for Anne. He had invited them to accompany himself and Mr Williams to his box at the Theatre Royal, Covent Garden.

For both sisters this was a daunting prospect, but especially so for Charlotte. She had never mixed in high society, as Anne had done in her posts as governess to both the Ingham and Robinson families, and she was worried that they would look ridiculously out of step with the other opera-goers. When George Smith arrived to collect them, her worst fears were confirmed. He was in full evening wear, including tails, whereas she and Anne were attired in the simple dresses they had arrived in. Charlotte was also self-conscious of the spectacles she had to wear for this event, and we can imagine her whispering to Smith throughout the evening of how she felt distinctly underdressed. Perhaps it is from this very early meeting between George Smith and Charlotte, and there were to be many more in the years ahead, that he formed his famous opinion of her, namely that 'she would have given all her genius and fame to be beautiful'.[16]

Anne, whose companion for the evening was Mr Williams, was much less self-conscious. She was used to being dressed plainly in the company of lords, ladies and gentlemen. Even so, she was seeing opulence on a scale that she had never seen before, both in the building itself and in the people who frequented it.

The building was huge and dominated the front of Bow Street, with Doric columns announcing the grand entrance hall. It was larger in size than today's Royal Opera House standing on the same site and had only been opened a year previously after an extensive redesign by Benedict Albano. There were 188 boxes in all, and Anne and Charlotte had to ascend the grand central staircase covered in red carpet to reach the box belonging to George Smith. A butler service was on hand to provide fine food and fine wine, but Anne was too enraptured in the opera itself. It was *The Barber of Seville* by Rossini, a composer admired by Anne, and one whose scores she had played on her piano.

She had seen performances of opera before, but not on this scale and not by performers of this virtuosity and brilliance. The famous 'Figaro's Aria' in particular would have been a thing of sheer delight to Anne; surely music and singing of this scale could only be a gift from God? When she had held that accusatory letter in her hand in the parsonage, she could not have imagined that on the following evening she would be seated in this grand opera house listening to music that made her heart soar. She leaned forward excitedly in her seat, as her drumming fingers kept time with the score.

Back in the Chapter Coffee House, Anne could not stop talking about the performance, analysing which singers had been best. From this, Charlotte was to write that there were some things that Anne would have liked better about the performance, but that was simply a reflection of the impact it had made on this music-loving woman. When we look back on Anne's life, here at least is one night that she would have found completely joyful.

Sunday morning arrived, and now Anne could indulge her other true passion in life. Mr Williams arrived to escort the sisters to church. Despite being in the shadow of St Paul's, Anne asked to be taken to St Stephen's church in Walbrook, which was home to the celebrated preacher Reverend George Croly. Anne had read of Croly's reputation for Christian charity and of his brilliant sermons, where he would talk of God's forgiveness and love for all. Alas, he was not there on that particular Sunday, but Anne found the evangelical service to her liking nonetheless.

On Sunday afternoon they were taken to dine at Mr Smith's house, or rather at his mother's house where he still lived, in Bayswater. They were introduced to the family as guests of honour, and such was the effect on Anne and her sister that they could barely eat any of the large meal that was set before them. After the meal they strolled through Kensington Gardens, marvelling at the beautiful lawns and flower beds, although in Anne's eyes, they could never match the beauty of the wild moorland flowers.

Monday was to be their last full day in London, and it was on this day that they simply had to visit Thomas Newby. It is likely that he knew what was coming, and that George Smith had already contacted him now that he had received irrefutable proof of Newby's duplicity. Charlotte must have been expecting Anne to renounce her contract with Newby and demand that he hand the rights over to George Smith, but once again she would prove to Charlotte that she was her own woman. Anne could talk with confidence when she had to, and she left Thomas Newby in no doubt of how distasteful she found his actions. Nevertheless, she would not break the contract with him, but instead insisted that she be allowed to write a preface to the second edition that would make clear her opinion on what Newby and the critics had been saying about *The Tenant of Wildfell Hall* and its author.

As they stormed out of the shamefaced Newby's office, Charlotte must have been bewildered by her sister's decision, but she was learning to bite her tongue when it came to Anne. To Anne, a contract was a contract; even if one side had broken it, she would not. Further to this, to break off from Newby would have been an insult to Emily, who had also accepted his terms. It must be endured.

Light relief was needed afterwards, and they went to a new exhibition at the Royal Academy, looking at masterpieces they had never dreamt they would see in person. Dinner followed at Mr Smith's and then tea at Mr Williams' house. This was to prove to be another musical highlight for Anne. Mr Williams had eight daughters, one of whom would become a celebrated opera singer, and on this occasion she sang with another guest who was present, the daughter of Leigh Hunt, the poet and publisher who had been a friend of Keats, Byron and Shelley. Encouraged by all present, it is likely that Anne was persuaded to join in with the singing on this occasion, enchanting her hosts with her soft yet sweet voice.

Every hour in London brought new joys for Anne; it was a world completely alien to the one she had known, yet one that was full of delights for all the senses. All too soon, the London adventure drew to an end. Tuesday morning saw them take one last visit to Cornhill on their way back to Euston train station. George Smith insisted on loading them with books to take back with them and asked them to stay for a few more days, but this they could not do for reasons they could not admit, even though the astute Smith may have guessed them. Anne and Charlotte had exhausted the funds they had come with, and consequently they had to travel by second class on their return train journey. They stayed overnight in Leeds, before arriving back in Haworth on Wednesday morning, heavily burdened with presents and books, and full of exciting stories that Emily insisted on hearing again and again.

It was to be Anne's one and only visit outside of Yorkshire, but there remained one more journey that she and Charlotte would take together. The storm clouds had gathered over the moors between Haworth and Keighley at the start of their travels, but now they were gathering over the parsonage itself.

16

THE END OF THE UNHAPPY SCAPEGRACE

'Pray for me, Helen!'
'I do pray for you – every hour and every minute, Arthur;
but you must pray for yourself.'
His lips moved, but emitted no sound; then his looks became
unsettled; and, from the incoherent, half-uttered words that
escaped him from time to time, supposing him to be now
unconscious, I gently disengaged my hand from his, intending
to steal away for a breath of fresh air, for I was almost ready to
faint; but a convulsive movement of his fingers, and a faintly
whispered 'Don't leave me!' immediately recalled me: I took his
hand again, and held it till he was no more … None can imagine
the miseries, bodily and mental, of that deathbed! How could I
endure to think that that poor trembling soul was hurried away
to everlasting torment? It would drive me mad! But thank God
I have hope – whatever fate awaits it, still, it is not lost, and God,
who hateth nothing that He hath made, *will* bless it in the end!

The Tenant of Wildfell Hall

1848 had started in promising fashion for Anne. She was now a published poet and novelist, and was working on a second novel. Whilst the year would bring personal triumphs for Anne, the excellent sales of *The Tenant of Wildfell Hall* and her journey to London among them, it would also bring struggles, despair and eventual tragedy.

One particular struggle that assailed Anne from the very start of the year was her own increasingly fragile health. The severe attack of asthma that she had suffered towards the end of 1846 had been as alarming for her family as it was for her. She dealt with it by sitting still, breathing shallowly, conserving every intake of oxygen and showing few outward signs of the internal battle being fought, a battle for life. Charlotte described it thus, in a letter to Ellen Nussey:

> She had two nights last week when her cough and difficulty of breathing were painful indeed to hear and witness, and must have been most distressing to suffer; she bore it, as she does all affliction, without one complaint, only sighing now and then when nearly worn out.[1]

These attacks occurred more frequently than usual during 1847, and the winter of that year was particularly bleak, bringing an unending succession of colds, accompanied by difficulty in breathing, throughout the first three months of 1848. Anne could feel that her mental powers were at their height, but her physical powers were growing ever more unreliable. Nevertheless, in a letter that Anne wrote to Ellen on 26 January 1848 she plays down her troubles:

> We are all cut up by this cruel east wind, most of us i.e. Charlotte, Emily, and I have had the influenza or a bad cold instead, twice over within the space of a few weeks; Papa has had it once, Tabby has hitherto escaped it altogether − I have no news to tell you, for we have been nowhere, seen no one, and done nothing (to speak of) since you were here − and yet we contrive to be busy from morning to night. Flossy is fatter than ever, but still active enough to relish a sheep hunt. I hope you and your circle have been more fortunate in the matters of cold than we have.[2]

There are two key things that Anne is hiding from Ellen in this letter. She says they have done nothing 'to speak of', and yet she had been occupied with something that she could not speak of – working on her new novel. This was certainly one of the matters that contrived to keep her busy from morning to night, and as Charlotte frequently warned her, the long evenings spent hunched over a candle, dredging up memories of events that had been hateful to witness were injurious to Anne's health. The other thing that kept them occupied, and which Anne would never allude to in a letter even if she did so in her novel, was the increasingly terrible situation with Branwell.

Branwell suffered from three character flaws throughout his life: arrogance, self-pity and an addictive personality; they intensified as he grew older and formed a deadly cocktail. Patrick Brontë was an enlightened father in many ways, providing an education for his daughters that was much more fulsome and rounded than could be expected at the time, yet it was still young Branwell who was given the best of everything. As the only boy among five sisters, he quickly grasped that he would be expected to be the breadwinner of the family, that he was the great hope of the Brontës. This was a role that he relished in his childhood, telling his sisters how he would be a great writer or a great artist, but as reality took hold in his adult years, he found the disillusionment hard to cope with.

Any setback seemed insurmountable to Branwell. He had the opportunity to enter the Royal Academy but could not bear to subject himself to the inevitable scrutiny and criticism that this would bring to his work. When he found that portrait painting wasn't as profitable as he had expected, he promptly gave it up. Rather than supervising the men under his command on the railway, he would spend days carousing in public houses and drawing sketches in his notebook. The promising child had turned into an adult that could not be relied upon to do even the simplest task, and nobody knew it better than him. He sought refuge in drink and then drugs.

Branwell had been intemperate since his teenage years, despite the appeals of Anne and Charlotte for him to avoid the temptations of drink. He would soon be relishing the taste of laudanum as well, and then came an addiction to opium itself. The effect of opium was liberating for Branwell: no longer was he a failure, no longer a disappointment to his family and himself; in effect, he was no longer himself at all, he was just a mind floating free of his body, with no earthly ties to weigh him down. He was still bright enough, at this point, to realise the damaging effects that opium addiction could bring. Going cold turkey, he weaned himself painfully off the drug, just as Lord Lowborough would do in *The Tenant of Wildfell Hall*.

At Thorp Green, however, a different temptation would prove even more powerful: the temptation of the flesh. Mrs Lydia Robinson was to be the most addictive substance of all to Branwell. He could not shake off the combination of love and lust, and he would in fact never try to do so. After his inevitable dismissal in the summer of 1845 he had immediately embarked upon his greatest drinking binge to date. In her diary paper of 1845, Anne wrote:

> Branwell has left Luddenfoot and been a Tutor at Thorp Green and had much tribulation and ill health. He was very ill on Tuesday but he went with John Brown to Liverpool where he now is. I suppose, and we hope, he will be better and do better in future.[3]

Branwell's 'illness' of course was the family code for his drinking binges. Within a week of his return to Haworth they had become so extreme, and his behaviour so erratic, that there were fears for his physical and mental health. The sexton John Brown, Branwell's friend and drinking partner, had seen first hand that Branwell's drinking was getting out of control, and he needed little persuading from Patrick to take Branwell away for a few days, in the hope that the change of scenery would do him good. This was the hope also expressed in Anne's letter, and at this point she felt confident that her brother could be weaned off of his love for wine and spirits, just as Helen feels confident about saving Huntingdon from the ravages of drink in chapter thirty of *The Tenant of Wildfell Hall*:

> I determined this [addiction to wine] should never be, as long as I had any influence left; and though I could not prevent him from taking more than was good for him, still, by incessant perseverances, by kindness and

firmness, and vigilance, by coaxing, and daring, and determination – I succeeded in preserving him from absolute bondage to that detestable propensity, so insidious in its advances, so inexorable in its tyranny, so disastrous in its effects.[4]

In the weeks after Branwell's return from Liverpool, Anne may indeed have felt that they had succeeded in preventing his complete bondage to drink, but an event was about to occur that would quash all hopes of that forever. Whilst Mrs Robinson may have enjoyed her affair with Branwell on purely physical terms, as an escape from the humdrum of everyday life and a last tribute to her fading looks, Branwell harboured hopes of a different kind. He had heard how the Robinson males invariably died young, and Reverend Edmund Robinson, lord of the manor of Thorp Green, was himself often in ill health due to his explosive temper and intemperate manner. If Branwell could bide his time, he would certainly outlive the man who stood between him and his dreams. This thought recurred to him in all his moments of sobriety, even after he had been dismissed from his position.

His drinking continued throughout the remainder of 1845 and into 1846, but while he was oblivious to life around him to the extent that he did not even know that his sisters had published a book of poetry, he had still not reached his lowest depths. He would often take to drinking in Halifax, where he would meet up with his good friend the sculptor Joseph Bentley Leyland, sometimes in company with his brother Francis Leyland, later to be a biographer of Branwell, Francis Grundy and other friends from his days with the railway. In Halifax he felt free of the confines of Haworth, free to do as he pleased without the risk of upsetting and scandalising his family. He even thought of taking this freedom to its two natural conclusions. On 28 April 1846, he wrote to Leyland and talked about plans to move abroad,[5] but in other correspondence he was already talking about how tired he was of life.[6]

On 26 May the event occurred for which Branwell had been waiting. Edmund Robinson had died suddenly, and now he could bring his love for Lydia into the open and even perhaps realise his ambition of marrying her. Branwell had complete faith in Lydia's love for him, so it seemed natural that she should want to marry him as soon as a suitable period of mourning had been completed. Once more, he was completely naive of the way the world really was. It never occurred to Branwell that his deep love was unreciprocated or that the distinction in social class between them would make such a union impossible. This should not have been a shock, as the matches Mrs Robinson strived to make for her daughters showed how she viewed marriage as merely a social form to improve one's situation in life. In this, we see that Anne understood Mrs Robinson much more than Branwell ever did.

The Thorp Green Hall coachman was dispatched post haste to Haworth, but when Branwell went to meet him at the Black Bull, the news was not at all what he had been expecting or hoping for. The coachman brought news from Mrs Robinson saying that her late husband had left a will stating that she could not marry Branwell, and that his estate was to be passed on to his children, under the administration of trustees. One trustee was Charles Thorp, the co-founder of Durham University, who, so the coachman avowed, had promised to shoot Branwell if he ever came near Lydia Robinson again.[7]

This news came as a devastating blow to Branwell. He pictured his erstwhile employer having one final laugh from beyond the grave as he prevented the union with Branwell that Lydia had so long craved. In fact, the whole story was a falsehood. Although it was not unheard of for wills at the time to contain such codicils, none such existed in the will of Edmund Robinson. The story had been invented by Lydia Robinson, possibly in collusion with Charles Thorp, to keep Branwell away from her and to stop the harassment that she was sure would ensue from him. It had all been a harmless fling to her; she could not help it if he had been unable to control his feelings in the same way. Edmund had been a useful stepping stone for Lydia Robinson, but she now had bigger fish to catch. Before long she had moved back to the Midlands of her childhood and had set her stall before the wealthy Sir Edward Dolman Scott, Member of Parliament for Lichfield. There was only one problem, Sir Edward was married. Lady Scott died in August 1848, and by November of that year, the former Lydia Robinson married Sir Edward. She was then 48, and he was 75.

All hope was now gone for Branwell. Throughout his life he had been a fantasist, a dreamer who imagined himself as a hero on a grand scale, but now reality had so uncompromisingly intruded. This was reinforced by a string of letters to Branwell between 1846 and 1848 from both Dr Crosby, the Thorp Green physician who was well known to Branwell, and Anne Marshall, who had been a friend of his sister Anne.[8] The message was always the same, there is no chance of a reunion with Lydia, she cannot see you, she is rebuilding her life. Branwell now embarked on a scheme not to rebuild his life but to end it.

Incapable of doing things in small measures, he now took to drinking on an epic, Byronic scale, and an old friend was added to his vices, as he returned to the solace of opium. In this first stage of his decline, he could still be rakish and charming. His Irish lilt and natural eloquence and ebullience made him a favoured raconteur at the Black Bull and the King's Head, and when further afield at his favourite Halifax watering holes he would often turn his questionable charms on the ladies. In a letter to Ellen of this time, Charlotte warns Ellen, then planning a visit, that she should be prepared to notice a change in Branwell, but she need not be afraid of his conduct towards her. If anything, Ellen is warned, she will find him 'smooth as oil'.[9]

As his drinking continued to gain in ferocity, however, and as opium addiction once more took hold, he started to lose his looks, eloquence and confidence. This is something that Branwell had been afraid of, but by now he was powerless to resist. Once more Anne reflects the dangers of drinking in the words of Huntingdon:

> Don't think, Helen, that I'm a tippler; I'm nothing at all of the kind, and never was, and never shall be. I value my comfort far too much. I see that a man cannot give himself up to drinking without being miserable one half his days and mad the other; besides, I like to enjoy my life at all sides and ends, which cannot be done by one that suffers himself to be the slave of a single propensity – and moreover, drinking spoils one's good looks.[10]

This was a promise that both Huntingdon and Branwell made, and yet both would fail to adhere to their own warning. By 1847, drink and opium were the only things of importance in Branwell's life, other than a half memory of a woman who had done him wrong, whether knowingly or unknowingly. He began to suffer the effects of delirium tremens, often fainting upon bar floors and having fits. When not drinking he slept during the day, and his nights were punctuated by screaming fits where he would rail against his visions and the terrifying demons he saw before him.

It was under these most trying of conditions that Anne and her sisters composed their masterpieces, and yet Anne could never shake off her love for her poor, fallen brother. Charlotte had by now washed her hands of Branwell, and for more than two years refused to speak to him, but his younger sisters could not turn off their emotions in such a way. Emily, by this time the strongest person in the parsonage, would regularly wait up for Branwell's homecomings, carrying him up the stairs in the wee small hours.

Anne, too, would like to look in upon Branwell when she retired to her bed, and on one occasion this saved his life. Branwell was beyond the point where he had the patience to read, but one night he attempted to look at a periodical by candlelight, with inevitable consequences. John Greenwood, the Haworth stationer well known to the Brontës, related the story as he heard it. Anne, upon looking into his room, had found that Branwell was asleep but had set his bed on fire. Anne tried to drag her brother out of the bed, but he was a dead weight and would not wake up. With the flames taking hold, Anne ran down the stairs and whispered to Emily for assistance. Emily hauled Branwell out of the bed and threw him into a corner, before she and Anne extinguished the flames with jugs of water.

They tried to hide this incident from their father, but it was impossible, and it led to him taking a typically brave decision. Branwell, he admitted ruefully, was not safe to be left on his own, so he would have to share a room with him. From here onwards Anne and her sisters often feared for their father's life, with Branwell screaming threats at his father and promising that in the morning at least one of them would be dead. Nevertheless, Patrick stood firm, although it meant that he was often completely deprived of sleep.

In his more lucid moments, Branwell would write to his friends Leyland and Grundy, bemoaning his ill health and wishing he could be dead. These letters show, as well as tell, of his illness.[11] The script often changes wildly in mid letter, and its untidiness reflects the confusion in his mind. His family had to face the facts: Branwell was not only a hopeless addict, he was also on the edge of insanity.

His daily threats and curses were not the only strain Branwell would place on his family. He would beg money off anyone who could spare it and then immediately spend it all on gin and opium. He ran up huge debts at Halifax inns, and on more than one occasion debt collectors turned up at the door to the parsonage. Patrick had no option but to make the payment or see his son be taken away to the debtor's gaol in York. We also read, from letters by both Branwell and Charlotte, that he was also getting money from another unspecified source, the 'old source' as it was called. This could have been from the Freemasons, as Branwell had been a member of Haworth's Three Graces masonic lodge, but is more likely to have been from Lydia Robinson herself, sent via the auspices of Dr Crosby.

In the midst of this domestic chaos, Anne still found time to write one of her most poignant and reflective poems. 'The Narrow Way' is dated 24 April 1848 and has become a popular hymn. She starts by exhorting:

> Believe not those who say
> The upward path is smooth,
> Lest thou should stumble in the way
> And faint before the truth.

She finishes by revealing the secret of true happiness:

> To labour and to love,
> To pardon and endure,
> To lift thy heart to God above,
> And keep they conscience pure,
> Be this thy constant aim,
> Thy hope and thy delight,

What matters who should whisper blame,
Or who should scorn or slight?
What matters, if thy God approve,
And if within thy breast,
Thou feel the comfort of his love,
The earnest of his rest?[12]

After this poem came her visit to London, and then to fulfil the agreement she had made with Thomas Newby, the composition of the famous preface to the second edition of her best selling novel. It took her nine days to write, as Anne wrestled with how much she would reveal and how much she would conceal. Finally she reached the same conclusion she always had, let all be revealed:

I would not be understood to suppose that the proceedings of the unhappy scapegrace with his few profligate companions I have here introduced, are a specimen of the common practices of society: the case is an extreme one, as I trusted none would fail to perceive; but I know that such characters do exist, and if I have warned one rash youth from following into the very natural error of my heroine, the book has not been written in vain.[13]

For Anne, watching her brother's decline was especially painful. Branwell made clear, amidst his incoherent ramblings, that his degradation was all down to Mrs Robinson, and while he could never wish her ill, he did wish he had never met her. The plain truth of this point could not be lost on a soul as sensitive as Anne. Without her efforts, he never would have met the cause of his downfall; she therefore saw herself as a sinner as much as her brother. In *The Tenant of Wildfell Hall* she describes how Huntingdon is unable to give up drink and how this finally kills him.[14] While writing these dread-filled scenes, she may have harboured some faint hopes that Branwell could be saved, but fact was about to emulate fiction.

By September 1848, Branwell's condition had greatly deteriorated. He would spend days on end in bed and was eating so little that he had become thin and shrunken. In the third week of September his friend Francis Grundy, who had grown worried at Branwell's failure to accept an invitation to meet him in Skipton, rode to Haworth and sent a message to the parsonage inviting Branwell to dine with him at The Black Bull. To Grundy's surprise it was Reverend Brontë who first came to meet him. Patrick thanked Grundy for the kindness shown to his son but warned him to expect a great change in Branwell.

The warning was well warranted. Before long Branwell shuffled and stumbled into the inn that he had so often frequented. Grundy described the appalling sight:

> A head appeared. It was a mass of red, unkempt uncut hair, wildly floating around a great, gaunt forehead; the cheeks yellow and hollow, the mouth fallen, the thin white lips not trembling but shaking, the sunken eyes, once small now glaring with the light of madness.[15]

This monstrous Branwell mumbled about being forced out of his bed, but a glass of brandy from Grundy restored him to something approaching his old self. He ate a meal, saying that it was the first he had enjoyed in many days. He also explained that he knew his death was coming, and that he was glad of it. This death, he professed one last time, would be entirely due to his doomed love for Lydia Robinson.

A chilling moment then occurred, showing the danger that Branwell was to himself and everyone around him. He produced from his sleeve a long knife that he kept hidden away. He revealed that he thought the invitation had actually come from Satan and that he had planned to stab whoever was waiting for him until Grundy's kind voice had restored some sanity to him just in time.

Grundy said goodbye to his hopeless friend, but as he left he turned and took one last look up the hill. Branwell was stood, stooped and shaking in the road, tears streaming down his face. He last walked the streets of Haworth on 22 September 1848, presumably to obtain more gin or opium. He could not mount the step leading from Main Street to Church Lane, and William Brown, brother of his friend John, had to carry him back to the parsonage. The next day, Branwell could not get out of bed, and the surgeon John Wheelhouse was called for. He pronounced it a hopeless case: Branwell was in the last days of his life.

Despite his decline over the previous twelve months, this came as a surprise to all concerned. Patrick, wiping away tears, began an unrelenting vigil by his bedside. Branwell had long since spurned any form of religious belief, yet now his father exhorted him to return to the faith and repent his sins while he still could. Anne and Emily were by his bedside, wiping the sweat from his fevered brow throughout the hours that passed by, and even Charlotte was now in attendance. At last, on 24 September, a change occurred. A peace seemed to descend upon Branwell, and he talked of how he wanted God's forgiveness and how he was sorry for the wrong he had done to his sisters, the sisters that he truly loved.

This was the first death that Anne had witnessed, and it was a moment of both terror and triumph. Her prayers had been answered at last, as she knew that they would. Patrick offered one final prayer for God's forgiveness, and Branwell was heard to whisper 'amen'.[16] With his last iota of strength, he pulled his starved body from the bed and collapsed into his father's arms. The man who had borne such promise, such expectation, had died aged 31.

17

THE UNBREAKABLE SPIRIT

But as above that mist's control
She rose, and brighter shone,
I felt her light upon my soul;
But now – that light is gone!
Thick vapours snatched her from my sight,
And I was darkling left,
All in the cold and gloomy night,
Of light and hope bereft;
Until, methought, a little star
Shone forth with trembling way,
To cheer me with its light afar –
But that, too, passed away.
Anon, an earthly meteor blazed
The gloomy darkness through;
I smiled, yet trembled while I gazed –
But that soon vanished too!
And darker, drearier fell the night
Upon my spirit then; –
But what is that faint struggling light?
Is it the moon again?

Kind heaven! increase that silvery gleam,
And bid these clouds depart,
And let her soft celestial beam
Restore my fainting heart!

'Fluctuations'

Branwell's living had cast a dark shadow over the parsonage that had stretched over a decade and intensified in the three years leading to his demise, but his death brought little respite as each remaining family member reacted in a different way.

Patrick Brontë felt the blow keenly, although he knew it had been coming. He had already seen his wife and two eldest daughters buried beneath the stone floor of his Haworth church, but as Charlotte revealed in a letter to W.S. Williams on 2 October, he found this death the hardest of them all to take: 'My poor father naturally thought more of his only son than of his daughters, and much and long has he suffered on his account – he cried out for his loss like David for that of Absalom – My son! My son! And refused at first to be comforted.'[1]

As Patrick held his son in his arms in his dying moment, it is natural that his mind should have gone back to that day at Thornton when he held him in his arms as a newborn baby. It had all been for nothing, but at last he was now at peace. From what we know of Patrick, it is unfair of Charlotte to accuse him of thinking more of his only son than of his daughters, but as often with Charlotte, her pronouncements on others are a clue to her own thoughts and actions.

Charlotte had resented the attention that Patrick had paid to Branwell during the last painful years of his life, believing him unworthy of help. She had turned her back on her closest childhood companion, and now she was overwhelmed by a sense of grief and an even greater sense of guilt. She had not said she loved him, not tried to talk him out of the dark pit into which he had descended, a location that she knew better than most. Like Branwell, she too had questioned the truth of her faith, been spurned by a person she loved and suffered crushing bouts of depression, and yet in his last years she had not even spoken to him. As death claimed Branwell, Charlotte collapsed on to the floor and was gripped by a grief-stricken illness that confined her to her room for a week.

In the immediate aftermath of Branwell's death, it was left to Anne to pick up the pieces. It was she who initially wrote to W.S. Williams on 29 September 1848, apologising for her sister's inability to reply to an earlier letter:

> My sister wishes me to thank you for your two letters, the receipt of which gave her much pleasure, though coming in a season of severe domestic affliction, which has so wrought upon her too delicate constitution as to induce a rather serious indisposition, that renders her unfit for the slightest exertion. Even the light task of writing to a friend is at present too much for her, though, I am happy to inform you, she is now recovering … I am, dear Sir, Yours Sincerely, A. Brontë [2]

Anne, who had long been suspected of having the most delicate constitution, was now shaking off the grief that she herself felt and acting as nursemaid to both her eldest sister and her father. Even now she could feel a fatigue growing within her, but she would not fail to do her duty. For Anne the death of her brother had come as a relief, for in the last moment he had sought the salvation that she and her father had urged upon him. We know well how much that meant to Anne; she would now be in no doubt that his soul was saved and forgiven, and that she would meet him again one day in a far better place.

Three years earlier, when Branwell's debauchery was approaching its zenith, she had looked ahead to this day, and her short poem 'The Penitent' now perfectly encapsulated her feelings:

> I mourn with thee, and yet rejoice
> That thou shouldst sorrow so;
> With angel choirs I join my voice
> To bless the sinners woe.
> Though friends and kindred turn away,
> And laugh thy grief to scorn;

I hear the great Redeemer say,
'Blessed are ye that mourn.'
Hold on thy course, nor deem it strange
That earthly cords are riven:
Man may lament the wondrous change,
But 'there is joy in heaven!'[3]

Branwell's repentance had not only saved his soul but Anne's as well. The sin she had brought upon herself by introducing her brother to Mrs Robinson, as well as the guilt she felt at having been powerless to prevent his descent into a self-made hell, was now wiped away.

Emily too had conflicting feelings. It was she who had cared for him, in her own way, in the last years; it was she who had carried him on her shoulders, quite literally. She could not help but be glad that he was free of torment, but one of her great purposes in life had been torn away from her. Her sisters still had their writing, but her great project was now at an end.

The cessation of Emily's writing after *Wuthering Heights* is a mystery that will always remain impossible to solve. All throughout her life she had been a voracious writer, even if her work was mainly on Gondal themes. Between September 1843 to May 1845 she had written in excess of twenty poems, many of them now considered masterpieces, but from the date of publication of *Poems by Currer, Ellis, and Acton Bell* she wrote just one more poem, 'Why Ask to Know the Date, the Clime?'

She had of course also written her great novel in that period, but the completion of it seems to have marked the end of her creative life. There are three possible reasons for this. The first is that she was horrified at the speculation that the publication of her work was bringing. Even though she had used the pseudonym of Ellis Bell, critics were making pronouncements on the author as a person, many of them wounding to her pride. Under such searing and often unfair scrutiny, the thrill of writing had lost its edge. It could also be that the collapse of Branwell had made her stop writing temporarily, her creative powers dimmed by anguish that she could admit to nobody.

The third possibility is that she did write further work, but that it was destroyed. Certainly we have a letter from Thomas Newby to Emily discussing the progress of a second novel, but no trace of such a work now remains. Newby's letter of 15 February 1848 tells Emily that she is right to take her time over this second novel, as if it surpasses her first it could cement her reputation as a great writer.[4] It may be questioned whether Newby, never the most reliable man, had got Ellis and Acton mixed up, and whether the letter was therefore intended for Anne, but if this was the case why did Emily keep it in her writing desk? It seems likely that Emily had at least thought of writing again when Branwell's struggle allowed it, when her muse returned. It was never to return.

Branwell's funeral took place on 24 September 1848. By that time his father had rallied in spirits, although Charlotte was still too ill to attend. As was traditional, the funeral service in memory of the deceased was held a week later on 1 October, and on this occasion all of the family were in attendance. At this service Emily was racked by a coughing fit that left her doubled up in the pew. As she removed the handkerchief from her mouth, she took one glance and then hid it swiftly away. On the solemn procession back to the parsonage she cast a glance at the familiar moors that had been such a delight to her. Nobody could have known that she would never walk outside again.

Emily was the tallest of the Brontë children, and in stark contrast to her sisters had always been in good health, so the illness that now took hold surprised everyone. In its first days, little was thought of it other than that she had a cold or influenza brought on by the low spirits that were understandable in the circumstances. Anne too had developed a cold and the familiar difficulty in breathing, and a letter from Charlotte to Ellen dated 29 October states, 'I feel much more uneasy about my sisters than myself just now. Emily's cold and coughs are very obstinate. Nor can I shut my eyes to Anne's great delicacy of constitution.'[5]

While Anne's illness appeared to abate, Emily's was making rapid progress. Every day her coughing fits were getting worse, she was eating little and growing thinner. To the family's horror, her illness was taking the same form as Branwell's. Dr Wheelhouse had certified that Branwell died from bronchitis and chronic marasmus, or wasting, but the underlying cause seems clearly to have been tuberculosis. Patrick knew these signs all too well, having watched his daughters Maria and Elizabeth die of the complaint, and he begged Emily to allow a doctor to be fetched. She refused.

Emily did not believe in the power of doctors, or 'quackery' as she called it, but trusted in her own force of will to heal herself. If she kept going, if she refused to bow under the yoke of illness, she would yet regain her health. Only Emily knew the pain and torment she was in, for she refused to acknowledge them herself. In fact, she retreated even further into herself, even from Anne, talking very little and simply smiling and nodding; she knew that her frail voice would be a sign of the weakness that she would not allow to be shown.

By the end of October it had become a grim farce, a mockery of reality. Emily would not countenance even an allusion to the illness that was becoming every day more apparent in her physical appearance. Charlotte wrote:

> She is a real stoic in illness, she neither seeks nor will accept sympathy. To put any question, to offer any aid is to annoy; she will not yield a step before pain or sickness till forced; not one of her ordinary avocations will she voluntarily renounce. You must look on her and see her do what she is unfit to do, and not dare to say a word.[6]

It was at this time that a reviewer in *The North American Review*, the well-respected E.P. Whipple, took it upon himself to severely critique the Bell brothers as a whole. As a form of light relief from the prevailing gloom, Charlotte read the review to her sisters, as she described in a letter to W.S. Williams on 22 November:

> What a bad set the Bells must be! What appalling books they write! Today as Emily appeared a little easier, I thought the Review would amuse her so I read it aloud to her and Anne. As I sat between them at our quiet but now somewhat melancholy fireside, I studied the two ferocious authors. Ellis, 'the man of uncommon talents, but dogged, brutal, and morose', sat leaning back in his easy chair drawing his impeded breath as best he could, and looking, alas! piteously pale and wasted; it is not his wont to laugh, but he smiled half-amused and half in scorn as he listened. Acton was sewing,

no emotion ever stirs him to loquacity, so he only smiled too, dropping at the same time a single word of calm amazement to hear his character so darkly portrayed. I wonder what the reviewer would have thought of his own sagacity could he have beheld the pair as I did.[7]

By the end of November Charlotte conceded what all knew but none could talk of: it seemed likely that Emily was sliding towards death. Upon hearing of her symptoms, a doctor had confidently diagnosed inflammation of the lungs. On 23 November, Charlotte wrote to Ellen:

> I told you Emily was ill in my last letter – she has not rallied yet – she is very ill: I believe if you were to see her your impression would be that there is no hope: a more hollow, wasted pallid aspect I have not beheld … In this state she resolutely refuses to see a doctor; she will give no explanation of her feelings, she will scarcely allow her illness to be alluded to. Our position is, and has been for some weeks, exquisitely painful. God only knows how all this is to terminate.[8]

By 7 December, Charlotte confessed to W.S. Williams that 'hope and fear fluctuate no more'.[9] Even so, Emily would not change her daily routine. She rose at 7 a.m. and by great effort would bring herself slowly down the central staircase, past the grandfather clock, until she reached the hall. From there she would stumble into the kitchen and begin her routine of cooking and cleaning, with Tabby Aykroyd no longer assisting but silently correcting the errors that Emily was making. She refused to return to her room until 10 p.m.

She also insisted on feeding the dogs as always. Martha Brown recalled how in the height of her frailty Emily collected some breadcrumbs and meat in her hands and walked towards Keeper and Flossy. A sudden gust of wind swept under the door, and so light and weak was Emily that it blew her against the wall. Reeling and nearly falling, she angrily waved away offers of help before proceeding to feed the pets as if nothing had happened.

Through all this Anne had to look on helpless. She too tried to persuade Emily to see a doctor or to take some of the homeopathic medicine that Charlotte had secured for her from W.S. Williams, but her sister would no longer listen to anybody. Silence reigned as Emily simply squeezed Anne's hand defiantly. It was a squeeze that spoke of sisterly love, a bond that could never be broken, but also of a will that would not be moved.

Anne herself had never been averse to taking medicine, but when Emily looked at her sister and remembered the torments she had passed through despite the medicine she took, her conviction that it was all quackery was strengthened. Even though the family's concerns were concentrated on Emily, she could see that her younger sister herself was ill and suffering a cold that made her too unable to leave the house. The task of walking the dogs now fell to Patrick's curate Arthur Bell Nicholls, who would do anything for the family and one member of it in particular. It was a task that would remain in his charge for many years.

Winter brought with it its routine storms and biting winds, but even in this dreadful and silent gloom there was a moment of light for Anne. Anne's former charges had never forgotten their governess and continued to write to her on an almost daily basis, much to the chagrin of Charlotte, who would forever associate them with Mrs Robinson and the decline of Branwell. This ongoing correspondence had been carefully hidden from Branwell lest it excite his passions too greatly, but now there was no need to hide it.

In early December there was a surprise visit to the parsonage. Charlotte answered the door, and found two well-dressed, obviously well-to-do ladies. It shows a lot for the love they bore her, in those days when transport to Haworth could be irregular and expensive, that Bessie and Mary Robinson, now Clapham, had come in person to see Anne. They had written to request a visit, but nobody had expected it to happen. As she revealed to Ellen, Charlotte was amazed when she walked into the room in which they were closeted: 'They seemed overjoyed to see Anne; when I went into the room they were clinging round her like two children – she, meantime, looking perfectly quiet and passive. Their manner evinced more levity and giddiness than pretension or pomposity.'[10]

The love of the Robinson girls for Anne could not be denied. She had been strict with them at times, but it had paid off. They were now young women whose lives would be lived under the influence of Anne Brontë, not Lydia Robinson, even though they would never see her again.

This brief happy day for Anne was soon followed by the darkest days she had known since the death of William Weightman. Charlotte, against Emily's express order, had consulted a leading homeopathy expert called Dr Epps, but Emily would make no attempt to try the medication he prescribed.

It can be asked whether Emily wanted to die, whether she was in effect willing it. Certainly it was not a subject she shrank from. Some of her greatest poems talked of deathbeds and the finality that death brings to all. In one of the most memorable moments in *Wuthering Heights*, she had looked forward to the possibility of an afterlife:

> Heaven did not seem to be my home; and I broke my heart with weeping
> to come back to earth; and the angels were so angry that they flung me
> out into the middle of the heath on the top of Wuthering Heights; where
> I woke sobbing for joy.[11]

Emily was certainly not scared of death, she had become scared of nothing, but she would also not willingly have left her beloved moors and her adored Anne behind. Emily would have chosen life if the chance came, but she gave herself up to nature, saying let the natural way of things proceed just as it does with all animals.

George Smith and W.S. Williams had sent books for Emily to read from Cornhill, but by December her eyesight had failed her, so Charlotte and Anne would take turns reading to her. On the evening of 18 December, the same day that she had been blown against the wall, Charlotte read an essay of Emerson to her, until she realised that Emily was no longer listening. She left her and pledged to finish the essay the next day, but one look at Emily's face in the morning told her that a change had taken place.

Emily, terribly gaunt and in great pain, insisted on walking down the stairs once more, although this time she was powerless to stop her sisters helping her. She was guided into the kitchen, where she attempted to resume her duties, but she found them impossible. She was blind, and there could be no more hiding from the truth.

'I will see the doctor now,' she said, and Martha Brown ran to fetch Dr Wheelhouse. Crushed by sorrow once more, Charlotte ran to the moors searching desperately for a sprig of heather to give to her sister. At last she found a piece, tiny and weather blown, and raced back to the parsonage. She approached Emily but found that she neither saw nor recognised the heather or Charlotte, who dissolved in tears before her.

The doctor had been and pronounced it a hopeless case: she was in the final stages of consumption. Emily grasped in the darkness for something, and Anne, sensing what she wanted, planted her black comb into her hands. Emily commenced combing her long hair, but the comb slipped from her fingers and fell into the fire. It can still be seen in the Brontë Parsonage Museum today, the middle section burned away. Emily's legs finally buckled and she fell to the floor. Anne, with help, lifted her sister on to the long black couch in the room where they had composed so many stories and poems together. She took Emily's hand and stroked it gently, just as Emily had done for her when she was a young child struggling to breathe. At two o'clock that afternoon, with her family around her, the 30-year-old Emily Brontë took her last breath.

There had been no final amen from Emily; indeed, she had not been capable of it. She did believe in eternal life, but not in the constraints of organised religion. Nevertheless, Anne was convinced that she too would be with the angels. Charlotte saw Emily's death as proof of the more than human powers her sister possessed. She had faced death unbowed, unbroken. She had refused to change in any way; it was as if her unbreakable spirit had defeated death.

The testimony of William Wood, Tabby's nephew, shows the depth of struggle that Emily had endured. As the village carpenter, it was William who made Emily's coffin. He said it was the narrowest he had ever made for an adult. Despite Emily's unusual height, it was just 16in wide.[12] Emily's funeral procession was led by her father and her beloved dog, Keeper, the ferocious mastiff she had tamed. Keeper sat in the family pew throughout the service, and after returning to the parsonage he stood for days on end howling outside the door to what had been Emily's room.

A year that had brought great literary acclaim and success had ended in tragedy. Death had claimed two of the Brontë children within three months of each other, but his work wasn't finished yet.

18

THE GLORIOUS SUNSET

I have no horror of death: if I thought it inevitable I think I could quietly resign myself to the prospect, in the hope that you, dear Miss Nussey would give as much of your company as you possibly could to Charlotte and be a sister to her in my stead. But I wish it would please God to spare me not only for Papa's and Charlotte's sakes, but because I long to do some good in the world before I leave it. I have many schemes in my head for future practise – humble and limited indeed – but still I should not like them to come to nothing, and myself to have lived to so little purpose.

Final letter to Ellen Nussey, 5 April 1849

It was a mournful Christmas Day in the Haworth Parsonage. Just twenty-eight years earlier it had seemed full of promise, and it was full of life: Patrick was thriving in his new parish with his wife, Maria; their children Maria, Elizabeth, Charlotte, Branwell and Emily were running around happily; and little Anne was in her cradle. Now she, Charlotte and Patrick were all that was left in a house full of ghosts.

Patrick had lost the daughter who had been almost a surrogate son to him, as well as managing the household as his wife would have done. He had declared Emily, 'my right hand, nay the very apple of my eye',[1] and now she too had been buried under the unfeeling church floor he had to tread.

Charlotte had witnessed the death of a sister that she had been in awe of. She had thought that Emily's strength would never be diminished, but she was wrong. This time she had no guilt to weigh her down, this time she would be strong, because she knew that she had to be. She saw that both her father and her sole remaining sister had taken the death very badly. Anne had become more silent, adopted indeed the silence that had enveloped Emily, as if she were preparing to martyr herself. The sister Anne had loved as much as anything the world could offer was gone; was she also now looking too fervently to the next world?

On 23 December 1848, Charlotte wrote a heart-rending letter to Ellen Nussey, which starts:

Emily suffers no more either from pain or weakness now. She never will suffer more in this world – she is gone after a hard, short conflict. She died on Tuesday, the very day I wrote to you. I thought it very possible then she might be with us still for weeks and a few hours afterwards she was in Eternity – yes, there is no Emily in Time or on Earth now. Yesterday, we put her poor, wasted mortal frame quietly under the church pavement. We are very calm at present, why should we be otherwise?[2]

A little later in the letter, however, Charlotte reveals why she was far from calm in reality, why she was again gripped by fear: 'I now look at Anne and wish she were well and strong – but she is neither.'[3]

Two days later, on Christmas Day, she wrote to W.S. Williams, again expressing both her grief and her concerns for Anne: 'My father and my sister Anne are far from well … The sight too of my sister Anne's very still but deep sorrow wakens in me such fear for her that I dare not falter.'[4]

At Charlotte's request, Ellen Nussey now came to stay at Haworth. As Charlotte said, she had never been needed more. She found the whole family in the grip of mourning and Anne in the grip of a disease that had been taking hold seemingly unnoticed since the time of Branwell's death, and that had probably been in place long before that.

Anne was coughing again, but she now had severe breathlessness upon any physical exertion. Her favourite white handkerchief with tiny red chevrons emblazoned upon it would often be brought from her mouth with larger red globules of blood, and she suffered from dreadful pains in her side. On 5 January, a leading physician called Dr Teale was called from Leeds. He was a specialist in lung diseases and tuberculosis. Ellen describes what happened on that day of sorrow:

> Anne was looking sweetly pretty and flushed, and in capital spirits for an invalid. While consultations were going on in Mr Brontë's study, Anne was very lively in conversation, walking around the room supported by me. Mr Brontë joined us after Mr Teale's departure and, seating himself on the couch, he drew Anne towards him and said, 'My *dear* little Anne.' That was all – but it was understood.[5]

Here at last we have a first-hand account of how Anne could not only talk when she wanted to, she could even be 'very lively in conversation'; alas, it was all a show. The brave façade of happiness was swept away in an instant, and tears flowed involuntarily from Anne's eyes as she lay back on the couch where her sister Emily had taken her last breath just two weeks earlier. The doctor had confirmed that Anne was in an advanced stage of consumption, and while treatments could perhaps slow down the progress, there was no hope of a cure.

Dr Teale prescribed cod liver oil and carbonate of iron, and he also took steps to prevent the further spread of the disease. Ellen was ordered to return home to Birstall, and Charlotte was told that she could no longer share a bed with Anne, as she had been doing since Emily's final illness had taken hold.

Anne had endured many trials and emerged triumphant, but now she was facing the greatest trial of them all, and she found the burden almost impossible to bear. Once more those dreadful religious doubts that had plagued her at Roe Head, and at low intervals throughout her life, returned, and more powerfully than ever. What if she was wrong about it all? What if there was to be no forgiveness for her? What if she would never meet Emily and Branwell in a better world? It was too awful to contemplate, but these thoughts filled every waking moment and prevented sleep at night.

In the midst of spiritual torment, and suffering terrible physical hardship, she turned one last time to the relief of poetry. The result is called 'Last Lines' and is her most powerful work; indeed, it's like no other poetry in the Brontë canon. Anne first started the composition on 7 January, two days after Dr Teale's all too final diagnosis:

A dreadful darkness closes in
On my bewildered mind;
O let me suffer and not sin,
Be tortured yet resigned.
Through all this world of whelming mist
Still let me look to Thee,
And give me courage to resist
The Tempter till he flee.
Weary I am – O give me strength
And leave me not to faint;
Say Thou wilt comfort me at length
And pity my complaint.
I've begged to serve Thee heart and soul,
To sacrifice to Thee,
No niggard portion, but the whole
Of my identity.
I hoped amid the brave and strong
My portioned task might lie,
To toil amid the labouring throng
With purpose pure and high.
But Thou has fixed another part,
And Thou has fixed it well;
I said so with my breaking heart
When first the anguish fell.
For Thou hast taken my delight

And hope of life away,
And bid me watch the painful night
And wait the weary day.
The hope and the delight were Thine;
I bless Thee for their loan;
I gave Thee while I deemed them mine
Too little thanks, I own.
Shall I with joy Thy blessings share
And not endure their loss?
Or hope the martyr's crown to wear
And cast away the cross?[6]

At this point Anne lay down her pen, physically and mentally she could face no more. She had talked of the fear of sinning, of succumbing to the tempter Satan himself by questioning in her heart the faith she had always clung to. Let me suffer any physical tortures, she says, let me be a martyr, but do not let me suffer this final indignity. This was the lowest point she could possibly reach, whatever else may lay in wait, and she could write no more. And yet, as we will see, she did later take the pen up again and give this remarkable work a completely different ending.

Anne, so used to hiding all emotion, was now powerless to stop this display of grief, and her mental anguish took a physical toll as well. On 13 January, Charlotte wrote once more to W.S. Williams to 'unburden her mind'. 'Anne and I sit alone and in seclusion as you fancy us, but we do not study; Anne cannot study now, she can scarcely read; she occupies Emily's chair – she does not get well.'[7]

This was the spiritual nadir for Anne, and her health had failed to the extent that any movement would bring a sharp, stabbing, almost unbearable pain. She was silent; her vision had worsened. All she desired was to sit in Emily's chair, nothing else was important to her but to feel some connection with her sister. It seems likely that these black thoughts would have hastened her end with wicked speed, but somehow the next two weeks saw a great change for the better.

At the lowest ebb a moment of light had burst in upon her. The words that she had heard from Reverend La Trobe returned to her, along with the thirty passages of the Bible that Helen Lawrence so confidently cites to her aunt in *The Tenant of Wildfell Hall.* There was hope, after all. There was more than hope: there was a certainty of redemption and salvation. It was as if a candle had been lit in the darkness, in a second the shadows receded and faith returned. It would not let Anne down again.

There was another source of inspiration that Anne called upon for her spiritual renewal, a letter she had received in December 1848 from the Reverend David Thom, an evangelical preacher from Liverpool. He had felt compelled to write to her in praise of *The Tenant of Wildfell Hall*, defending it against the accusations of ungodliness that some critics had branded upon it. He also praised its use of the doctrine of universal salvation and affirmed it was one that he too firmly believed in. She had received other appreciative letters from readers, but this one was very special to her, so much so that even in the midst of torment following Emily's death, and while struggling with her own as yet undiagnosed illness, she replied to him. The letter is dated 30 December 1848, and she begins by pleading ill health for her delayed reply. She then writes:

> I have seen so little of controversial Theology that I was not aware the doctrine of Universal Salvation had so able and ardent an advocate as yourself; but I have cherished it from my very childhood – with a trembling hope at first, and afterwards with a firm and glad conviction of its truth. I drew it secretly from my own heart and from the word of God before I knew that any other held it. And since then it has ever been a source of true delight to me to find the same views either timidly suggested or boldly advocated by benevolent and thoughtful minds; and I now believe there are many more believers than professors in that consoling creed … I thankfully cherish this belief; I honour those who hold it; and I would that all men had the same view of man's hopes and God's unbounded goodness as he had given to us.[8]

This belief that she cherished so much, this 'controversial theology' that could only be hinted at, had been tested to the utmost, but at the final battle it emerged triumphant. Her father and sister could not fail to notice the difference. Her face took on an enigmatic smile, she talked again, and more freely than ever before. Anne's health even showed signs of improvement, her walking was improving and she now took delight in reading once more. And, almost incredibly, she returned to 'Last Lines' and crafted a new ending. To the original poem of fear and despair, Anne added a further twenty-eight lines that create a stark contrast:

These weary hours will not be lost,
These days of passive misery,
These nights of darkness anguish tost
If I can fix my heart on thee.
Weak and weary though I lie,
Crushed with sorrow, worn with pain,
Still I may lift to Heaven mine eyes,
And strive and labour not in vain,
That inward strife against the sins
That ever wait on suffering;
To watch and strike where first begins
Each ill that would corruption bring,
That secret labour to sustain
With humble patience every blow,
To gather fortitude from pain
And hope and holiness from woe.
Thus let me serve Thee from my heart
Whatever be my written fate,
Whether thus early to depart
Or yet awhile to wait.
If Thou shouldst bring me back to life
More humbled I should be;
More wise, more strengthened for the strife,
More apt to lean on Thee.
Should Death be standing at the gate
Thus should I keep my vow;
But, Lord, whate'er my future fate
So let me serve Thee now.[9]

This section is not only different in character to the first half of 'Last Lines', it is also written in a firmer, more confident hand, giving a clear delineation of where Anne put down the work and then recommenced it. The top of the manuscript reads 'Jan 7th', and at the bottom she has written 'Finished. Jan. 28, 1849'. We gain, therefore, a great insight into the struggle that she went through over this three-week period. She has moved from anger and doubt, a period where she questions all her beliefs, to a time of acceptance and redemption. She has regained mastery of her body and spirit, and never more would the 'dark night of the soul' have any power over her.

Anne was still in great pain, although this could fluctuate from day to day, giving herself and her family joy on one day and despair on the next, but now she would internalise it as she had always done. Taking Emily as an example, she would not allow pain and illness to beat her. With what little time God had given her, she would not complain and allow self-pity to intrude.

A key difference between Emily's struggle and that of Anne is that Anne allowed herself to submit to medical treatment, and indeed she actively sought it out. Whilst the end result was inevitably the same, it did allow her to enjoy brief periods where the ravages of consumption were less intense, and it prolonged her life for weeks.

Recognising Anne's willingness to receive help, in stark contrast to Emily, Charlotte's kindly publisher made an offer. George Smith had been charmed by the gentle and modest genius Anne on her visit to London, and he took a keen interest in the Brontë family as a whole. After receiving a letter from Charlotte detailing Dr Teale's diagnosis, Smith wrote to the parsonage, offering to pay at his own expense for one of the very best consumption experts in London, Dr John Forbes, to visit Anne and provide a suitable treatment. Patrick was loathe to accept favours, but in this case he would have accepted any help that he thought could prove effective. He realised, however, that the initial diagnosis was undoubtedly correct and that even this great doctor could do no more than Dr Teale had done. The offer was politely declined, but Charlotte wrote to Dr Forbes describing Anne's condition and the subsequent prescription. Forbes wrote back saying that he was aware of Dr Teale and trusted his judgement, and that he too would have prescribed cod liver oil in this instance.[10] There was nothing more to be done.

Anne continued to take the medicine, but the taste was disgusting to her. She complained that it smelled and tasted like train oil, but she still forced herself to consume it for as long as she could. Eventually she could take it no longer, every attempt to swallow the oil was making her sick, and she was rapidly losing weight to an alarming degree. Other medicines were substituted, of which Anne believed 'Gobold's Vegetable Balsam' to be particularly efficacious, and she also used a respirator that Ellen had bought for her.

Whatever was suggested to Anne, she tried most willingly. Every step was a labour of Hercules for her, yet she would make herself take them, effacing grimaces with the sweet smile that could capture hearts. Throughout these months a change occurred in Charlotte too. She saw now that she had misjudged her youngest sister all her life, and she looked with wonder upon Anne's patient faith and resilience. The love that had lain dormant since childhood resurfaced, and she finally accepted how much Anne meant to her. She was the final link to their past, she could not be allowed to go the way of the others. As Charlotte later wrote in a touching elegy, Anne was the one who Charlotte would have died to save.[11]

There was one treatment that Anne longed to try, and in her usual calm and measured way she continued to urge its trial. Dr Teale had said that removal to a warm climate could bring about good results for sufferers of consumption, but only if it was undertaken before the disease reached its final climax. As the wintry winds subsided at last, Anne was impatient to put the plan into action.

Charlotte was less sure of the wisdom of this course of action. She saw how thin Anne was becoming, how the slightest exertion could be almost too much for her. Surely, she thought, Anne could not survive any such journey? We must wait, she told Anne, until the weather becomes warmer and until your strength returns a little. And so they waited, all the time knowing that each day could bring the change they most dreaded.

Anne's quiet persistence continued, and at her behest Charlotte finally consulted Dr Teale on this matter in April. It was not the reply that Charlotte had hoped for: he saw no problem in taking Anne to the coast when the weather improved, and he even went so far as to suggest Scarborough, a resort known for its healing powers.

'Thank you Lord,' Anne said in silent prayer when she read the letter from her doctor. It was the precise answer she had wanted, and of course no better location could be found for her. She would see Scarborough once more, watch the raging sea once again. Her spirits soared, yet the illness continued to gain hold. Once more, Anne was told that she would have to wait for better weather and better health. Each night she fought this declaration, not by protestations but by prayer. If God willed it, she would get to Scarborough.

Despite this resignation, Anne also knew that she needed an ally if she was to get to Scarborough, and there was only one suitable candidate. Ellen Nussey, thinking to bring some temporary relief to Charlotte and her father, had suggested in March that Anne come to stay with her in Birstall and be cared for by her sisters. Charlotte was horrified by this idea, telling Ellen that she could not bear it if Anne was to die away from her at Brookroyd. Nevertheless, a month later Anne would write to Ellen herself, asking her to accompany Charlotte and her to Scarborough. If Ellen agreed to this plan, she reasoned, Charlotte would be much more likely to accept it. Ellen affirmed that she would be willing to help, and so Anne wrote again explaining her plan.

The letter was written on 5 April 1849. It is written on two sheets of small paper, one of which has a thick black border, showing that Anne was still in mourning for Emily. The letter, unlike some of Anne's other letters, is written in cross letter style. This means that lines are written both horizontally and vertically, so that the page has to be turned around after reading to obtain the rest of the message. This was a relatively common practice at the time, as it saved on the cost of paper and postage, but it seems strange that Anne should have chosen the method for this particular letter, as at this time she had more money than she had ever had before and knew that she would have very little time left in which to spend it. Anne's godparent, Fanny Outhwaite, had not seen her often, but she had never stopped thinking of her and had provided moments of financial assistance to the Brontë family throughout her life. Fanny had died on 14 February 1849 and had left Anne the substantial amount of

£200 in her will.[12] It was from this bequest that Anne intended to fund the journey to Scarborough.

Anne's final letter is a masterpiece of patience, faith and compassion. Despite the physical pain we know she was suffering, it is written cross style in a very straight, clear and legible hand. Now a key treasure at the Brontë Parsonage Museum, the sight of it has been known to reduce a reader to tears, so brave was the emaciated young woman who wrote it. It reads:

My dear Miss Nussy,

I thank you greatly for your kind letter, and your ready compliance with my proposal as far as the will can go at least. I see however that your friends are unwilling that you should undertake the responsibility of accompanying me under present circumstances. But I do not think there would be any great responsibility in the matter. I know, and every body knows that you would be as kind and helpful as any one could possibly be, and I hope I should not be very troublesome. It would be as a companion not as a nurse that I should wish for your company, otherwise I should not venture to ask it. As for your kind and often repeated invitation to Brookroyd, pray give my sincere thanks to your mother and sisters, but tell them I could not think of inflicting my presence upon them as I now am. It is very kind of them to make so light of the trouble but trouble there must be, more or less – and certainly no pleasure from the society of a silent invalid stranger – I hope however that Charlotte will by some means make it possible to accompany me after all, for she is certainly very delicate and greatly needs a change of air and scene to renovate her constitution. And then your going with me before the end of May is apparently out of the question, unless you are disappointed in your visitors, but I should be reluctant to wait till then if the weather would at all permit an earlier departure. You say May is a trying month and so say others. The earlier part is often cold enough I acknowledge, but according to my experience, we are almost certain of some fine warm days in the latter half when the laburnums and lilacs are in bloom; whereas June is often cold and July generally wet. But I have a more serious reason than this for my impatience of delay; the doctors say that change of air or removal to a better climate would hardly ever fail of success in consumptive cases if the remedy were taken in time, but the reason why there are so many disappointments is, that it is generally deferred till it is too late. Now I would not commit this error; and to say the truth, though I suffer much less from pain and fever than I did when you were with us, I am decidedly weaker and very much thinner, my cough still troubles me a good deal, especially in the night, and, what seems worse than all I am subject to great shortness of breath on going up stairs or any slight exertion. Under these circumstances I think there is no time to be lost. I have no horror of death: if I thought it inevitable I think I could quietly resign myself to the prospect, in the hope that you, dear Miss Nussey would give as much of your company as you possibly could to Charlotte and be a sister to her in my stead. But I wish it would please God to spare me not only for Papa's and Charlotte's sakes, but because I long to do some good in the world before I leave it. I have many schemes in my head for future practise – humble and limited indeed – but still I should not like them to come to nothing, and myself to have lived to so little purpose. But God's will be done. Remember me respectfully to your mother and sisters, and believe me, dear Miss N.

Yours affectionately,

Anne Brontë[13]

Her signature, the last words she would ever write, is scrunched up into the corner of the fourth side of paper. Anne had run out of room, she was running out of time, but she had said all she had to say. It is a letter full of piquancy, one of the most touching moments being her wish for a little more time so that she could 'do some good in the world' and her belief that she had lived 'to so little purpose'. Her characteristic humility survived until the very last, but the world would later judge her efforts in a different and greater light.

This humility can make one think of the Beatitudes of Jesus at the sermon on the mount ('Blessed are the humble, for they shall inherit the earth'), but the letter and Anne's attitude at this time, the dusk of her life, is also redolent of another piece of scripture, and one that Anne would have been very familiar with. Surely in these times of trial she found comfort in turning to a passage she would have heard again and again at every Easter celebration: Matthew, Chapter 26. Jesus is in the Garden of Gethsemane with his disciples. He tells them to wait for him as he goes off to pray, knowing that his torture and death is just hours away. Here is the passage in the King James version that Anne would have used:

> Then cometh Jesus with them unto a place called Gethsemane, and saith unto the disciples, 'Sit ye here, while I go and pray yonder'. And he took with him Peter and the two sons of Zebedee, and began to be sorrowful and very heavy. Then saith he unto them, 'My soul is exceeding sorrowful, even unto death: tarry ye here and watch with me.' And he went a little farther, and fell on his face, and prayed, saying, 'O my Father, if it be possible, let this cup pass from me: nevertheless not as I will, but as thou wilt.'[14]

The corresponding passage from St Luke also adds how Jesus prayed so hard and was in such turmoil that he sweated drops of blood. These are the prayers that Anne used during her darkest moments in January, with the blood falling not from her forehead but her mouth. Anne's letter to Ellen closes just as the prayer of Jesus had finished. She asks if it be possible for the cup of death to be taken away from her, 'but God's will be done'.

What were the 'humble and limited schemes' that Anne had in mind that would never come to fruition? Undoubtedly she was talking of another book, or even a series of books, and there can also be little doubt that Anne would have used her writing as a means of instructing people how to live a better life. Perhaps, emboldened by the support of people such as Reverend Thom, she would have written an overtly religious book or one that attacked the hypocrisy of some of the more severe preachers in the Church? As with the passing of all great writers, we shall never know what we lost.

Anne's heartfelt letter to Ellen had the desired effect. Her objections expressed in an earlier letter, probably at the prompting of Charlotte, were overcome. May it must be, and plans were now put into place. Charlotte wrote to Margaret Wooler, who since giving up teaching had bought a house in Scarborough, for advice. Miss Wooler, who remembered her former pupil Anne well and fondly, offered to let them use her house free of charge while she was away, but Anne objected. The house was near to the North Bay, but Anne held fondest memories of the South Bay, where she had stayed before. In the end, there was only one possible location. They booked a suite at the exclusive Wood's Lodgings, accommodation that Anne had stayed in with the Robinsons, at the section named 'No. 2, The Cliff'. It was certainly expensive by the Brontës' usual standards, but thanks to Fanny Outhwaite, Anne covered the costs for herself, Charlotte and Ellen.

As May arrived and the day of departure grew nearer, Charlotte became more and more troubled. Anne's cough was getting worse not better, and she was getting weaker and thinner by the day. 'I must go,' Anne would say, 'I must see the sea again.' Such was Anne's present condition that Charlotte thought she must warn Ellen, just as Patrick had warned Grundy before he met Branwell in his final days. On 1 May, Charlotte wrote: 'She is very much emaciated, far worse than when you were with us; her arms are no thicker than a little child's. The least exertion brings a shortness of breath. She goes out a little every day, but we creep rather than walk.'[15]

By 12 May, however, Charlotte was writing to Ellen once more in a slightly more positive light. Cooler weather had arrived, and strangely enough it seemed to be beneficial to Anne's condition. Charlotte even writes that 'I still hope that if she gets over May she may last a long time.'[16] Unusually for Charlotte, this letter wasn't completed and posted on the same day, a sign of the physical and mental strain she was under. It finished with a postscript dated 14 May that reads, 'Anne was very ill yesterday. She had difficulty of breathing all day, even when sitting perfectly still. Today she seems better again. I long for the moment to come when the experiment of the sea-air will be tried. Will it do her good? I cannot tell. I can only wish.'[17]

The fluctuations in health continued, but at last Charlotte was resolved not to block Anne's journey to Scarborough if it was at all possible; it was obvious that there was no hope to be had in Haworth: something different must be tried. The date of departure had been set for 23 May. On that day, Ellen arrived, as had been arranged, at Keighley railway station to wait for the sisters. They did not turn up, and Ellen later wrote of her fear as she saw two coffins being unloaded from a train. The day was growing late, and Ellen returned home to Birstall, a distance of nearly 20 miles, with a heavy heart.

On the next day, Ellen set off early and travelled directly to Haworth. Arriving at the parsonage, she was surprised to see a carriage outside the door. Charlotte ran to her old friend and embraced her, explaining that Anne had been so ill the day before that she could barely leave her bed, but there had been a slight upturn again that morning. Looking into the carriage, Ellen saw Anne, dreadfully thin, already sitting there. Flossy was on her lap receiving one last cuddle, before Martha Brown took the dog away with her tail curled sadly between her legs and her head damp from Anne's kisses and tears.

Patrick and old, faithful Tabby Aykroyd were watching out of a window. They had already said their last goodbyes, and Patrick would later write that he knew as the carriage pulled away that he would never see his youngest child again. Once the coach had set off, to the surprise of Charlotte and Ellen, Anne seemed to revive a little in both body and spirit. She was so close to her goal now, it was as if she could hear the sea calling to her; nothing could stop her.

Unable to walk any distance on her own, Anne found no shortage of people volunteering to help her whenever it was necessary. She was carried from her carriage to the train at Keighley and then out of the carriage at York. She was easy to carry: she was as light as a feather.

Fearing that the journey would be too arduous to be completed in one stage, the sisters and Ellen had agreed to stay overnight in York. Accommodation was arranged at the George Hotel in Coney Street, across the River Ouse from the railway station. The hotel has long since closed, but the original archway and window can be seen still, forming part of a shop on what is now a bustling street full of local shoppers and tourists.

On Friday morning a bath chair was hired for Anne, and she was pushed through the streets by Charlotte and Ellen in turn. Anne had explained to her sister how people dressed up in their finest for holidays in Scarborough, so one priority was to purchase suitable clothing. A list was made of the clothing needed, and it read: 'Bonnet. Corsets. Stockings black silk. Dress. Gloves. Ribbon for neck.'[18] To Charlotte the shopping trip seemed like a mockery under their present circumstances, but Anne insisted upon it, as well as insisting upon paying for the goods, and she was not now to be denied any of her wishes.

One building in York she longed to see more than any other was York Minster. It was a grand Yorkshire church, and one that this Yorkshire woman loved above all others. After being wheeled towards the entrance, Anne took a few faltering steps inside. Unable to walk far, she sat down on one of the back rows and glanced up at the ceiling. Ellen afterwards noted down in great detail the events of the last few days of the life of a woman who had become a real friend to her, and it is thanks to her moving and beautifully written testimony that we know much of what came to pass in York and Scarborough.

Anne spent a long time silently contemplating the ornately decorated bosses and struts, the carved angels and the stained-glass windows. It was, as it had been for centuries, a supremely beautiful scene. Her face was radiant, and it was as if she had been overcome by a profound joy. She whispered one half-finished sentence: 'If finite power can do this, what is the …'[19]

Overcome by emotion, Anne was unable to finish the sentence, and Charlotte placed her back into the bath chair and wheeled her away, fearing that this contemplation of an earthly paradise was about to hasten her exit to another one.

On the next day they made the journey to Scarborough, and with each mile that passed Anne grew happier and more talkative. She pointed out the countryside that she knew and talked of the happy times she had spent there, even in the summer that she had shared with poor Branwell.

Number 2, The Cliff had been prepared just as Anne and Charlotte had wished, and they also had the services of a housemaid named Jane Jefferson. The two bedrooms were upstairs, and below was a lounge with a large window. Anne was helped to it, and she stood looking down far below to the beach and the sea. She had changed, but the sea had not. It was strong and constant; it would be forever the same when Anne had gone, when generations after her had gone. She smiled and nodded her head. Yes, this gave her hope, even as she approached the end of her life. In the grandeur of these surroundings built to glorify God, she felt an affirmation that all was as she always thought, or at least hoped, it would be. All that she had read in scripture was true. What was to inevitably come would bring with it the mercy and salvation she had always dreamed of.

Charlotte wrote immediately to W.S. Williams, stating that the lodgings were comfortable and Anne was in the window looking down on the sea. 'She says if she could breathe more freely she would be comfortable at this moment – but she cannot breathe freely.'[20]

Anne's spirits were greatly raised, but her health would obstinately not respond. Little matter, she would follow Emily's example and refuse to be a slave to her illness. That Saturday morning she asked to be taken to the spa baths, across the marvellous bridge that she so loved. Once there, she asked to be left alone in the baths with an attendant, insisting that Charlotte and Ellen go off to enjoy some of the wonderful sights she had told them about. They of course objected vigorously, until they perceived that their objections were upsetting Anne. She was an invalid, true, but she did not want to be treated as one. They left her soaking in the thermal waters and waited anxiously at the lodgings for her return.

It was a distance of around 500 metres from the bath house to No. 2, The Cliff, and Anne, spurning the help that was offered from the spa, had determined to walk it herself, slow painful step by slow painful step. She had reached the gate when she collapsed exhausted to the floor, but still Anne would not be defeated. Mrs Jefferson, who had seen the fall, and would afterwards tell Charlotte about it, had rushed to assist Anne, but she was waved away. Anne rose slowly to her own feet, wheezing with each exertion, and then walked in under her own power.

In the afternoon, her breathing had eased a little once more, and Anne asked if she could be taken down to the beach. This was arranged, and Anne then paid for a donkey ride. Worried that the boy would drive the donkey too hard, and hating as always any cruelty to one of God's creatures, she took the reins herself and drove off slowly along the beach. Once again, she had told Ellen and Charlotte not to follow her, and this time Charlotte understood why. She wanted to be alone with her thoughts: she had a lifetime of living to do in a handful of minutes.

Stopping the donkey, Anne rested and looked once more about her. Yes, she smiled, nature was wonderful, the world was good. Emily had been right about that as she had about many things, if only she could have found the sustaining faith that Anne had. In the still silence of Scarborough beach she thought back to the scene towards the end of *Agnes Grey* set in this exact location. Agnes had been waiting, and her man had come. Now she had the conviction that her man was waiting, she could almost feel his presence walking along the beach just as she had imagined it. She turned the donkey around and made her return journey. The time for waiting was over. Later on, that evening, Anne was taken across the bridge to the spa once more, looking around the gardens before returning.

On the next morning, a Sunday, Anne asked to be taken to church. With unusual gentleness Charlotte told her that was out of the question. She then asked Charlotte and Ellen to go, and leave her there, but they would not hear of leaving her. It was then that Anne realised the toll that the exertions and excitement of the last day had taken. 'Do you think we should try to get back to Haworth now?' she asked. Charlotte asked Anne what she wanted to do, but in answer she turned her head once more and looked down at the sea. Anne's choice was made, and Charlotte squeezed her sister's hand. She would die in Scarborough.

Why did Anne make this choice? Certainly it was a town that she held great affection for, featuring it in both her novels. She was also enough of a pragmatist to know that even if she tried to return to Haworth, she may not have made it. At the heart of her decision, how-ever, was one final act of selfless bravery, and it was also at the forefront of her mind when she had lobbied to be brought to the resort. Yes, if God willed it the healing waters of Scarborough could still have saved her, but at heart she knew that her moment to take the cup had come. Her father was then 72 years old, and he had seen four of his children buried in Haworth, including two in the last year. Anne wanted to save Patrick the grief of having to see another child die in front of his eyes so soon after he had watched Branwell and Emily perish. This last act of kindness was to spare him the horror that Anne worried he might not withstand.

Whilst church was now out of the question, she asked to be taken to the beach one more time. She sat on a seat quite alone, having urged her companions to visit the Pomona concert hall. After being brought back to the lodgings she turned and took one last breath, shallow and struggling as it was, of sea air. All was done now as it had to be done; a calmness descended.

Ellen recalled that the Sunday evening heralded a spectacular gold and red sunset over the bay:

It closed with the most glorious sunset ever witnessed. The castle on the cliff stood in proud glory gilded by the rays of the declining sun. The distant ships glittered like burnished gold; the little boats near the beach heaved on the ebbing tide, inviting occupants. The view was grand beyond description. Anne was drawn in her easy chair to the window to enjoy the scene with us. Her face became illuminated almost as much as the glorious sun she gazed upon. Little was said, for it was plain that her thoughts were driven by the imposing view before her to penetrate forwards to the region of unfading glory.[21]

A glorious sunset over the bay, a little boat bobbing on the tide, and with her back to us, Anne looking out over it. Here was the physical fulfilment of the picture she had drawn nearly a decade earlier. She had thought it was a sunrise looking out at a life to come, now she realised it had been a sunset looking over a life that was passing.

Monday morning, 29 May arrived, and Anne tried to walk down the stairs but found that she could no longer manage it. Ellen attempted to carry her, but found it a far from easy task. As they reached the last step, Anne's body flopped forwards, and their heads clashed. A shocked Ellen, thinking that her friend had died in her arms, dropped her into an armchair, at which point Anne stirred and Ellen apologised. 'Don't be sorry,' said Anne, 'it could not be helped, you did your best.'[22]

Once more Anne was placed in the window, and then at eleven she announced that she felt a change coming on. A doctor was called for, and Anne, worried now about the burden she was placing on Charlotte and Ellen, asked him if there was a possibility she could return to Haworth.

The doctor looked awkwardly towards Charlotte for guidance, but in a calm voice Anne asked him to tell her the truth. She was told that she had entered her dying hours, at which Anne thanked him for his honesty and kindness and sent him away.

The doctor returned on two more occasions, on the hour marks, to observe how things were passing. He was amazed at how calm Anne remained and later told Charlotte, who then related it to W.S. Williams, that 'in all his experience he had seen no such death-bed, and that it gave evidence of no common mind'.[23]

Anne continued to gaze out of the window, the silence broken only by the ticking of a clock, but she could no longer see what was in front of her. Turning her head she once more asked Ellen to look after Charlotte as a sister and then said she believed she was now passing out of this world into heaven. There was a calm, steady ecstasy in her voice.

We can imagine how sights long since seen, voices long ago heard, came now to Anne's mind. She saw her sister Maria reading to her, Branwell presenting her with a picture of a fairy-tale castle, her aunt was giving her a goodnight kiss, she was a child again receiving the dancing doll from papa, Rossini's overture was playing in the background, she called out to Flossy who was chasing after some sheep, and then she heard the words of comfort and strength that James la Trobe had given her. She felt fingers entwined in hers, it was Emily comforting her as a child, William Weightman's hand wiped away with tenderness a stray lock of hair from her face.

Her reverie was broken by the sound of crying. Charlotte had reached the depths of despair, and her grief could be held back no more. If only Charlotte could know that there was no need for grief. Anne uttered her last words: 'Take courage, Charlotte, take courage.'[24]

At two o'clock on Monday, 28 May 1849, with bravery, stillness, certainty and love, Anne Brontë died.

THE LEGACY LIVES ON

Because the road is rough and long,
Shall we despise the skylark's song,
That cheers the wanderer's way?
Or trample down, with reckless feet,
The smiling flowerets, bright and sweet
Because they soon decay?
Pass pleasant scenes unnoticed by,
Because the next is bleak and drear;
Or not enjoy a smiling sky,
Because a tempest may be near?
No! while we journey on our way,
We'll smile on every lovely thing;
And ever, as they pass away,
To memory and hope we'll cling.
And though that awful river flows
Before us, when the journey's past,
Perchance of all the pilgrim's woes
Most dreadful – shrink not – 'tis the last!
Though icy cold, and dark, and deep;
Beyond it smiles that blessed shore,

Where none shall suffer, none shall weep,
And bliss shall reign for evermore!

'Views Of Life'

The doctor came one last time, to certify the death. Charlotte remained slumped in a chair, almost insensible to the world, with Ellen and Mrs Jefferson taking care of the necessary arrangements. Charlotte had decided, in accordance with what she knew Anne's wishes were, to have her sister buried in Scarborough, rather than causing extra grief to their father by having the body transported back to Haworth.

Thus it is that Anne is the only Brontë not buried under the floor of St Michael and All Angels' church, Haworth. She was buried on 30 May in St Mary's churchyard, at the head of a small section adjacent to the main churchyard itself. Anne's grave looks down to the sea below and above her is the hill leading to Scarborough Castle, the setting that Anne had chosen for Mr Weston to propose to Agnes Grey.

St Mary's was being renovated at the time, so although Anne was buried there the funeral service itself was held at Christ church on Vernon Road. The doctor who had visited Anne in her final hours was so moved and impressed by her conduct that he offered to come to the funeral, but Charlotte politely said no, Charlotte and Ellen would be all the mourners she would need. When they reached Christ church, however, they found one more person was already in attendance. It was Margaret Wooler, who must have been alerted to the news by either Charlotte or Ellen or read the notice that appeared in a Scarborough newspaper, paying final respects to one former pupil and providing comfort for another.[1]

Patrick had been expecting the news that Charlotte sent to him. He tried to comfort his only remaining daughter now, telling her that he had known he would not see Anne again and ordering Charlotte to spend some time at the coast recuperating before returning home. She and Ellen spent a further week in Scarborough, before Charlotte journeyed alone to the nearby resorts of Filey and then Bridlington.

Arranging the funeral and headstone had been more than Charlotte could bear, and so with her customary kindness and pragmatism, Ellen filled the void. Unfortunately, not wishing to question Charlotte at such a delicate time, when her mental anguish was at a dangerous new height, some of the information Ellen provided to the stonemasons was incorrect. It was 1852 before Charlotte could bring herself to visit the grave, and she found that there were five errors on the headstone. She paid to have these corrected, but one still remains. The headstone now reads: 'She died aged 28, May 28th 1849'. She was, in fact, 29.

The official cause of Anne's death was given as 'consumption – six months',[2] but it seems likely that the tuberculosis, then referred to as consumption, had Anne in its grip long before then. In 1972, the eminent doctor Professor Philip Rhodes published a study called 'A Medical Appraisal of the Brontës', which sheds new light on the illnesses that accounted for Anne, Emily and Branwell.

The first Brontës to die of tuberculosis were Maria and Elizabeth. Both contracted it at that hotbed of illness, Cowan Bridge, and died within six weeks of each other after returning to Haworth. Haworth itself was, as we have seen, a community where deadly epidemics were an annual occurrence and where life expectancy was much lower than in surrounding areas, and yet the main killers there were cholera and typhoid rather than tuberculosis, a primarily urban disease. This makes it an anachronism that five of the six Brontë children should die of the disease. The relative seclusion and insularity peculiar to the Brontë children meant that they would not have been as exposed to these illnesses and would therefore not have built up a resistance in the way that other children did. When Maria and Elizabeth came into contact with tubercular pathogens at Cowan Bridge their bodies simply had no means of fighting them off.

During their decline at Haworth, both children would have come into regular contact with their brother and sisters, and it seems probable that all the Brontës gained their first exposure to tuberculosis at this time. Anne's recurring bouts of breathlessness and flu throughout her life may not have been purely a symptom of her asthma but of underlying tuberculosis. Even with these latent low-level doses of the disease in their systems, the events of 1848 and 1849 suggest that there was another particularly virulent strain introduced to the household, and there's one location that is extremely likely to have been the source: London.

London was then the largest city in the western world with a rapidly growing population; conditions were rife for the spread of tuberculosis. Charlotte had travelled more widely and frequently in the previous years, and so she may have had greater natural resistance to the disease, but Anne, who had often suffered illnesses and was deemed to be in 'delicate' health, was at great risk from the pathogens that were all around her in the capital. Those days at the Chapter Coffee House were among the happiest of her life, but they could also have been responsible for the wave of death that was to come to the parsonage.

Branwell's body was already greatly weakened by his addictions to alcohol and opiates, and so the pathogens that his sister unwittingly brought back from London would kill him within three months of her return. Emily had lived an increasingly solitary life in the preceding years, even retaining her standard aloofness during her time in Brussels, and so would have had very little resistance against the massive dose of tuberculosis that was now within her home. She took it upon herself to be nursemaid to Branwell, spending time in close proximity to him, and in so doing she signed her own death warrant. From then on, it was only a matter of time before Anne too succumbed to the same illness. This dreadful, yet unstoppable, chain of events was summed up over a century later by Professor Rhodes:

> Anne perhaps was the most amiable and affable of all the Brontës, but it seems likely that it was the exposure to the pathogens of the big city that killed her, and it is probable that it was she who brought home the infection which killed Branwell and Emily before her.[3]

If Thomas Newby had not made that spurious claim about the identity of Acton Bell, causing George Smith to send his letter to Haworth, the Brontë story could have been very different. As it is, Charlotte was left alone and bereft, and she took it upon herself to act as literary executor for her sisters, much to the detriment of Anne's reputation.

We know that Emily and Anne wrote large amounts of Gondal prose, yet none of it survives. We also know that there must have been many more letters, poems and possibly diary entries from both sisters that are no longer in existence, although hope always springs eternal that more of Anne's letters may resurface one day, particularly of that long and fruitful correspondence with the Robinson girls of which not a trace can currently be found.

Sadly for lovers of literature, and students of the Brontës' lives, it seems that much of this material belonging to Anne and Emily was destroyed either before or after their deaths, and the most likely culprit for this was Charlotte.

Charlotte herself admitted to some of these actions. After the deaths of Anne and Emily, she prepared new editions of their poetry and prose. Sometimes she would amend the work as well, as in Charlotte's version of *Wuthering Heights* where she softened Joseph's dialect to make it easier to understand for readers outside of Yorkshire. She also carefully selected which works she thought were likely to enhance her sisters' reputations and which weren't. Of going through Anne's papers she writes, 'In looking over my sister Anne's papers, I find mournful evidence that religious feeling had been to her but too much like what it was to Cowper.'[4] William Cowper was an extremely popular eighteenth-century poet, but he suffered so greatly from religious doubt brought on by his struggle with Calvinist doctrines that he spent two years in an insane asylum. Charlotte adds that finding this 'evidence' would be 'too distressing, were it not combated by the certain knowledge that in her last moments this tyranny of a too tender conscience was overcome'.[5]

Once more, Charlotte seems to misunderstand her sister's feelings. It is true that Anne often struggled with religious doubts, but she had found a way to conquer these doubts, and her strong faith would give her a happiness and inner calm that Charlotte herself could never find.

Charlotte took it upon herself to be judge, jury and indeed executioner of her sisters' works. Two years after their death, she wrote:

It would not be difficult to compile a volume out of the papers left me by my sisters, had I, in making the selection, dismissed from my consideration the scruples and the wishes of those whose written thoughts these papers held. But this was impossible; an influence, stronger than could be exercised by any motive of expediency, necessarily regulated the selection. I have then, culled from the mass only a little poem here and there.[6]

With so much material that we know to have existed now missing, we must make our own judgement on how 'little' this culling was. Some have said that it may have been Emily and Anne themselves who destroyed their work as their deaths approached, but this can be questioned. Emily, who undoubtedly was unwilling for her name to enter the public domain, would not even admit she was ill until hours before her death, and Anne had pledged to put her work before the world, to expose the truth, warts and all, whatever the public may think of it.

In Charlotte's 1850 'Biographical Notice of Ellis and Acton Bell', the veil was finally lifted. She named her sisters to the world, yet at the same time she commenced her control of their reputation. She and her sisters had been hurt by the criticism that had been levelled at them, and she would now defend them in the way she thought best. Unfortunately, this was not by letting their writing do the talking, but by portraying them as simple, uneducated women who did not know what they were doing; if they had offended anyone, they had done so accidentally. Charlotte knew this analysis to be erroneous, of course, but she considered it the best path to take.

Whilst these actions may be understandable, if not completely condonable, her conduct towards *The Tenant of Wildfell Hall* would immeasurably damage Anne's reputation. We have seen how little regard Charlotte had for the novel, and in fact she suppressed its re-publication after Anne's death. By 1850, she was working with Smith, Elder & Co. on a reprinted collection of her sisters' works, but on 5 September 1850 she wrote to W.S. Williams:

'Wildfell Hall' it hardly appears desirable to preserve. The choice of subject in that work is a mistake – it was too little consonant with the character, tastes, and ideas of the gentle, retiring, inexperienced writer. She wrote it under a strange, conscientious, half-ascetic notion of accomplishing a painful penance and a severe duty. Blameless in deed and almost in thought, there was from her very childhood a tinge of religious melancholy in her mind … As to additional compositions, I think there would be none as I would not offer a line to the publication of which my sisters themselves would have objected.[7]

This last line is telling. The obvious inference is that there are, or were, other works, but Charlotte did not think Anne and Emily would have liked them to be published. For this reason poetry, prose and letters from Anne and Emily, perhaps even the beginnings of a successor to *Wuthering Heights* hinted at by Newby, were consigned to the ashes.

The story of the Brontë sisters did not end with Anne's death. Even during Anne's illness, Charlotte had started work on her second novel for Smith, Elder & Co., *Shirley*. This was followed by a further novel, *Villette*, borrowing from her time in Belgium, and *The Professor*, which would finally be published posthumously.

Shirley is of particular interest to Brontë lovers, as in it Charlotte gives a portrait of her sisters in the guise of its two heroines. Shirley Keeldar is Emily and Caroline Helstone is Anne. In Chapter 9 of the novel, the character Jessy Yorke, herself based on Martha Taylor, the sister of Charlotte's friend Mary, describes Caroline, by which we can read Anne, thus:

'She is nice; she is fair; she has a pretty white slender throat; she has long curls, not stiff ones – they hang loose and soft, their colour is brown but not dark; she speaks quietly, with a clear tone; she never makes a bustle when moving; she often wears a gray silk dress; she is neat all over.'

Shirley was started in 1848 when all three sisters were healthy, but it was completed in very different circumstances. It is believed that Charlotte had planned to kill the character of Caroline in the book, but by the time she reached the fatal Chapter 24, entitled 'The Valley of the Shadow of Death', Anne herself had died. Charlotte could not bear to see her die again; in print, at least, she could save her, even though it meant changing the course of the book itself. Throughout the chapter Caroline is dying, seemingly of tuberculosis, but in a moving twist she miraculously recovers and goes on to live a happy life and eventually marry the man she loves.

Charlotte was deeply affected by Anne's death, and she suffered frequent bouts of illness and depression. With the encouragement of her publishers, however, she became less reclusive and began to make appearances in London literary society, making friends of writers such as William Thackeray, Elizabeth Gaskell and Harriet Martineau. In the last year of her life, Charlotte was to find the happiness that had so long eluded her.

Arthur Bell Nicholls, her father's curate, proposed to her in 1853, but Charlotte was shocked and rejected him outright, and Patrick was also furious at his assistant's impertinence. Charlotte writes of how Nicholls then resolved to leave for Australia as a missionary. She wrote to Ellen of his last sermon at Haworth. He stood shaking in the pulpit, unable to speak, before the congregation had to help him out of the church, many of them in tears. Charlotte later found him outside the church 'sobbing as women never sob'.[8]

In the end, Nicholls moved not to Australia but to another parish. He refused to give in and continued to write to Charlotte and her father. A year later he returned to Haworth, and Charlotte, moved by his persistence if still professing little liking for him, accepted his proposal. In June 1854 they married and went on honeymoon to Arthur's native Ireland. To her surprise, Charlotte enjoyed married life and fell in love with her husband. She soon became pregnant, but as all too often in the Brontë story, her happiness was to be short lived. Charlotte suffered hyperemesis gravidarum, or excessive morning sickness. After weeks of wasting away she became physically unable to eat or drink. Her distraught husband of less than a year was by her bedside as she died, aged 38, on 31 March 1855. Patrick Brontë had outlived all of his six children.

Charlotte had become highly regarded, and even famous, in her own lifetime, something that neither Anne nor Emily would ever experience, but her actions regarding *The Tenant of Wildfell Hall* would see Anne relegated to her sister's shadow for over a century. Anne's second novel had been hugely successful, selling far more copies than *Wuthering Heights*, but at the height of its success it disappeared from public view. *The Tenant of Wildfell Hall* was not reintroduced until ten years after Anne's death and four years after Charlotte's, by which time it had largely been forgotten about, even by the growing numbers of Brontë lovers, many of whom were already making literary pilgrimages to Haworth.

On the occasions when this work of brilliance was spoken of, it was often by people who regurgitated Charlotte's view that it was a mistake that did not deserve to be published, a book altogether too coarse and brutal. This view continued, largely unchecked, for over 100 years. Even many supposed supporters of Anne would not think of challenging this prevailing view of *The Tenant of Wildfell Hall*.

Sir Linton Andrews was a journalist and academic, and chairman of the Brontë Society for twenty-four years from 1945. He was seen as a champion of Anne at this time, and yet even he said that Anne had been too coarse, too unrealistic in her portrayal of Huntingdon. In 1965 he writes that 'A father determined to teach his little son to drink wine, gin and brandy, to use foul language, and to hate and despise his mother, seems over-drawn.'[9]

It is a view that few people today would concur with. In Sir Linton's cosy post-war world it seemed absolutely impossible that a man would allow his child to swear, let him drink or encourage him to hate his estranged wife. Anne was in this, as in many things, well ahead of her time.

A talent as great as Anne's could not stay in the shadows forever; she was much more than just an appendix to the story of Charlotte and Emily. One of the earliest signs of a reappraisal was *Anne Brontë: A Biography*, written in 1959 by Winifred Gérin. Gérin would later also write biographies of Branwell, Emily and Charlotte, and she was awarded the OBE for services to literature, but her first act was to restore the reputation of Anne.

Anne was also discovered and lauded by a new generation of feminist writers and scholars in the latter half of the twentieth century. They recognised both of her novels, but especially *The Tenant of Wildfell Hall*, as proto-feminist works of fiction. In a time when women had a clearly defined role, one of servitude and domesticity, Anne refused to be confined to the societal norms. She used her books to promote equality of the sexes, a more rounded education for girls and greater rights for married women.

This recognition of Anne as a pioneering feminist writer dates back as far as 1913, when the writer and suffragette May Sinclair stated that the slamming of Helen's door against her husband in *The Tenant of Wildfell Hall* had reverberated throughout Victorian England.[10] It has reverberated ever since, bringing her to the attention of a new generations of fans.

Elizabeth Langland's *Anne Brontë: The Other One*, published in 1989 and part of a series of books on women writers, took a feminist critique of Anne's work, revealing how insightful and revolutionary it had been. Emily and Charlotte created wonderful and powerful works of fiction, novels that will forever be read and loved, but Anne turned an unflinching spotlight upon the world as it truly was: 'Thematic innovations place her in the forefront of feminist thought in the nineteenth century even as her formal and technical innovations demand that we look again at her contribution to the English novel.'[11]

To 1840s polite society, it was unthinkable that a woman should have the final say on whom she married, but not to Anne, and not to her character Helen Lawrence:

'He is come on a very important errand – to ask your hand in marriage, of your uncle and me.'

'I hope my uncle and you told him it was not in your power to give it. What right had he to ask *anyone* before me?'[12]

Helen makes a very unfortunate choice of course, and a revelation at the start of Chapter 34 was particularly shocking to many readers: 'It is not enough to say that I no longer love my husband – I HATE him! The word stares me in the face like a guilty confession, but it is true: I hate him – I hate him! – But God have mercy on his miserable soul.'[13]

These lines were truly unique in 1838, they must have led to many a gasp among readers, and they still have power today, the power of truth. It was the truth that Anne always sought in her writings, and it is the truth in her work that is helping it secure a resurgence in her popularity. Readers across the world are now placing Anne where she belongs, alongside her sisters Charlotte and Emily, and in the very first rank of nineteenth-century writers.

Who knows what further revelations time will bring? We may find long hidden letters or poems, or even a photograph. One possible photograph of Anne recently came to light, and if genuine it is the only photographic portrait of both Anne and Emily. It was found in a Paris collection and shows three sisters posing in front of a brick wall. On the back is written: 'Les Soeurs Brontë'. The photograph has proved controversial, not to say divisive. It is a photograph on glass, and such technology was not available until the 1850s, after Anne and Emily had died. However, many earlier daguerreotypes were copied on to glass in this period, and the picture has a faint mark around its periphery and distortion in the corners as though it is a copy of a picture that had originally been in a frame.

The three girls in the photograph are purported to be Charlotte, looking directly into the camera with piercing eyes, and next to her Emily with her arm around the shoulders of Anne, both of whom are looking towards Charlotte. Some say the ladies do not resemble the portraits we have of the Brontës, while others see very close resemblances to both descriptions and pictures of the sisters and to undisputed photographs of their cousins, the Branwells. A close-up inspection of the eyes and nose of the 'Charlotte' figure in the photograph shows a remarkable similarity to the same features in Branwell's 'pillar portrait'. Some have noted that 'Charlotte' and 'Emily' have hats, rather than bonnets, that were not worn in England in the 1840s, yet photographs from Belgium, where the sisters had spent time, dating from this decade show women with very similar head wear. It will be impossible to prove the authenticity one way or the other, but it makes a fascinating conundrum for Brontë lovers.

Anne Brontë is an intriguing if enigmatic woman, and her quest for honesty and truth, come what may, led her to reveal a lot of herself in her writing. In many ways we can understand Anne better than even Charlotte did, who from the earliest years was blinded to the talent that her sister possessed. Was she really perpetually calm and quiet? We hear Ellen say that Anne could talk very well when she had to. Charlotte portrayed Anne as being dour and sad, yet Anne's novels are full of wit and humour, and her character was attractive enough to win the lifelong love and affection of her pupils in the Robinson household. Anne herself writes, under the guise of Helen: 'Smiles and tears are so alike with me;

they are neither of them confined to any particular feelings: I often cry when I am happy, and smile when I am sad.'[14]

Anne, through great self-control, often hid her feelings in real life, only to release them in her writings. For this we can all be grateful. Anne continues to win new fans, and successive generations are finding that Anne speaks directly to them, and of their concerns, far more than either of her sisters. Anne Brontë was a great writer, but much more than that, she was a woman full of love for humanity, full of hope for the future and full of courage.

NOTES

PROLOGUE

1. Smith, Margaret (Ed.), *The Letters of Charlotte Brontë, Volume 2*, p.94

CHAPTER 1

1. Barker, Juliet, *The Brontës*, p.172
2. On the occasion of Charlotte's honeymoon, see chapter 19
3. Barker, Juliet, *The Brontës*, p.2
4. Green, Dudley, *Patrick Brontë Father Of Genius*, p.13
5. Green, Dudley, *Patrick Brontë Father Of Genius*, pp.59–60
6. Manuscript now held in the Leeds University library special collection
7. Brontë, Anne, *Agnes Grey*, p.3
8. Gérin, Winifred, *Anne Brontë*, p.2
9. Green, Dudley, *Patrick Brontë Father Of Genius*, p.70
10. Gérin, Winifred, *Anne Brontë*, p.1

CHAPTER 2

1. Green, Dudley, *Patrick Brontë Father Of Genius*, pp.78–9
2. Green, Dudley, *Patrick Brontë Father Of Genius*, p.79–80
3. Green, Dudley, *Patrick Brontë Father Of Genius*, p.82–4
4. On 27 November 1821, Patrick wrote to John Buckland: 'During many years, she had walked with God; but the great enemy, envying her life of holiness, often disturbed her mind in the last conflict.' Barker, Juliet, *The Brontës*, p.104
5. 'Miss Branwell was, I believe, a kindly and conscientious woman, with a good deal of character, but with the somewhat narrow ideas natural to one who had spent nearly all her life in the same place. She had strong prejudices, and soon took a distaste to Yorkshire.' Gaskell, Elizabeth, *The Life Of Charlotte Brontë*, p.96
6. Rhodes, Philip, 'A Medical Appraisal Of The Brontës', *Brontë Society Transactions 1972*, pp.101–2
7. Barker, Juliet, *The Brontës*, p.105
8. 'I know of no ties of friendship ever existing between us which the last eleven or twelve years has not severed or at least placed an insuperable bar to any revival.' From Mary Burder's letter to Patrick Brontë, 18 August 1823. Green, Dudley, *Patrick Brontë Father Of Genius*, pp.97–8
9. Barker, Juliet, *The Brontës*, p.111
10. Brontë, Charlotte, *Jane Eyre*, p.45
11. Gaskell, Elizabeth, *The Life Of Charlotte Brontë*, p.104
12. Gérin, Winifred, *Anne Brontë*, p.20
13. Gérin, Winifred, *Anne Brontë*, p.24
14. Brontë, Charlotte, *Jane Eyre*, p.65
15. Gaskell, Elizabeth, *The Life Of Charlotte Brontë*, p.98
16. Gérin, Winifred, *Anne Brontë*, p.26
17. Neufeldt, Victor A. (Ed.), *The Works Of Patrick Branwell Brontë: 1837–1848*, p.413–4

CHAPTER 3

1. Gérin, Winifred, *Anne Brontë*, p.13
2. Brontë, Anne, *Agnes Grey*, pp.25–6
3. Harland, Marion, *Charlotte Brontë at Home*, p.18
4. Barker, Juliet, *The Brontës*, pp.130–2
5. *Leeds Mercury*, 11 September 1824
6. Smith, Margaret (Ed.), *The Letters of Charlotte Brontë, Volume 2*, p.403

CHAPTER 4

1. Gaskell, Elizabeth, *The Life of Charlotte Brontë*, p.94
2. Brontë, Charlotte, *The History of the Year*, 12 March 1829
3. *Ibid.*
4. *Ibid.*
5. Leyland, Francis, *The Brontë Family*, pp.63–4
6. Gérin, Winifred, *Anne Brontë*, p.49
7. Brontë, Charlotte, *Jane Eyre*, p.4
8. Brontë, Anne, *The Tenant of Wildfell Hall*, p.381
9. *Ibid.*
10. Alexander, Christine, Introduction to *Tales of Glass Town, Angria and Gondal*, p.28
11. Alexander, Christine and Sellars, Jane, *The Art Of The Brontës*, p.155 manuscript now held in the Brontë Parsonage Museum, Haworth
12. Alexander, Christine, *Introduction to 'Tales Of Glass Town, Angria And Gonda'*, pp.19–20
13. The Brontës, *Tales of Glass Town, Angria, and Gondal*, pp.441–4
14. The Brontës, *Tales of Glass Town, Angria, and Gondal*, pp.453–4
15. The Brontës, *Tales of Glass Town, Angria, and Gondal*, pp.489–90

CHAPTER 5

1. Green, Dudley, *Patrick Brontë Father of Genius*, p.223
2. *Ibid.*
3. A summary and explanation of the report and its findings can be found in *Haworth in the Brontë Era, B.H. Babbage's Visit to Haworth*, published in Keighley in 1998
4. Atkinson, E., *Haworth in the Brontë Era, B.H. Babbage's Visit to Haworth*, p.5
5. Atkinson, E., *Haworth in the Brontë Era, B.H. Babbage's Visit to Haworth*, p.7
6. Lister, Philip, *Ghosts & Gravestones of Haworth*, p.12
7. Brontë, Anne, *Agnes Grey*, p.4
8. Gaskell, Elizabeth, *The Life of Charlotte Brontë*, pp.180–1
9. Brontë, Anne, *Agnes Grey*, p.83
10. Greenwood, Robin, *West Lane and Hall Green Baptist Churches in Haworth in West Yorkshire: Their Early History and Doctrinal Distinctives*, p.93
11. Green, Dudley, *Patrick Brontë Father of Genius*, p.133, manuscript of John Greenwood's diary now held in the Brontë Parsonage Museum
12. The Brontës, *Tales of Glass Town, Angria, and Gondal*, pp.486–7

CHAPTER 6

1. Gérin, Winifred, *Anne Brontë*, p.233
2. Smith, Margaret (ed.), *The Letters of Charlotte Brontë, Volume 1*, pp.129–30
3. Gérin, Winifred, *Anne Brontë*, p.74
4. *Ibid.*
5. Brontë, Anne, *Agnes Grey*, p.11
6. Gérin, Winifred, *Anne Brontë*, p.68
7. Lemon, Charles, *Early Visitors to Haworth: From Ellen Nussey to Virginia Woolf*, p.6
8. Gérin, Winifred, *Anne Brontë*, p.67

9. Gérin, Winifred, *Anne Brontë*, pp.67–8
10. Gérin, Winifred, *Anne Brontë*, p.67
11. Barker, Juliet, *The Brontës*, p.236
12. Green, Dudley, *Patrick Brontë Father of Genius*, p.140
13. Gaskell, Elizabeth, *The Life of Charlotte Brontë*, pp.133–5
14. Smith, Margaret (ed.), *The Letters of Charlotte Brontë, Volume 1*, p.140
15. The Brontës, *Tales of Glass Town, Angria, and Gondal*, pp.453–4
16. The Brontës, *Tales of Glass Town, Angria, and Gondal*, pp.165–6
17. The Brontës, *Tales of Glass Town, Angria, and Gondal*, p.163
18. Smith, Margaret (ed.), *The Letters of Charlotte Brontë, Volume 1*, p.144
19. Smith, Margaret (ed.), *The Letters of Charlotte Brontë, Volume 1*, p.154
20. Brontë, Charlotte, *Jane Eyre*, pp.25–6

CHAPTER 7

1. Green, Dudley, *Patrick Brontë Father of Genius*, p.142
2. *Fraser's Magazine for Town and Country*, Volume 38, July–December 1848, pp.193–5
3. Smith, Margaret (ed.), *The Letters of Charlotte Brontë, Volume 1*, p.174
4. *Ibid.*
5. Brontë, Anne, *Agnes Grey*, pp.7–8
6. Brontë, Anne, *Agnes Grey*, p.12
7. Smith, Margaret (ed.), *The Letters of Charlotte Brontë, Volume 1*, p.189
8. *Ibid.*
9. Brontë, Anne, *Agnes Grey*, p.37
10. Brontë, Anne, *Agnes Grey*, p.22
11. Smith, Margaret (ed.), *The Letters of Charlotte Brontë, Volume 1*, p.189
12. From the diary of Gertrude Elizabeth Brooke, *Mirfield Parish News*
13. Brontë, Anne, *Agnes Grey*, p.27
14. Brontë, Anne, *Agnes Grey*, p.22

CHAPTER 8

1. Smith, Margaret (ed.), *The Letters of Charlotte Brontë, Volume 1*, p.191
2. *Huddersfield Daily Examiner*, 29 December 2014
3. Brontë, Anne, *Agnes Grey*, p.42
4. *Leeds Mercury*, 15 February 1840
5. Hibbs, Helier, 'Was there a Fire at Thorp Green Hall?', *Yorkshire Archeological Journal 79*, p.334
6. Brontë, Anne, *Agnes Grey*, p.48
7. The Brontës, *Tales of Glass Town, Angria, and Gondal*, pp.488–9
8. The Brontës, *Tales of Glass Town, Angria, and Gondal*, pp.489–90
9. The Brontës, *Tales of Glass Town, Angria, and Gondal*, p.489
10. The Brontës, *Tales of Glass Town, Angria, and Gondal*, p.489

CHAPTER 9

1. Chitham, Edward, *A Life of Anne Brontë*, p.67
2. *The Durham University Calendar, For 1842*, appendix p.IV
3. *Leeds Intelligencer*, 23 June 1838
4. Chitham, Edward, *A Life of Anne Brontë*, pp.80–2
5. Smith, Margaret (ed.), *The Letters of Charlotte Brontë, Volume 1*, pp.223–4
6. Smith, Margaret (ed.), *The Letters of Charlotte Brontë, Volume 1*, p.228
7. Smith, Margaret (ed.), *The Letters of Charlotte Brontë, Volume 1*, p.247
8. Barker, Juliet, *The Brontës*, p.325
9. Brontë, Patrick, *A Funeral Sermon for the Late Rev. William Weightman, M.A.*, p.5
10. Smith, Margaret (ed.), *The Letters of Charlotte Brontë, Volume 1*, p.211
11. Smith, Margaret (ed.), *The Letters of Charlotte Brontë, Volume 1*, p.279
12. Charlotte and Emily were at school in Brussels, see Chapter 10
13. Brontë, Patrick, *A Funeral Sermon for the Late Rev. William Weightman, M.A.*, p.7
14. Smith, Margaret (ed.), *The Letters of Charlotte Brontë, Volume 1*, p.261
15. Smith, Margaret (ed.), *The Letters of Charlotte Brontë, Volume 1*, p.229

16. *Ibid.*
17. Barker, Juliet, *The Brontës*, p.339
18. Bell, C., E. and A., *Poems by Currer, Ellis, and Acton Bell*, p.140 (published in this collection under the alternative title of 'Appeal')
19. *The Durham University Calendar, For 1842*, p.21
20. *The Durham University Calendar, For 1842*, p.63
21. *The Durham University Calendar, For 1842*, appendix p.v
22. Barker, Juliet, *The Brontës*, pp.402–3
23. Brontë, Patrick, *A Funeral Sermon for the Late Rev. William Weightman, M.A.*, p.2
24. Brontë, Patrick, *A Funeral Sermon for the Late Rev. William Weightman, M.A.*, pp.6–7
25. Brontë, Patrick, *A Funeral Sermon for the Late Rev. William Weightman, M.A.*, p.8
26. Brontë, Patrick, *A Funeral Sermon for the Late Rev. William Weightman, M.A.*, p.7
27. *Ibid.*
28. *Leeds Intelligencer*, 29 October 1842
29. The plaque is still within the church of St Michael and All Angels, Haworth. The inscription reads, 'This Monument was erected by the inhabitants in Memory of the Late WILLIAM WEIGHTMAN Who died September 6th, 1842, aged 26 years [he was actually 28] And was buried in this church On the tenth of the same month. He was three years Curate of Haworth And by the congregation and parishioners In general was greatly respected For his orthodox principles, active zeal, moral habits, learning, mildness, and affability.'

CHAPTER 10

1. Brontë, Anne, *Agnes Grey*, p.114
2. Brontë, Anne, *Severed and Gone*, written April 1847, manuscript now held in the Brontë Parsonage Museum, Haworth
3. Brontë, Anne, *Agnes Grey*, p.113
4. Brontë, Anne, *Agnes Grey*, p.114

5. Barker, Juliet, *The Brontës*, p.409
6. The Brontës, *Tales of Glass Town, Angria, and Gondal*, p.489
7. The Brontës, *Tales of Glass Town, Angria, and Gondal*, p.488
8. On 19 July 1841, Charlotte wrote to Ellen Nussey: 'I was well aware indeed that Aunt had money – but I always considered that she was the last person who would offer a loan for the purpose in question. A loan however she has offered or intimated that she perhaps will offer in case pupils can be secured … I do not expect that Aunt will risk more than 150£ on such a venture.' Manuscript now held in the Brontë Parsonage Museum, Haworth
9. Smith, Margaret (ed.), *The Letters of Charlotte Brontë, Volume 1*, p.268
10. Smith, Margaret (ed.), *The Letters of Charlotte Brontë, Volume 1*, p.269
11. Green, Dudley, *Patrick Brontë Father of Genius*, p.150
12. Barker, Juliet, *The Brontës*, p.395
13. Just one example is found in Charlotte's letter to M. Heger of 8 January 1845: 'I know that you will lose patience when you read this letter. You will say that I am over-excited – that I have black thoughts etc. So be it Monsieur. I do not seek to justify myself, I submit to all kinds of reproaches – all I know is that I cannot – I will not resign myself to the total loss of my master's friendship – I would rather undergo the greatest bodily pains than have my heart constantly lacerated by searing regrets.' This, and the manuscripts of other letters to M. Heger, is now held by the British Library, London.
14. Barker, Juliet, *The Brontës*, p.367
15. *Ibid.*
16. Langland, Elizabeth, *Anne Brontë: The Other One*, p.7

CHAPTER 11

1. Gérin, Winifred, *Anne Brontë*, p.195
2. Smith, Margaret (ed.), *The Letters of Charlotte Brontë, Volume 2*, p.224
3. Barker, Juliet, *The Brontës*, p.461
4. *Ibid.*
5. Barker, Juliet, *The Brontës*, p.460

6.   Barker, Juliet, *The Brontës*, p.150
7.   Orel, Harold, *The Brontës: Interviews and Recollections*, pp.61–2
8.   Brontë, Anne, *Agnes Grey*, p.109
9.   Brontë, Anne, *Agnes Grey*, p.91
10. Smith, Margaret (ed.), *The Letters of Charlotte Brontë, Volume 2*, p.92
11. *Sheffield Daily Telegraph*, 29 December 1881
12. The Brontës, *Tales of Glass Town, Angria, and Gondal*, p.492
13. The Brontës, *Tales of Glass Town, Angria, and Gondal*, p.490
14. Brontë, Charlotte, *Biographical Notice of Ellis and Acton Bell*, p.1
15. Brontë, Charlotte, *Biographical Notice of Ellis and Acton Bell*, p.2
16. Bell, C., E., & A., *Poems by Currer, Ellis, and Acton Bell*, p.10

CHAPTER 12

1.   *Halifax Guardian*, 5 June 1841
2.   Bell, C., E. and A., *Poems by Currer, Ellis, and Acton Bell*, p.155
3.   Barker, Juliet, *The Brontës*, p.580
4.   Smith, Margaret (ed.), *The Letters of Charlotte Brontë, Volume 1*, p.530
5.   Hargreaves, G.D. 'The Publishing of "Poems by Currer, Ellis and Acton Bell"', *Brontë Society Transactions 1969*, p.298
6.   The Brontës, *Tales of Glass Town, Angria, and Gondal*, p.492
7.   Brontë, Anne, *The Tenant of Wildfell Hall*, p.4
8.   Brontë, Anne, *The Tenant of Wildfell Hall*, p.3
9.   Brontë, Anne, *Agnes Grey*, p.152
10. *Ibid.*
11. Brontë, Anne, *Agnes Grey*, p.153
12. *Ibid.*
13. Moore, George, *Conversations in Ebury Street*, p.221
14. *Ibid.*
15. Brontë, Charlotte, *Biographical Notice of Ellis and Acton Bell*, p.3

CHAPTER 13

1. Gaskell, Elizabeth, *The Life of Charlotte Brontë*, p.305
2. Brontë, Charlotte, *Biographical Notice of Ellis and Acton Bell*, p.2
3. Gaskell, Elizabeth, *The Life of Charlotte Brontë*, p.325
4. 'I should like to know if Mr Newby often acts as he has done to my relatives, or whether this is an exceptional instance of his method. Do you know, and can you tell me anything about him?' Smith, Margaret (ed.), *The Letters of Charlotte Brontë, Volume 1*, pp.561–2

CHAPTER 14

1. *The Examiner*, 19 February 1848
2. Quoted in an advert placed by Thomas Cautley Newby in *The Athenaeum*, 25 December 1847
3. *Atlas*, 22 January 1848
4. Gérin, Winifred, *Anne Brontë*, p.233
5. *Atlas*, 22 January 1848
6. Brontë, Anne, *The Tenant of Wildfell Hall*, p.4
7. Letter to Ellen Nussey, 4 October 1847, manuscript now held in the Brontë Parsonage Museum, Haworth
8. *Ibid.*
9. Brontë, Anne, *The Tenant of Wildfell Hall*, p.12
10. Brontë, Anne, *The Tenant of Wildfell Hall*, p.118
11. Brontë, Anne, *The Tenant of Wildfell Hall*, p.378
12. Brontë, Anne, *The Tenant of Wildfell Hall*, p.138
13. *Ibid.*
14. Smith, Margaret (ed.), *The Letters of Charlotte Brontë, Volume 1*, p.521
15. *Ibid.*
16. Brontë, Anne, *The Tenant of Wildfell Hall*, p.340
17. See, for example, Charlotte's letter to Ellen Nussey, 13 December 1846: 'It was merely the arrival of a Sherrif's Officer on a visit to Branwell – inviting him either to pay his debts or take a trip to York – of course his debts had to be paid. It is not agreeable to lose money

time after time in this way but it is ten times worse to witness the shabbiness of his behaviour on such occasions.' Smith, Margaret (ed.), *The Letters of Charlotte Brontë, Volume 1*, p.507

18. Brontë, Charlotte, *Biographical Notice of Ellis and Acton Bell*, p.5

CHAPTER 15

1. Gérin, Winifred, *Anne Brontë*, p.261
2. *Spectator*, 8 July 1848
3. *The Rambler*, September 1848
4. *Morning Post*, 14 August 1848
5. *Ibid.*
6. *Ibid.*
7. *The Examiner*, 29 July 1848
8. Brontë, Charlotte, *Biographical Notice of Ellis and Acton Bell*, p.4
9. Gérin, Winifred, *Anne Brontë*, p.261
10. Barker, Juliet, *The Brontës*, p.557
11. Charlotte gave a detailed recollection of this scene, and her time in London, in a letter to Mary Taylor on 8 September 1848. Smith, Margaret (ed.), *The Letters of Charlotte Brontë, Volume 2*, pp.111–5
12. Smith, George, *A Memoir: With Some Pages of Autobiography*, p.91
13. *Ibid.*
14. Gérin, Winifred, *Anne Brontë*, p.269
15. Hargreaves, G.D., 'The Publishing of "Poems by Currer, Ellis and Acton Bell"', *Brontë Society Transactions 1969*, p.298
16. Smith, George, *A Memoir: With Some Pages of Autobiography*, p.91

CHAPTER 16

1. Smith, Margaret (ed.), *The Letters of Charlotte Brontë, Volume 1*, p.507
2. Letter to Ellen Nussey, 26 January 1848, manuscript now held in the Brontë Parsonage Museum, Haworth
3. The Brontës, *Tales of Glass Town, Angria, and Gondal*, p.492

4. Brontë, Anne, *The Tenant of Wildfell Hall*, pp.204–5

5. Gérin, Winifred, *Anne Brontë*, p.238

6. 'I am too hard to die and too wretched to live.' Branwell's letter to Joseph Bentley Leyland of June 1846.

7. Gérin, Winifred, *Anne Brontë*, p.238

8. Barker, Juliet, *The Brontës*, p.494

9. Smith, Margaret (ed.), *The Letters of Charlotte Brontë, Volume 1*, p.524

10. Brontë, Anne, *The Tenant of Wildfell Hall*, p.151

11. Manuscripts of Branwell's later letters, showing the variance in hand-writing, are held in the Brontë Parsonage Museum, Haworth

12. *Fraser's Magazine*, December 1848

13. Brontë, Anne, *The Tenant of Wildfell Hall*, p.4

14. Brontë, Anne, *The Tenant of Wildfell Hall*, pp.344–5

15. Orel, Harold, *The Brontës: Interviews and Recollections*, p.56

16. Smith, Margaret (ed.), *The Letters of Charlotte Brontë, Volume 2*, p.124

CHAPTER 17

1. Smith, Margaret (ed.), *The Letters of Charlotte Brontë, Volume 2*, p.122

2. Letter to W.S. Williams, 29 September 1848, manuscript now held in the British Library, London

3. Bell, C. E., and A., *Poems by Currer, Ellis, and Acton Bell*, p.44

4. Gérin, Winifred, *Anne Brontë*, p.259

5. Smith, Margaret (ed.), *The Letters of Charlotte Brontë, Volume 2*, p.130

6. Smith, Margaret (ed.), *The Letters of Charlotte Brontë, Volume 2*, p.132

7. Smith, Margaret (ed.), *The Letters of Charlotte Brontë, Volume 2*, p.142

8. Smith, Margaret (ed.), *The Letters of Charlotte Brontë, Volume 2*, p.145

9. Smith, Margaret (ed.), *The Letters of Charlotte Brontë, Volume 2*, p.147

10. Smith, Margaret (ed.), *The Letters of Charlotte Brontë, Volume 2*, pp.152–3

11. Brontë, Emily, *Wuthering Heights*, pp.120–1

12. Gérin, Winifred, *Emily Brontë*, p.259

CHAPTER 18

1. Green, Dudley, *Patrick Brontë Father of Genius*, p.133
2. Smith, Margaret (ed.), *The Letters of Charlotte Brontë, Volume 2*, p.157
3. *Ibid.*
4. Smith, Margaret (ed.), *The Letters of Charlotte Brontë, Volume 2*, p.159
5. Barker, Juliet, *The Brontës*, p.581
6. The manuscript of this poem is held in the Brontë Parsonage Museum, Haworth. It was published posthumously by Charlotte in 1850. It was Charlotte who gave the previously untitled poem the title of 'Last Lines', and added the note: 'I have given the last memento of my sister Emily; this is the last of my sister Anne: These lines written, the desk was closed, the pen laid aside – for ever.'
7. Smith, Margaret (ed.), *The Letters of Charlotte Brontë, Volume 2*, p.167
8. Letter to Reverend David Thom, 30 December 1848, manuscript now held in Princeton University Library, New Jersey
9. The manuscript of this poem, clearly showing the point at which the poem was set down and then taken up again, is held in the Brontë Parsonage Museum, Haworth
10. Gérin, Winifred, *Anne Brontë*, pp.304–5
11. 'There's little joy in life for me, And little terror in the grave; I've lived the parting hour to see, Of one I would have died to save.' The opening lines of 'On the Death of Anne Brontë', written by Charlotte on 21 June 1849
12. Smith, Margaret (ed.), *The Letters of Charlotte Brontë, Volume 2*, p.208
13. Letter to Ellen Nussey, 5 April 1849. Manuscript now held in the Brontë Parsonage Museum, Haworth
14. Matthew 26: 36–9, King James Bible
15. Smith, Margaret (ed.), *The Letters of Charlotte Brontë, Volume 2*, p.205
16. Smith, Margaret (ed.), *The Letters of Charlotte Brontë, Volume 2*, p.208
17. *Ibid.*
18. As recorded in Charlotte Brontë's cash-book, now held in the Brontë Parsonage Museum, Haworth
19. Nussey, Ellen, *A Short Account of the Last Days of Dear A.B.*, p.2. Manuscript now held in King's School Library, Canterbury

20. Smith, Margaret (ed.), *The Letters of Charlotte Brontë, Volume 2*, p.213
21. Nussey, Ellen, *A Short Account of the Last Days of Dear A.B.*, p.2. Manuscript now held in King's School Library, Canterbury
22. Barker, Juliet, *The Brontës*, p.593
23. Smith, Margaret (ed.), *The Letters of Charlotte Brontë, Volume 2*, p.220
24. Nussey, Ellen, *A Short Account of the Last Days of Dear A.B.*, p.10. Manuscript now held in King's School Library, Canterbury

CHAPTER 19

1. Barker, Juliet, *The Brontës*, p.595
2. Barker, Juliet, *The Brontës*, p.594
3. Rhodes, Philip, 'A Medical Appraisal of the Brontës', *Brontë Society Transactions 1972*, p.108
4. Brontë, Charlotte, Introduction to *Selections Of Poems By Acton Bell*, published 1850
5. *Ibid.*
6. Brontë, Charlotte, Introduction to *Selections of Poems by Ellis Bell*, published 1850
7. Smith, Margaret (ed.), *The Letters of Charlotte Brontë, Volume 2*, p.581
8. Smith, Margaret (ed.), *The Letters of Charlotte Brontë, Volume 3*, p.168
9. Andrews, Sir Linton, 'A Challenge by Anne Brontë', *Brontë Society Transactions 1965*, p.28
10. Sinclair, May, Introduction to *The Tenant of Wildfell Hall*, published 1914
11. Langland, Elizabeth, *Anne Brontë: The Other One*, p.60
12. Brontë, Anne, *The Tenant of Wildfell Hall*, p.108
13. Brontë, Anne, *The Tenant of Wildfell Hall*, p.243
14. Brontë, Anne, *The Tenant of Wildfell Hall*, p.101

SELECT BIBLIOGRAPHY

Alexander, Christine and Sellars, Jane, *The Art of the Brontës* (Cambridge University Press, 1995)

Alexander, Christine (ed.), *Tales of Glass Town, Angria, and Gondal* (Introduction) (Oxford World's Classics, 2010)

Atkinson, E., *Haworth in the Brontë Era, B.H.Babbage's Visit to Haworth* (Keighley, 1998)

Barker, Juliet, *The Brontës* (Weidenfeld & Nicolson, 1994)

Brontë, Patrick, *A Funeral Sermon for the Late Rev. William Weightman, M.A.* (Halifax, 1842)

Chitham, Edward, *A Life of Anne Brontë* (Blackwell, 1991)

Dinsdale, Ann, *The Brontës at Haworth* (Frances Lincoln, 2006)

du Maurier, Daphne, *The Infernal World of Branwell Brontë* (Penguin, 1972)

Gaskell, Elizabeth, *The Life of Charlotte Brontë* (Penguin Classics, 1985)

Gérin, Winifred, *Anne Brontë* (Allen Lane, 1959)

Gérin, Winifred, *Charlotte Brontë* (Oxford University Press, 1967)

Gérin, Winifred, *Emily Brontë* (Oxford University Press, 1971)

Green, Dudley, *Patrick Brontë Father of Genius* (The History Press, 2008)

Greenwood, Robin, *West Lane and Hall Green Baptist Churches in Haworth in West Yorkshire: Their Early History and Doctrinal Distinctives* (Whitley Bay, 2005)

Grundy, Francis, *Pictures of The Past* (Griffith & Farrar, 1879)

Harland, Marion, *Charlotte Brontë at Home* (Kessinger Publishing, 2010)

Ingham, Patricia, *The Brontës* (Oxford University Press, 2008)

Langland, Elizabeth, *Anne Brontë: The Other One* (Palgrave Macmillan, 1989)

Lemon, Charles, *Classics of Brontë Scholarship* (The Brontë Society, 1999)

Lemon, Charles, *Early Visitors to Haworth: From Ellen Nussey to Virginia Woolf* (The Brontë Society, 1996)

Leyland, Francis, *The Brontë Family* (Hurst & Blackett, 1886)

Lister, Philip, *Ghosts & Gravestones of Haworth* (Tempus, 2006)

Miller, Lucastra, *The Brontë Myth* (Jonathan Cape, 2001)

Moore, George, *Conversations in Ebury Street* (William Heinemann, 1930)

Neufeldt, Victor A. (ed.), *The Works of Patrick Branwell Brontë*, Volume 3, 1837–1848 (Taylor & Francis, 2015)

Orel, Harold, *The Brontës: Interviews and Recollections* (Palgrave Macmillan, 1996)

Smith, George, *A Memoir with Some Pages of Biography* (Cambridge University Press, 2012)

Smith, Margaret (ed.), *The Letters of Charlotte Brontë (Volumes 1–3)* (Clarendon Press, 1995)

Spark, Muriel, *The Essence of the Brontës* (Peter Owen, 1993)

The versions of books by the Brontë sisters referred to in the notes are as follows:

Bell, C., E. and A., *Poems by Currer, Ellis, and Acton Bell* (Aylott & Jones, 1846)

Brontë, Anne, *Agnes Grey* (Wordsworth Classics, 1998)

Brontë, Anne, *The Tenant of Wildfell Hall* (Wordsworth Classics, 1994)

Brontë, Charlotte, *Biographical Notice of Ellis and Acton Bell* (Smith, Elder & Co., 1850)

Brontë, Charlotte, *Jane Eyre* (Wordsworth Classics, 1999)

Brontë, Charlotte, *Selections of Poems by Acton Bell* (Smith, Elder & Co., 1850)

Brontë, Charlotte, *Selections of Poems by Ellis Bell* (Smith, Elder & Co., 1850)

Brontë, Emily, *Wuthering Heights* (Penguin Classics, 1985)

INDEX

Visit our website and discover thousands of other History Press books.

www.thehistorypress.co.uk

WITHDRAWN

WITHDRAWN

WITHDRAWN